'*Obsolete* is both a rallying cry and a toolkit for change. Now more than ever, leaders and shareholders at every business, in every industry, need to think differently about how people, profit and the planet intersect if they are going to thrive long into the future. It's not just the right thing to do, it's the smart thing to do. This book offers lessons from business leaders at the forefront of change and provides practical advice for people who want to join the movement.'

Douglas Lamont, Chief Chocolonely at Tony's Chocolonely, Co-Chair
of Better Business Act, and Former CEO of Innocent Drinks

'*Obsolete* is full of the kind of thinking that totally disrespects everything they teach you in business school – however naïve that may sound. Instead, it invites the reader to imagine how running a business has the power to change the trajectory of our planet and contribute to the lives of the people that live here. It can be mind-blowing to see what happens when you drop all the "bizniz" in your business.'

John Schoolcraft, Chief Creative Officer at Oatly AB

'At COP21 David Attenborough declared that, "a new industrial revolution is essential" and in this book, Chris shares example after example of those solution focused pace-setting Change Brands leading that much-needed revolution. Perfectly paced, packed with real-world insights and inspiration. This is going to be a well-thumbed keeper for all aspiring change-makers.'

Michelle Carvill, author of Can Marketing Save the Planet?

'A powerful call to action with a simple behaviour change at its heart – change the world by changing where people spend their money.'

Richard Shotton, author of The Choice Factory *and Founder of Astroten*

'*Obsolete* is a manifesto for modern capitalism. Many believe capitalism is part of the problem, this book shows that it can also be the solution. But legacy brands beware – change is now your day job.'

Tara Austin, Host of Nudgestock and Partner, Ogilvy Behavioural Science Practice

'The world needs businesses to be at their best, more so now than ever. *Obsolete* is a masterclass in how brands can harness their power to drive meaningful change. A must-read for all founders and business leaders.'

Andy Fishburn, Managing Director, Virgin Start-Up

'*Obsolete* is a timely wake-up call for brands and businesses trying to come to terms with a rapidly changing world. For all those businesses having sleepless nights about new brands emerging in their market and eating their lunch, this is essential reading.'

Mark Sinnock, Global Chief Strategy, Data and
Innovation Officer, Havas Creative Group

'We should never underestimate the power we have as consumers to create change. How do we do that? By supporting Change Brands and buying from them. It really is that simple. This book shows you who they are and why it's so important to think before we buy.'

Sahar Hashemi OBE, entrepreneur, author and Founder of Buy Women Built

'*Obsolete* is essential reading for those who believe business should be part of the solution – not just part of the problem. It doesn't just emphasize that the way we spend our money can change the world, it's a blueprint for how you can create your own Change Brand and build businesses that regenerate our planet.'

Leo Rayman, CEO & Founder of EdenLab

'*Obsolete* covers with optimism the chance we all have to reinvent capitalism for the better – and an inspiring blueprint of Change Brands – including our own Tony's Chocolonely, Oatly, Wild, Who Gives a Crap – leading the way in showing good business and good ethics can and should sit hand-in-hand.'

Ben Black, Head of FMCG Investing, Verlinvest

'*Obsolete* is essential reading for those eager to drive global change through everyday choices, highlighting how Change Brands can make both a difference and a profit. Discover how your wallet can help to shape a better world.'

Zoe Scaman, Founder of Bodacious Studios and Keynote Speaker

'Marketing has the opportunity and challenge to lead the biggest shift in the consumer economy the world as yet seen, essential if we are to live sustainability and improve the quality of people's lives. *Obsolete* shows how inspirational new brands are, challenging the status quo, offering more sustainable choices in everyday product categories, and stimulating competition and innovation that will accelerate this sustainability shift.'

Stephen Woodford, Chief Executive of the Advertising Association

'The circular and sustainable economy is surely the innovation opportunity of a generation. "Change how people spend their money, and you can change the world", Chris Baker rightly proclaims with passion and experience, and not a moment too soon. He brilliantly shows many ways it can be done – and how to avoid some of the pitfalls, especially if you don't have a blank page to start from. *Obsolete* is a theory of change and a handbook for brands with integrity to pull it off!'

Sebastian Munden, Chair of WRAP, co-author of Sustainable Advertising: How advertising can support a better future, *and former CEO of Unilever UK & Ireland*

'At a time when brand equity can be devalued within minutes, it's refreshing to learn about why companies and consumers should invest in it in the first place. A must read for any aspiring change-makers.'

Oli Harris, Managing Director, Venturebeam

'In a world where brands hold more power than governments, *Obsolete* is a must-read for anyone wanting to make a positive impact on society.'

Anna Vogt, Chief Strategy Officer at VML

'The power to drive real change is in the consumer's hands. This book perfectly highlights the challenges and opportunities for brands wanting to disrupt and drive systemic change in their industry!'

Guy Hayler, Co-Founder and CCO, Blue Earth

'What started with a cup of coffee has the potential to become a game-changing global movement. *Obsolete* shows you how to change the world by changing how people spend their money.'

Cemal Ezel OBE, Founder & CEO, Change Please

Obsolete

How Change Brands are Changing the World

Chris Baker

BLOOMSBURY BUSINESS
LONDON · OXFORD · NEW YORK · NEW DELHI · SYDNEY

BLOOMSBURY BUSINESS
Bloomsbury Publishing Plc
50 Bedford Square, London, WC1B 3DP, UK
29 Earlsfort Terrace, Dublin 2, Ireland

A catalogue record for this book is available from the British Library

Library of Congress Cataloging-in-Publication data has been applied for

ISBN: 978-1-3994-1665-8; eBook: 978-1-3994-1664-1

2 4 6 8 10 9 7 5 3 1

Typeset by Deanta Global Publishing Services, Chennai, India
Printed and bound in Great Britain by CPI Group (UK) Ltd, Croydon CR0 4YY

MIX
Paper | Supporting
responsible forestry
FSC
www.fsc.org   FSC® C171272

To find out more about our authors and books visit www.bloomsbury.com and sign up
for our newsletters

'You never change things by fighting the existing reality'

*'To change something, build a new model that makes the existing model **obsolete**'*

Buckminster Fuller
Writer, futurist, inventor, architect

To Maggie, Jasper, Delphi and Katy.
My reasons why.

Contents

PART ONE

Why Change Brands Matter and How They're Changing the World

CHAPTER ONE

Humanity's Most Powerful Invention

'The best time to plant a tree was twenty years ago.
The second-best time is now.'

Ancient Chinese Proverb

A great quote, and one you've probably heard before. But it's also one we perhaps took a little bit too literally when we came up with the idea for our brand – Serious Tissues – in late 2019. I've got three young kids, Maggie, Jasper and Delphi, and combined with the other three founders, we've got eight children who were in primary school or younger. Yes, we've been busy!

We had become increasingly concerned about climate change. The more we read, the more it became crystal clear that the world our children were going to inherit as adults would be vastly different to the one that we all grew up in. We wanted to do something about it, rather than stand by and be powerless.

A lot has been written about the importance of tree planting as a potential solution to climate change. Clearly it is not a 'silver bullet' that will solve the problem all on its own. There is debate around exactly how much of the world's carbon emissions large-scale tree planting programmes can capture, but one thing is clear: we need to plant a serious amount of trees if we're to limit global warming to anywhere near the 1.5°C target outlined in the Paris Agreement signed in 2015 at COP21. In a world where we need trees more than ever, there was one obvious place to look to make an impact. A product that billions of people use multiple times every single day: the humble toilet roll.

The vast majority of toilet paper sold across the world is made from trees. Trees that have spent 20 or 30 years growing to maturity and capturing carbon along the way, that are then cut down, pulped and made into toilet paper. At least a million trees are cut down every day for toilet paper.* Given the current situation, turning a tree into what must be the ultimate single-use product is almost criminal, especially when alternatives exist.

Armed with this knowledge, we created Serious Tissues. A toilet paper brand with the commitment to plant a tree for every single roll we sell. Our rolls are made from 100 per cent recycled paper, primarily recovered from office paper and post-consumer use paper, so no trees are harmed in the process. We're also plastic-free and locally made in the UK to keep down the shipping footprint that you get with a bamboo solution transported from China.

We help people make a simple switch that makes a real difference. A switch that may feel small but is actually hugely significant. Someone switching their toilet paper to us for a year would plant over 100 trees, their own personal forest, just by changing their loo roll.

In the three years since our launch, we've planted over 1.2 million trees all over the world and are on course to plant another million in 2024 as we continue to grow rapidly and more and more customers make sustainable switches.

It's just the beginning. As we start to open up more supermarket relationships and corporate partnerships (we're already available in Ocado and providing toilet roll for a lot of big companies including CBRE, Estee Lauder and AXA), we access a much bigger market. If we can get a 1 per cent share of the UK toilet roll market, we'd be

---

* Environmental Impacts of Traditional Toilet Paper Usage – Edge Australia. https:// drive.google.com/file/d/1IOBDcixSgD5Lgz2gT3UmPb0i4EIvI4bs/view

planting over 4 million trees and turning over £18.6 million each year.* And that's just in the UK.

If we go back to our quote at the start of this chapter and look at the 20-year timeline for Serious Tissues, the potential impact becomes seriously exciting. Looking at a mid-range growth estimate, by the time my youngest daughter is 21, we'd have planted over 100 million trees. I'm sure you'll agree, this is a mind-blowing figure. While we might not be able to change the world just by changing how people wipe their bums, hopefully this will prove to be a serious contribution in staving off the worst effects of climate change.

My reasons why © Chris Baker

A Change is Brewing

Serious Tissues wasn't the first time that we saw that asking people to make very small but highly significant changes in their buying

---

* The total UK toilet roll market is estimated to be worth £1.86 billion in 2024 – Statista. https://www.statista.com/outlook/cmo/tissue-hygiene-paper/united-kingdom?currency =GBP

habits could make a real difference to some of the world's biggest problems.

Working in Central London at the time, it was impossible to miss the growing number of homeless people on the streets. Recent statistics suggest there are over 300,000 people who are homeless in the UK alone, with about 3,000 sleeping rough on any given night and the rest living in temporary accommodation, with a large proportion of those being families.*

One day between meetings, I was sat in a coffee shop in Covent Garden and there was a homeless man sat out the front. The problem had become so commonplace that homeless people were becoming invisible. People walked straight past this man asking for change – ignoring him, pretending to be on their phone. Tapping their pockets to say they had no change and then walking straight into the coffee shop to spend £3 on a skinny latte. If you were in his shoes, it would be impossible not to feel disconnected from the rest of society.

Something wasn't right about this journey and seeing it happen time and time again sparked an idea. There had to be an opportunity to disrupt this journey. What if we could use that £3 spent on coffee to tackle the problem of homelessness? What if we could train homeless people as baristas in a modern update on *The Big Issue* model?

So, with the support of the creative agency I was working for at the time, FCB Inferno, we took the idea to *The Big Issue* magazine. They loved it but they said, 'We're a magazine publisher, not a coffee business so you'll need to find a coffee partner.' In a beautiful moment of serendipity, I was living in Peckham in Southeast London at the

---

* Shelter, 2023. https://england.shelter.org.uk/media/press_release/at_least_309000 _people_homeless_in_england_today#:~:text=At per cent20least per cent20309 per cent2C000 per cent20people per cent20homeless per cent20in per cent20England per cent20today per cent20 per cent2D per cent20Shelter per cent20England

time and met Cemal Ezel and Rich Robinson, who had just set up a coffee roastery called Old Spike Roastery that was working with homeless people and they were looking to expand. We decided to combine forces and throw the weight of the agency and *The Big Issue* behind a new kind of coffee brand.

It was important to create a brand that didn't feel like 'charity coffee'. The idea of a coffee 'from the streets' didn't exactly tickle the taste buds. With that in mind, the plan was always to leverage all the premium cues of a speciality coffee brand and make the mission to tackle homelessness a more subtle part of the journey. Cemal found a piece of street art by an Australian artist called Meek (albeit often attributed to Banksy) that was called 'Begging for Change'. This captured exactly the sentiment we were looking to bring to life with the brand and so, with an added dose of British politeness, 'Change Please' was born. A premium coffee brand that would sell coffee to tackle homelessness.

'Begging for Change' by Meek and a Change Please coffee © Meek,
Begging for Change, 2004 / Change Please

Here, the real step change was the move to a Job First model, rather than a Housing First model. The traditional way to tackle homelessness is to try and give someone a home – the clue is in the name. But this is often just a sticking plaster on the problem and doesn't tackle any of the root causes. Where Change Please is different is that it takes a Job First approach. The homeless person, found through a network of charity partners, gets a job that pays them a Living Wage. They learn a skill as a barista that builds their confidence. And on top of that, they get help with housing, therapy and support throughout the whole process. But the real game changer is the self-esteem boost they get with the new role. Instead of people walking past them as they sit on the streets asking for change, they are coming to them on the same level, asking them for something they value: a great cup of coffee to fuel them through their day. This rise in confidence and constant social interaction proved transformational for the first few baristas Change Please worked with – and has been ever since.

'There's a quote from my favourite film, *A Bronx Tale*, that sums up homelessness,' Cemal explains. '"The saddest thing in life is wasted talent." You've got people that can contribute, can make a difference, can give back to society and be part of our system. But for one reason, whether it's their own or someone else's, they've got into a negative spiral and gone out on the streets. And regardless of what people are going to tell you, 95 per cent of people don't want to be there and they're not faking it, and around 45 per cent of those people want to leave that situation and can work. So, when you start looking into all of this, you realize this is just huge waste and there's an opportunity to make a big difference.'

So, in late 2015, we launched Change Please, with a single coffee cart in Covent Garden, just down the road from that original coffee shop. The idea struck a major chord. On the back of a one-page press release we were featured on BBC and ITV News, across numerous radio stations and press titles including the *Telegraph*, *The Times*, the *Guardian*, *Metro* and *Vice* with a combined reach of over 600 million people. This coverage, that other brands would have paid thousands of pounds for, also generated over 2.6 million social media impressions. This sort of exposure and share of voice is almost unheard of with the tiny budgets we were operating with, but it just goes to show that when you have an idea that offers a solution to a problem a lot of people care about, a small voice can turn into a powerful echo.

Change Please was asking people to simply change where they bought their coffee to give someone else a chance to turn their life around. We were asking them to turn right and get their coffee from Change Please rather than turning left and getting it from a massive chain like Starbucks or Costa. Another simple change but one that could make a significant difference.

The quality of the coffee was always of the utmost importance to Cemal to address the potential elephant in the room of the association between coffee and homelessness. 'One of the biggest challenges we've seen is that people feel that there's got to be some sort of compromise. The images and labels that come to mind when you're thinking of homeless people doesn't necessarily correspond with a high-quality product so we've always gone above and beyond to make sure the quality of the product is fantastic first and foremost. One of the biggest things we hear after people drink our coffee is that they say with a sense of surprise, "oh wow, that does taste really good" and that's the wrong way round, but it proves we're getting the product side right. And we don't just say it now, we've won nine Great Taste Awards, which is testament to the effort we've made on that side of the business.'

The business grew quickly, driven by the absolute force of nature that is Cemal. His passion for both the problem and the intricacies of creating a great cup of coffee is contagious and has been the fuel behind the growth of the brand. One cart in Covent Garden quickly grew to ten across London. A Sainsbury's and Tesco supermarket listing followed and numerous businesses changed their in-house coffee supplier. Change Please is now the coffee served on Virgin Atlantic, in David Lloyd Clubs and across numerous WeWork sites around Europe. It is the coffee served in AstraZeneca UK, so may have played a small role in developing the Oxford Vaccine and it may soon be the first coffee served in Space on board Virgin Galactic. It's also now available in 22 countries including France, Australia and the US, with the model transferring seamlessly to other countries facing a similar problem with homelessness. Change Please have also partnered with major brands including Colgate, HSBC and Nespresso to combine forces to help people battling homelessness, exploring a range of different ways of making an impact that we cover later in this book.

Thousands of homeless people have been helped by Change Please in a little over eight years. Hundreds of lives changed, just by changing the coffee you drink. And it's still very early days for the brand. As the number of cafés grow, more corporates change their coffee supplier and more supermarkets add Change Please to their shelves, the more people it can help and the bigger impact it has on the problem of homelessness.

In the words of one of the brilliant Change Please trainees, Liam: 'I feel part of a movement, part of a change in society. Everyone is part of a bigger thing. I am not just someone who makes the coffee, we are Change Please.'

A Growing Movement

Everywhere you look, it is increasingly possible to see all sorts of different brands and businesses making a positive difference to the world through their products. Big companies and small companies in almost every sector you could imagine are disrupting markets with the promise of a positive impact. But it's more than just a few unrelated success stories dotted here and there, it is a growing movement of companies with a lot in common. A rising tide of change baked intrinsically into business models.

We're living in a world that's crying out for change. It feels like there are more problems than ever so any product that sets out to make a difference is likely to strike a chord with the audience. People are increasingly looking for brands and businesses that have a positive impact on the world around them, rather than contributing to problems. This is especially true among younger generations who are set to inherit major spending power in the next decade.

Allbirds have built a serious foothold in the sportswear market as the world's most sustainable trainer with $266.25 million in sales.* Ecosia have planted over 200 million trees by using advertising revenue generated by people switching their search activity from Google. Tony's Chocolonely have raised awareness of modern slavery and child labour in the cocoa supply chain with their delicious chocolate while hitting $162 million in revenue in 2023. Vinted, the marketplace for preloved clothes, reached €371 million in 2022 with an offering that combined a more sustainable way to build your wardrobe with affordability and a way to make a bit of extra cash. They pushed back against fast fashion and the amount of clothing ending up in landfill, but key messages related to style and cost as key motivators.

Oatly has been a runaway success story in this space since former CEO Toni Petersson and Chief Creative Officer John Schoolcraft joined in 2012. They turned an oat milk product that had come out of a Swedish university and was selling primarily through health food shops into a brand that has become a cultural phenomenon, taking on Big Dairy and changing the milk preferences of millions

---

* Allbirds results, September 2023

of people across the world. Despite reaching unicorn status and returning revenue of $783 million in 2023, when I asked John what he was most proud of, it was the impact they've made, 'That we could create something that society could benefit from. That switching from cow's milk to oat milk reduces the carbon footprint of that milk significantly, anywhere from 44 per cent to 76 per cent less depending on where it is distributed,* and that every single product we sell in place of cow's milk is a win for the planet.'

Oatly's packaging before and after the rebrand that
would ignite their growth © Oatly

These companies have built highly successful businesses that operate globally by having a positive impact on the world's problems. Look at almost any category out there and someone is

---

* Based on studies across the US, Europe and China of Oatly's best-selling Barista product

shaking up the market with an offering that sets out to make a positive difference.

Brands are emerging everywhere that are disrupting the status quo in a new way and making the most of this shift in audience mindset. Technology, value and improved service have all been major market disruptors in their time. Virgin built a multi-billion-dollar empire on the basis of trying to fix a problem with the customer experience. FMCG (Fast-Moving Consumer Goods) brands have thrived by creating a problem in the consumer's mind and then looking to solve it with anti-ageing, teeth-whitening, fat-shredding products. But nowadays brands have their sights set much, much higher: they're aiming to tackle the world's biggest problems. And it's not like there is a shortage of problems to solve.

We are at the start of the next major market disruption, that of 'social disruption'. Disrupting entire categories with innovative business models that combine an issue people care about with a product they love. This 'social disruption' is an irresistible force that is almost impossible for legacy brands to fight off as attitudes continue to shift and consumers demand more. Audience attitudes are changing to reflect this. Sustainability is a key consideration driver in numerous purchases and continues to grow in importance. The ethics of a company, their impact on the planet and their 'purpose' has become far more prominent.

Corporate Social Responsibility in a large corporate is no longer the domain of the 'hemp-wearing hippy' down the corridor and they don't just support a charity or cause because the 'chairman's wife watched a documentary on pandas'. Impact has become as core to the operation of a business as a company's website. It is of fundamental importance and it's only going to grow as we stand on the cusp of the largest inter-generational transfer of wealth ever seen across the next couple of decades. Positive impact was less of a consideration for older generations, but it is a key part of the mindset of Gen Z (those born between 1997 and 2012) and younger age groups and will make a huge difference to the brands they choose to spend their money on.

This change is gathering momentum, and it doesn't even need every single consumer out there to change their buying habits. Cost, convenience and preference remain key factors in what people buy and that's not going to change any time soon. But when just a small proportion of the spend in these multibillion-dollar categories starts moving away from the status quo towards these brands, they start to look very closely at their own operations. Losing market share is an incredible catalyst for big companies to pick up the pace where previously they might have been dragging their feet. The catalyst is well and truly amongst the pigeons.

Faced with the direct choice between buying a coffee that will help someone off the streets, or one from a company not paying any tax in that country, what will you choose? If you can choose between toilet roll that cuts down trees versus one that plants trees, in today's world, the choice is easy. Then there's cleaning products that clean up the planet as well as your kitchen. The choice for the consumer is straightforward and the opportunity for these brands to challenge the established order is enormous.

More and more of these brands are emerging in all sorts of sectors and having real success as they build their businesses and become acquisition targets for the big players. Liquid Death, smol, Oatly, Tesla, Vinted, Who Gives A Crap, Flo Tampons, Wild Deodorants, Gener8 Ads, Oddbox, Beyond Meats... the list goes on. Even Michelle Obama is getting in on the act as co-founder of PLEZi Nutrition, a drink brand for kids that provides a healthier alternative to high-sugar options. Numerous brands all making their mark on the world, disrupting the status quo and making a positive difference. And this is just the beginning.

The rising tide of Change Brands

The Rise of Change Brands

These 'Change Brands' are seeing increased demand and are growing rapidly across geographies. They are winning business from the legacy brands who have dominated for years and becoming clear and present threats to their business. Change Brands are this decade's 'Challenger Brands' and they're going to change the world, one sale at a time.

The idea of the 'Challenger Brand' was popularized by Adam Morgan and his book, *Eating the Big Fish: How Challenger Brands Can Compete Against Brand Leaders*, first published in January 1999. Since then, it's become a hugely pervasive idea in business with small brands taking on a range of challenger behaviours in order to topple market leaders. It's such an established idea that big brands have even started to try and 'act like a challenger', despite their size, to stay relevant and compete.

Change Brands take a lot of what's great about Challenger Brands but go a step further. They're not just looking to disrupt a category and grow rapidly, they're also looking to make a real impact on some of the biggest problems facing society through the tools of business.

Change Brands are growing much faster than the rest of the market. Sustainable brands have driven 55 per cent of FMCG growth in the US despite only accounting for 19 per cent of the market.* They are also able to command a price premium of 40 per cent reinjecting value to many commoditized and stagnating sectors. And it's not just sustainability driving growth. According to BCorp research from October 2022, B Corps, companies who need to demonstrate their social and environmental impact, are growing their turnover faster than traditional businesses (27 per cent vs 5 per cent) and employee headcount (14 per cent vs 1 per cent). Even the big players are trying to get on the bandwagon. Unilever's sustainable living brands grew 69 per cent faster than the rest of their business. Change Brands are disrupting every single category out there – cars, trainers, tampons, coffee, cleaning products, chocolate, banking, advertising, deodorant – and no sector is safe from social disruption.

It's not like the marketplace doesn't need shaking up a little bit. Just 11 companies own almost every food, drink and

---

* NYU Stern Center for Sustainable Business – Sustainable Market Share Index (2020)

household brand that we buy in the supermarket and make more than a billion dollars a day in sales.* Mars, Coca-Cola, PepsiCo, Unilever, Procter & Gamble and the others shown in the graphic below own and operate hundreds of brands that dominate our shopping baskets across every country on the planet. The scale of Unilever's brands mean they are used by 3.4 billion people across the world every single day.† At the time of this stat, taken from their annual report in 2021, that means 43 per cent of the 7.9 billion people on the planet at that time were using a Unilever product on any given day. PepsiCo have 23 brands that do more than US$1 billion in annual sales. These 11 businesses are part of a food sector worth over $10 trillion in 2024,‡ almost 10 per cent of the entire global economy. In fact, they have such a colossal footprint that any small positive changes in their operations can have an enormous impact on the planet, for both good and bad.

And this market dominance extends into many other sectors. Just a handful of car companies control almost every vehicle on the roads. AB InBev are responsible for around two in every five beers drunk globally. The Big Five tech players hold an unhealthy dominance of what we do online and the devices we use to interact with the digital world. Without any pressure from the outside, they'll just continue along on their merry way, keeping costs down,

---

* Greenpeace – Behind the Brands, 2016 https://www.behindthebrands.org/images/ media/Download-files/bp166-behind-brands-260213-en.pdf. Based upon the Forbes 2000 list at www.forbes.com/global2000/list/. Regarding revenues (sales without deducting costs) and taking into account 2011 data (except for Mars, as only 2010 data were available), the top ten food and beverage companies earned $418.08 billion in 2011, which is equivalent to $1.145 billion a day.

† Unilever Annual Report 2021 – https://www.unilever.com/files/92ui5egz/ production/75f31d18a2219004f4afe03e37ccd2a3b383472f.pdf

‡ Statista, 2023

maximizing profits, hunting growth from new variants and creating products people don't really need.

The 11 companies that dominate the brand landscape © Capital One Shopping

Change Brands Change Other Brands

Without being challenged from outside on their behaviour, these dominant, legacy brands will just keep on doing what they're doing, making baby steps towards sustainability but not at the expense of all-important profits and growth targets.

As Change Brands grow and legacy brands come under pressure through losing sales or distribution, these established companies are forced to look at how they can inject purpose and impact into their own brands but often this proves an impossible task that draws derision from customers and shareholders. What's the social purpose of a shampoo, or a bag of sweets? Or a jar of mayonnaise?

There is also a temptation among legacy brands to try and polish their sustainability credentials to meet the shift in attitudes of their customers, while not making the changes required to back up those claims. This is known as 'Greenwashing' and has the potential to backfire. It is increasingly prominent across so many categories and while it's great that brands recognize they need to make shifts, marketing is rarely the first place to start. In fact, it's probably the worst. Consumers are increasingly seeing through this practice and it does more harm than good – many would think that Coca-Cola's sponsorship of the United Nations COP27, as the world's worst plastic polluter and major consumer of fossil fuels, seemed remarkably ill-judged. As was their attempt to position Innocent Smoothies (one of their brands) as solving the problem of single-use plastic with cute animals singing about recycling despite contributing millions of bottles to the problem each year. Fast fashion is also notorious for its environmental impact and, in 2022, H&M were shown up to be among the worst offenders with more than half of their ethical claims on their own environmental scorecards 'shown to be misleading, and in many cases, outright deceptive'*. Consumers are becoming increasingly tuned into these tenuous attempts to massage the facts and slow progress from big brands on issues people care about is becoming more and more untenable.

---

* https://qz.com/2180075/hm-showed-bogus-environmental-higg-index-scores-for-its-clothing

Change means cost to these companies. It seriously upsets the apple cart, disrupting the bottom line and finely tuned margins. Change Brands and changes in public opinion drive legislation changes that hurt these companies. Would the rest of the automotive industry really have moved so fast towards electric vehicles (EVs) if Tesla hadn't sent shockwaves through the sector?

If Cheeky Panda and Serious Tissues can do plastic-free packaging, why can't Andrex? If smol, Homethings and Ocean Saver can remove the water from cleaning products to reduce the shipping footprint, why can't Flash? If Flo can make biodegradable tampons, then why can't Tampax get rid of those plastic applicators? If other brands can make giant strides away from plastic, why can't Coca-Cola? Legislation around packaging, HFSS food (High Fat, Salt or Sugar) and the Internal Combustion Engine have been accelerated by other brands showing that what was previously considered 'impossible' is far from it.

Change Brands are having a substantial impact on the world. They're changing people's behaviour in a simple yet significant way that makes a real difference to the world we all live in. Millions of trees planted, tonnes of plastic packaging saved, reductions in harmful chemicals, unhealthy ingredients and carbon-intensive practices and attention brought to all kinds of worthy causes.

People are going to spend that money anyway, so if they can spend it on a product or service that positively impacts a problem they care about, then it becomes an absolute no-brainer. Clearly these brands need to reach a scale where they can be easily accessible on the high street or supermarket shelf, as well as being competitive when it comes to price, and this is no easy task. But when they do, they become an irresistible force that the existing brands that dominate these sectors need to acknowledge and react to.

A lot of brands are going to die in the next decade, becoming obsolete in the face of changing consumer demands. At the very least, some of the outdated models and production practices underpinning these brands will cease to exist. Making a positive impact is no longer a 'nice-to-have' for your brand, it's a must-have. It's table stakes in the battle for future consumer spend and without it, you might as well not play the game.

Now I'm not saying every single existing brand is going to be wiped off the face of the earth. These are huge brands with millions of customers, a lot of financial muscle and many positive brand associations built up in people's minds. But the way they do business will have to change. Models that prioritize profit over everything else will become obsolete as new models begin to emerge.

Change Brands are going to continue to ramp up the pressure on the status quo players who are moving slowly on issues that people care about. If these legacy brands don't change the way they do things fast, keeping pace with outside challengers, they may well find themselves consigned to the scrap heap.

Move the Money, Change the World

If you're thinking about how little old you can do something to change the world, the answer is perhaps closer to home than you think.

The change (probably) won't come by changing who you vote for. You might get to vote once every four or five years and perhaps 10–15 times in your lifetime. Depending on where you live and the electoral system in place, your vote may make a difference to the outcome of the election, the leaders we end up with and the policies they pursue. But more than likely, it won't.

The change might come from going out and protesting. Activism serves a vital purpose. It makes leaders pay attention and moves the conversation, shifting what's called the 'Overton Window' of political discourse to make new solutions more palatable and give them a chance to become mainstream policy. But protests can be ignored. Once that initial spike of energy dissipates, the ripples on the pond die down and the news cycle moves on to the next crisis, has it really made a difference?

You could get angry. Have an argument with someone sat on the other side of an issue and try and change their attitudes and behaviour. But our beliefs are a fundamental part of our identity that we've invested a lot of time into, and often inherited from previous generations, so rather than bringing someone round to your way of thinking, it's likely to lead to arguments, raised heckles and a more deeply entrenched position. In a world swimming with information (and disinformation), our confirmation bias means we can always find a source that confirms what we already believe that we can use to 'win' against the other side. This kind of arguing gets us nowhere and leads to a society more divided than ever.

The change is going to come about much more slowly and quietly and it will be driven by humanity's most powerful invention. Not the wheel, the aeroplane, religion, nuclear power, the iPhone or peanut butter.

Looking back at our thousands of years on the planet, it is clear that money is our most powerful invention. Money makes things happen. It's the invention that drives the growth of nations and companies, unlocks innovation and fuels progress. Money has solved countless problems in the past, leading to progress in life expectancy, disease prevention and education. It has helped countries recover from war, famine and pandemics and is probably the most powerful tool we have in the fight against climate change. Money is the closest we've come to inventing time travel, borrowing against a hypothetical future to make our lives better in the present.

Money is the ultimate unifying force in the world. It transcends politics. No matter your worldview, race, religion or location, the need for money is universal. It bestows status and power, it helps us buy the things we need for survival, it makes life easier.

That coin or note sat in your pocket, or more accurately now, the card or phone app that we use to buy things, carries more power than you can possibly imagine. Each of us spends money every single day on a wide variety of things: food, drink, clothes, transport, housing and entertainment. The average American spends $199 each day when you tot this all up (around $72,967 each year).[*] That means the entire US population spends over $15 trillion annually, accounting for 68 per cent of Gross Domestic Product (GDP) in the first quarter of 2024.[†] UK consumers collectively spend £1.6 trillion every year, 60 per cent of the nation's GDP of £2.687 trillion.[‡] Consumer spend accounts for the majority of spend in almost every economy on earth at 63 per cent on average[§] and is forecast to reach US$77 trillion a year by 2029.[¶]

Consumer spend is the most powerful lever we have to tackle the world's biggest problems. Moving just 1 per cent of consumer spend to Change Brands would make an enormous difference. In the UK, 1 per cent would mean £16 billion each year. In the US, that 1 per cent would mean $150 billion flowing to brands that are making a positive impact on society and the planet each year. Globally, that 1

---

* Statista Research Department. May 2024. https://www.statista.com/statistics /247455/annual-us-consumer-expenditures/#:~:text=In per cent202022 per cent2C per cent20the per cent20average per cent20annual,totaled per cent20to per cent2072 per cent2C967 per cent20U.S. per cent20dollars.

† U.S. Bureau of Economic Analysis.

‡ House of Commons Library 2024. https://commonslibrary.parliament.uk/research-briefings/sn02783/ https://commonslibrary.parliament.uk/research-briefings/sn0278 7/#:~:text=GDP per cent20by per cent20Expenditure,compared per cent20with per cent20the per cent20previous per cent20quarter.

§ The Global Economy.com https://www.theglobaleconomy.com/rankings/household _consumption/

¶ Statista – Jan 2024 https://www.statista.com/forecasts/1160305/consumer-spending-forecast-in-the-world#:~:text=The per cent20global per cent20total per cent20consumer per cent20spending,a per cent20new per cent20peak per cent20in per cent202029.

per cent shift would add up to over $700 billion. We don't need to move all the money, just a tiny shift of one or two per cent would be genuinely world-changing. Starting to move the money from companies that contribute to problems to those that are part of the solution is the fastest way to change the world.

Looking at things this way puts the power firmly in the hands (and pockets) of the consumer. This is one of the reasons there is a keyboard button on the front cover of this book – it's in our power to press it and drive change in the world.

Instead of making a lot of noise to try and change government policy, or drive change through an election result, a collective shift in consumer spend can drive change in society from the bottom up. It can force through legislation change and make politicians reconsider their priorities. And the great thing is, you don't even need to leave the house! You can change the world without even needing to change out of your favourite pyjamas.

How our money is spent has more potential to change the world than how we vote or almost anything else we can possibly do with our time on this planet.

Every transaction can act as a vote for the world you want to live in. Putting convenience and availability to one side, if the option presents itself to meet your needs with a brand making a positive difference to the world, then spending the money in your pocket in the right way is the start of that change. The more transactions that go to Change Brands, the bigger the impact these brands can have.

Every single purchase you make with a Change Brand is a marginal gain towards a better world. Another tree planted. Another plastic bottle, deodorant can or toothpaste tube saved from landfill or the ocean. Another meal to a family battling poverty. Another chance for someone trying to get off the streets. Another vote for slavery-free chocolate. Another house powered by the sun and the wind. While these brands may cost a little more initially, once they reach scale and increase distribution, their prices fall quickly and they can compete on something closer to a level playing field – and that's when their impact can grow exponentially.

If the brands and businesses that are having success and capturing an ever-growing amount of dollars, pounds, euros, yuan and yen are the ones making a positive difference in the world, this can only be a good thing. They become the businesses that financial markets and investors put their money behind; the brands dominating our supermarket shelves and ad breaks. They get the chance to work with politicians to shape legislation because power and money go hand in hand.

It may seem like a long shot to say that these brands can become the default option, rather than the outsider, but an increasingly well-trodden path is starting to form. It's straightforward to develop a brand and take it to market through a range of ecommerce platforms. People are more open to new brands through the rise of Direct to Consumer propositions and Amazon. Sustainability and social impact are becoming increasingly key purchase drivers across a range of categories and for more and more people. One per cent market share in these enormous categories is enough to be taken very seriously and is more in reach than ever.

This book will walk through the rise of Change Brands. It will talk about the impact they're having on the world and why now is the right time for these brands to rise. We'll also unpack the effect these brands are having on legacy brands, putting them under increasing pressure and forcing them to change their ways or be made obsolete. The second part of the book will walk through the key steps in creating a Change Brand and growing it to a point where your impact meets your ambition.

We'll hear from some brilliant founders and leaders of Change Brands, gaining an insight into their incredible journey so far and their ambitions for the future. We'll hear about the journey they were on before launching their brands, the spark that led to the creation of their brand and business and the trials and tribulations along the way. This will give us a valuable insight into what it takes to turn a powerful idea into a successful business with the power to change the world.

It's vitally important that the debate isn't a one-sided one. We need to consider what it's like within these massive multinational organizations and why, despite positive change becoming increasingly prominent on the agenda, these businesses aren't moving faster. So, to make sure we understand the challenges from both sides, we'll also hear from our very own spy in the camp of big FMCG companies. 'Agent Change' holds a prominent role within one of the big 11 companies mentioned earlier in this chapter and their input has been invaluable in ensuring we have a balanced argument.

We are stood on the cusp of a decade of disruption. A huge window of opportunity for Change Brands to really shake things up and move society forward. The chance is there to use humanity's most powerful invention to change things and tackle major issues, proving an alternative model of capitalism that can work for everyone along the way.

The cumulative power of money and consumerism, pointed in the right direction, can make a major dent in the world's problems rather than add to them. Because if enough people change how they spend their money, we really can change the world.

CHAPTER TWO

Change How You Spend Your Money, Change the World

'It always seems impossible, until it is done.'

Nelson Mandela

Change how people spend their money to change the world. Sounds simple, doesn't it? Well, it's certainly simpler than the alternatives.

Trying to persuade companies to move away from a model and entire system that prioritizes shareholder return and profit above all else is a seriously difficult task. How do you change an entire system where all the incentives are aligned to growth, profitability and share price? The same is true of trying to get government alignment to change legislation to bring about positive change and better business practices. Getting a single national government to do this amidst a web of vested interests, self-preservation and political ideologies is no mean feat. And then building global alignment across hundreds of governments with their own national interests and internal challenges is mind-boggling in its complexity. Just look at the repeated failure of global legislation on climate change despite decades of conferences to try and build a consensus.

How about changing what regular people do? Surely that is something that is in our power? Businesses and governments do have a tendency to pass the buck and expect people to make changes. Putting the onus on the consumer to change when they won't make changes themselves. But driving significant, lasting behaviour change at a population level to try and get us past some of the thornier issues facing humanity is extremely complex. Billions of people, emotional, irrational and unpredictable. Each one facing their own challenges in life and playing the cards they are dealt, while being expected to remember all these little changes and behaviours to make the world a better place.

Trying to change the behaviour of billions of people to find a way to minimize the effects of climate change, for example, is close to an impossible task. How do you change the behaviour of 8 billion people? And individual actions are only a tiny part of the change required to get us on the right path.

Millions upon millions have been spent on getting us to recycle more, turn off light switches and reduce food waste. 'Nudges' have been introduced to try and encourage us to do the right thing. Implementing nudges has become a bit of a cop-out for politicians when passing legislation or tackling the thornier side of a problem is deemed too hard or the people affected are too powerful. A little prompt to nudge us in the right direction might help and will perhaps deliver some incremental improvement. But we can't nudge our way past climate change.

Changing behaviour is hard. Humans are creatures of habit whose behaviours have evolved over millennia. We spend most of our time on autopilot. We love to take the easy option, follow the familiar and take the path most travelled. Behavioural science has shown that we are predominantly emotional in our behaviour, not rational, which makes us wonderfully unpredictable. Life is hugely complex and it's difficult to cut through the noise and make a meaningful difference. A campaign might get people to change their behaviour once, or for a short time, but will it lead to lasting behaviour change?

The same is true in the case of other positive outcomes. Major campaigns to encourage people to exercise more, smoke less, eat healthier, have safer sex... the list goes on. There's a day for this behaviour change. A month for another one. An influencer telling me to do something. Campaign after campaign imploring me to live a better life and change what I do. For my own sake, for my kids, for the planet. But putting fruit by the checkout rather than chocolate isn't going to end obesity.

There's a whole world of academia and business consultancy dedicated to changing behaviour (something I've been a part of for the last decade). Daniel Kahneman and Richard H. Thaler won the Nobel Prize in Economic Sciences (2002 & 2017 respectively) for shedding fresh light on the incredibly tricky task of changing human behaviour. It's a vitally important sector. A discipline with the noble ambition to change human behaviour for the better, for the sake of all of us. But changing human behaviour is hard. It takes a lot of time, considerable resources and the ability to keep doing it year after year. Government priorities change, charities need to move on to the next issue. And then we slide back to square one.

We're often trying to fight the tide of evolution. Attempting to change behaviours developed over thousands of years that have played a big part in our survival. In the past, our preference for high-calorie foods was a useful survival tool to see us through any period of food scarcity, but nowadays fuels the rising tide of obesity. But people already buy toilet paper. They already drink coffee, eat chocolate, wear shoes, chew gum, clean their houses, use tampons, drive a car, surf the internet and brush their teeth.

And they probably always will.

We're just talking about getting them to change the brand they buy to one that's a little bit better. And it doesn't have to be every single time they buy something, just start buying brands that are part of the solution and change will start to happen. These transactions quickly add up to something much bigger. This sort of behaviour change is far easier than driving major lifestyle changes around sustainability and health. In fact, people are already doing it every day. Competition is the lifeblood of the capitalist system. We're not saying we want consumers to buy more or buy less, we're saying spend that money in a slightly smarter way. With a brand that is part of the solution, rather than part of the problem.

This kind of tiny behaviour change is something we can genuinely achieve. Pick one brand over another, it's as simple as that. If brands that offer a better option or a positive impact exist in a category and they're easily available to people, it becomes a no-brainer to switch. A good product that meets your needs and makes you feel good at the same time. This sort of switch goes with the flow of human behaviour rather than fighting the tide and trying to cut through the endless noise and complexity of life.

By getting people to simply make these tiny behaviour changes of just picking up one brand rather than another in the supermarket or when shopping online, we also start a conversation about other changes that they can make. If they're happy with one easy and equivalent alternative to what they've bought in the past, they're likely to be more open to others. Oat milk might lead to sustainable toilet roll and cleaning products; it could also lead to picking up a more ethical beer, coffee or water brand next time you're out and about. Changing the food your dog eats could lead to picking up meat alternatives in the supermarket.

In the early days of Change Please, we created the below infographic that showed the breakdown of the £3 you were spending on your coffee. By showing the two options side by side, and that 54 per cent of the spend on a Change Please coffee went towards changing the life of someone affected by homelessness, it became a win-win. When faced with the choice of buying your coffee from a massive corporation, or buying it from Change Please and helping someone off the streets, for most of us the choice becomes an easy one. Clearly it is vital to deliver a good cup of coffee, at the right price and where people need it, but when all other things are equal, the right choice is obvious.

Cemal Ezel, the Change Please CEO, has an interesting perspective on this. 'As soon as we're asking them to do something they wouldn't normally do, that's when there's friction. It needs to taste great, not cost them any more and be easily available. When it meets all that criteria, the table stakes in the category, it becomes the most obvious choice and the ultimate no-brainer. They get a great cup of coffee and also feel like they're doing good. It reflects well on them and their own sense of identity and they come back again the next day. They look for more ways to support your mission and they talk to their friends about it.'

Original Change Please infographic © Change Please

By approaching it this way, that simple change becomes an easy choice for people to make time and time again. And there are more and more of these businesses offering simple choices and better options that can have a positive impact on the world.

These small changes can create a beautiful butterfly effect. As people become more open to trying new things and listening to the messages these brands are putting into the world, change starts to happen. They feel that sense of reward and achievement that comes with making a positive change. This can then have a knock-on effect on attitudes and the bigger behaviours we discussed earlier in the chapter. It could encourage people to reconsider the car they drive, the bank they use, where their pension currently sits or how often they fly. By starting small and showing that ethical, sustainable and impactful options can be just as good, if not better, than their current choices, we start the ball rolling on a much bigger change. Effectively changing the world by stealth from inside their kitchen cupboard, slowly making these choices the norm, rather than the exception.

When this change starts to gather momentum and money starts to move, those in positions of power and influence have to sit up and take notice. Businesses react to losing share and have to make changes to their supply chain or marketing. Politicians can see it is possible to do things differently in business, whether that is changing packaging, tackling exploitation in a supply chain or moving to electric vehicles, and they then feel emboldened to pursue a change to legislation.

The Magic Number

We also don't need the entire population to change to make a real difference. With the amount of money in these categories, a few percentage points of market share are enough to make people sit up and take notice. These markets are worth billions of dollars every single day and the success of a brand is based on their understanding of consumer trends and behaviours.

The global toilet paper market is enormous. It's currently worth US$107 billion every year and is growing at around 6 per cent.[*] The

---

* Statista, 2023

US and UK markets are worth $17.5 billion of that. Until the last few years, the status-quo brands have had things pretty easy. Toilet roll, predominantly made from trees, has been wrapped in plastic and piled high in every supermarket across the world and sold at a healthy margin. But toilet paper made from trees is on borrowed time. Cutting down a tree to turn it into the ultimate single-use product is bordering on insanity in a world where we need trees more than ever.

The world is crying out for more sustainable options and recycled and bamboo players have come in and offered an alternative. There are numerous brands who have made a dent in those huge market shares of the status quo. Beyond Serious Tissues, a comparatively small player on the global stage, bamboo brands like Who Gives A Crap, Cheeky Panda and Cloud Paper have built sizeable businesses in multiple countries around the world, fuelled by disruptive brand positioning and a more sustainable option.

At present Who Gives A Crap have over 250,000 subscribers in the UK, buying on average two boxes a year at £48 a go is £24 million in sales and their retail sales are growing fast. Cheeky Panda have reached a 1 per cent share in the UK. In combination with the other players in the space, this means tens of millions in consumer spend flowing away from the major players to Change Brands. This has meant the big brands have had to react. For example, Andrex have introduced double-length rolls and Cushelle have removed the cardboard tube to reduce the amount of carbon used in transporting toilet roll and improve their sustainability story. Regina have launched a 'bamboo' product to counter this shift, but the reason for the inverted commas is that while it says bamboo on the front of the pack, the roll is only 10 per cent bamboo and 90 per cent virgin pulp – a pretty shameless piece of greenwashing to tap into the shift in consumer spend. This proves that when money starts to move, so do the big players.

A compelling piece of research by Harvard Professor Erica Chenoweth shows that what she terms 'civil disobedience' is the most powerful way of changing society and influencing world politics. The study of over 300 social movements between 1900 and 2006 showed that there is a magic number of 3.5 per cent of the population needing to participate for real change to happen.* Non-violent campaigns of civil disobedience were much more likely to achieve change than violent campaigns.

Civil disobedience can take multiple forms, from protests to general strikes to consumer boycotts. One key reason for their success is for the ease of participation. Those who would generally shy away from law breaking find it easier to join a protest or change what they buy. This sort of civil disobedience meant that it was far easier to get people on board, with four times more participants on average (200,000) than the average violent protest at 50,000.

There's an interesting historical precedent in showing the power of changes in consumer spending as part of the anti-apartheid movement in South Africa. The people behind the movement realized that while Black citizens had most of the economic buying power, that money flowed to businesses owned by the White elites. To hit them where it hurts, they organized a total boycott of products from White-owned businesses. A few months of this practice and it had created an economic crisis among the white elites that left them in total panic and so they demanded the Apartheid government do something about it. The South African leader, P.W. Botha, resigned and the reformist F.W. De Klerk took his place as President, leading to the first free elections in the country. The consumer boycott

---

* Chenoweth & Stephan (2012), Why Civil Resistance Works: The Strategic Logic of Non-Violent Conflict (Columbia University Press) https://cup.columbia.edu/book/why-civil-resistance-works/9780231156820

ultimately played a major role in the end to segregation in the early 1990s and shows that if you move the money, you change the world.

Another historical example of the power of consumer spending was as part of the abolitionist movement to end the slave trade. A key component of the success of the movement was the boycott of goods produced by slaves in the West Indies, particularly sugar, to undermine the economics of the slave trade. The Abolitionists created a tea set, complete with the sugar bowl pictured below, that advocated for people to switch their sugar from the West Indies to 'East India sugar' (from South-East Asia, particularly Indonesia and the Philippines), which was slavery-free. Imagine the stir this sugar bowl would have caused in polite society in England over 200 years ago.

It is estimated that at its peak in the mid-1820s, between 300–400K people were participating in the switch, leading to a huge drop in sales. Given the adult population at the time was a shade over 10 million, the magic number of 3.5 per cent (or 350K people) was reached. The success of the boycott, alongside other activism, ultimately contributed to the passing of the Slavery Abolition Act in 1833.

East India Sugar bowl from the British Museum © British Museum

Now while these two examples show the power of consumers boycotting, or not spending their money, with certain businesses to effect change, we are now seeing the power of positive movements of money and the transformative effects it can have. Boycotting a business or continuing to buy a particular product in support of an issue you care about is also far easier than going on repeated protests and hassling your local politician. Doing it this way is as easy as making a trip to the supermarket, or even easier if you subscribe to a great Change Brand online for home delivery.

In the case of toilet paper in the UK, the combination of that group of Change Brands is likely to have comfortably reached the magic 3.5 per cent mark when it comes to market share, with millions of people shifting the brands they buy. Collectively, these brands have made a major positive impact. Apart from the millions of trees saved by not cutting them down for a recycled or bamboo option, these brands also have a positive forward impact. To date, Serious Tissues have planted over 1 million trees and Who Gives A Crap have donated millions to sanitation charities through their impact across the world. Their growth has also driven the positive shifts we're seeing from the competitors described earlier and this simply wouldn't have come about if not for Change Brands disrupting the market.

As a brand setting out to drive a change, 3.5 per cent feels like a very achievable number. In these huge markets, a percentage point or two is worth tens of millions, if not billions, and it genuinely matters to the legacy brands. While it's not easy to win a percentage point or two from these established and well-resourced brands, it is possible with the right proposition and far easier than it was a couple of decades ago.

The Customer is King

One of the reasons why this approach is so powerful is because the big Fast-Moving Consumer Goods (FMCG) companies are marketing-led organizations who place the customer at the heart of key decisions. If they see a change in behaviour, they will move to address it. Agent Change describes what it's like inside one of the big players: 'A lot of the big successful CPG [Consumer Packaged Goods] companies are marketing-led organizations. Yes, they've got incredible supply chain capabilities, but culturally, they tend to be marketing-led. It's about the brands. It's very consumer centric.' This means that if people start spending their money differently and buying different brands, the big companies will very quickly sit up and take notice.

But being customer-led can also stand in the way of progress. If people aren't changing their behaviour, it makes it very easy to stick with what they've always done and protect the status quo. Agent Change continues: 'There's a danger in the kind of rationale that says we have to follow what the consumers want. So, if consumers don't want this then it's very difficult for us to do it. And if consumers do want it, then we will be there like a flash and we will make it happen because that's what we do. We meet consumer needs and we delight consumers.'

Clearly changes in consumer behaviour can be powerful in effecting change in business and getting other companies to act but this same tool can also be used to make a case not to act. Agent Change describes the downsides of a customer-led culture: 'The reality is there is the potential to negate our responsibility by relying on that idea. We're not going to solve anything by waiting for consumers to prioritize it being solved. Consumers do want things to be more sustainable and healthier and all that good stuff but today, they need something affordable. Today, they don't want to take risks. They want to buy something that they know they like and know their kids like... Yes, they do want it to be sustainable. But you know, it's fourth on the list. And it's difficult to see how that changes on a day-to-day basis.'

The desire is certainly there within big organizations to become more sustainable. Agent Change describes how the culture has shifted fundamentally in the decade they've been in the role: 'The company I joined seven years ago is not the same company it is now. The awareness of these issues is much higher and the desire to act is fundamentally different.' They go on: 'And it's not all down to altruism. The reality is the very expensive advice that is being given to CEOs around the world at the moment is that shit is about to get real and things are gonna start falling apart. That's what the expensive advice says, not from NGOs [Non-Governmental Organizations], but from massively capitalist consultancies and institutions.'

The need to make a shift is there for all to see and as a result, there's lots of people who want to make a real difference and drive these businesses to be more sustainable but making major shifts to the supply chain are plagued with difficulty (more on this later). This means that pilots and trials become an important tool in demonstrating progress, but they can also work both ways. It's relatively easy for big companies to introduce a pilot of a new product within a particular geography or retailer rather than rolling it out more widely. They might trial a new packaging solution or a new variant. For example, Coca-Cola have trialled removing the label from their Sprite bottles to make them easier to recycle. Unilever have trialled refills in cleaning and also had a compressed deodorant trial a few years ago to reduce the size of the product to reduce its packaging and shipping footprint. Pilots serve an important purpose for big companies: they allow them to demonstrate their commitment to sustainability and other positive shifts and merchandize them internally. It keeps the more sustainability focused employees aligned and engaged with the bigger mission. If it's a success, it makes a good case for positive shifts because consumers have responded positively.

But if a pilot fails, it does the opposite and makes a case to keep things the same. To maintain the status quo, take the path of least resistance and not invest millions in changing the supply chain. And it seems to me that there are always more failures than successes. The narrative surrounding Unilever's cleaning refill pilots is that it didn't work. Similarly, the move to compressed deodorant was seen as a major fail on their part. Some consumers might moan about Coca-Cola's move to bottle tops that are attached to the bottle to make recycling more straightforward. Is a little bit of negativity among a few people enough to call the whole thing off?

The cynic in me would suggest it almost makes life easier if pilots fail and there's no imperative to make changes. A case of 'the consumer didn't want it so we don't need to worry'. But if these pilots and launches aren't supported properly with marketing spend and the right messages, then they are almost destined to fail. And maybe that's the intention: create the appearance of driving progress while strengthening the case to do nothing.

I think we're seeing a case of cognitive dissonance at a corporate level in these huge organizations. Cognitive dissonance is defined as the mental discomfort that results from holding two conflicting beliefs, values or attitudes. It's a bit like someone who knows all the health risks of smoking but justifies it by saying they only smoke socially, or when they're stressed. Or they say their 'grandma smoked 20 a day and lived to 85'. The desire is clearly there in big companies to make positive shifts in their impact on the world but they also want to continue to sell a lot of their product, get promoted and take home a healthy bonus at the end of the year. They can justify it to themselves by saying the pilot failed, or that consumers aren't ready, but there is the opportunity for them to lead the consumer rather than follow. In Agent Change's words, 'Producers have to take responsibility. Regulators have to take responsibility. We can't just say it's down to the consumer.'

And who knows, if they lead the way in a category, rather than slavishly following what the consumer seems to want, it might turn into a competitive advantage. Listening too hard to consumers can become a straitjacket. Apple co-founder Steve Jobs famously said: 'People don't know what they want until you show it to them' to illustrate the limitations of consumer research and then there's the old Henry Ford quote that's always trotted out: 'If I had asked people what they wanted, they would have said faster horses.'

Change Brands can be more visionary than big companies. Instead of incremental improvements that nudge things forward, they can take leaps and create something truly ground-breaking. They can move quickly, ride waves in culture and react to shifts in attitudes to carve out unique propositions that address some of the biggest problems in the world. Let's look at some of the brands who have built a major foothold in their markets and have the big players sitting up and taking notice.

A Bad Taste in the Mouth

While working on the TV show *Keuringsdienst van Waarde* (Quality Control Service) in 2003, the Dutch journalist Teun van de Keuken was shocked to learn that child labour and modern slavery is alarmingly widespread in West Africa. Across the region, there are over 1.5 million children working in farms, with many doing dangerous jobs like working with pesticides or clearing fields with machetes. The average prevalence of child labour in the cocoa industry is 46.7 per cent, meaning 1 in every 2 children in cocoa growing households is affected.[*] This

---

[*] NORC – University of Chicago: Assessing progress in reducing child labour in cocoa production in cocoa growing areas of Côte d'Ivoire and Ghana. 2020

is particularly shocking because over 70 per cent of the cocoa used to make the world's chocolate originates from four West African countries – Ivory Coast, Ghana, Nigeria and Cameroon – with more than 60 per cent coming from the Ivory Coast and Ghana.

So, what could van de Keuken do about it? At first, he turned himself into the authorities for eating chocolate and tried to get a judge to convict him of driving child slavery. While this made great content on the TV show and struck a chord with viewers, he was keen to go further. In Series Two of the documentary in 2005, he launched Tony's Chocolonely by producing 5,000 slavery-free chocolate bars. It was a huge success, with more than double the original run being sold in a month. What was originally another publicity stunt became the foundation for an incredible Change brand that would disrupt the chocolate industry in a big way.

Douglas Lamont, now Chief Chocolonely at Tony's (previously CEO at Innocent Drinks), said, 'It wasn't supposed to be a company, it was supposed to be a documentary. Series Two became a bit like *The Apprentice*, with them trying to make a chocolate bar, but then it actually sold and they went "oh shit, we've got a business here!"' It really shows what can happen when an idea captures the public imagination.

Lamont continues: 'They realized they were journalists who didn't know how to run a business, so they got people in to run the business. Maintaining that original idea of raising awareness and pushing for change in West Africa, while running a successful business became a beautiful combination. But, I love the fact that it kind of happened by accident. The mission came first. We're an impact company that makes chocolate, not a chocolate company that makes impact.'

A delicious selection of Tony's Chocolonely © Tony's Chocolonely

It turns out that almost all chocolate consumed around the world and made by huge companies like Mars, Nestlé and Mondelez has an element of slavery somewhere within the supply chain and people are waking up to that fact. Bellissimo, a Swiss chocolate brand, inadvertently confirmed this when they took legal action against Tony's in 2007 stating that 'slave-free chocolate doesn't exist'. But the judge didn't agree, and Tony's won the case. Giving more oxygen to the reason the brand existed in the first place and highlighting the problem so embedded in the sector.* Tony's refined their mission to focus on the goal of 'together, we'll make 100 per cent slave-free the norm in chocolate', rather than claiming they were already 100 per cent slave free. They acknowledged there was still a long way to go and they would continue the fight.

Tony's Chocolonely now started really living up to their tagline 'Crazy about chocolate, serious about people'. Moving from

---

* Dutch News Feb 2007. https://www.dutchnews.nl/2007/02/sweet_revenge-2/

targeting people's eyeballs to targeting their tummies. By changing how people buy chocolate, they could make a big difference to the problem of modern slavery. In selling their chocolate, they could guarantee a higher and fairer price to their suppliers so they could work hard to eradicate slavery in the supply chain. They also make a difference with The Chocolonely Foundation, funded by a dedicated 1 per cent of Tony's annual turnover, that focuses on activities that fall outside of the direct supply chain, such as increasing access to schools and water pumps.

Their work on the ground within the supply chain has already been proven to be effective. Douglas Lamont says, 'When you run this model over three years and you give families a living income, child labour rates go down from the typical 46 per cent in any given farm to less than 4 per cent over three years. And that's again where the power of data comes in. It might not persuade consumers but in the conversation with retailers and legislators it's really powerful.'

He continues, 'We're talking about farmers being able to earn a living income of around $3 a day, up from $1.50, we're not talking about giving them all a Mercedes. When you run that over millions of cocoa beans and consider that the cocoa cost in an average bar is only about 15 per cent of the total cost price, it's a tiny jump in total costs.'

Given the positive impact on millions of families, that tiny increase in cost is inconsequential and it's difficult to see why big companies aren't starting to make the change: 'The big corporates have spent a long time saying, "we're on the side of consumers and if we put the prices up, the people won't be able to afford it and everyone needs chocolate". But as soon as the commodity prices in the world increased and their margins are under threat, they just increase the price by 25 per cent and the consumers continued to buy.' The recent rise in food shopping prices with the big players passing on the cost to consumers is proof that people will pay more.

Tony's rapid growth is another case in point that shows people are happy to pay more for something they believe in. Lamont continues, 'Yes, we're more premium on the shelf, but we're the fastest-growing chocolate brand in the UK right now. And probably one of the fastest-growing chocolate brands in the world.' They've been a huge success story on the back of this powerful brand story that people genuinely care about and the price premium hasn't got in the way.

In 2017, 12 years after the launch, they've reached a 20 per cent market share in the Netherlands and are now the fastest-growing chocolate bar in the UK, establishing themselves as the fourth most popular chocolate brand after Galaxy, Lindt and Cadbury.* They now have five lead markets, Netherlands, UK, USA, Germany and Austria and are distributed globally. In 2023 they hit $162 million in global sales. They're now making a major dent in the world's biggest chocolate market – the US – with listings in all the major retailers including Target and Walmart and even John Oliver taking up their cause with a lengthy segment heroing Tony's and knocking the traditional chocolate manufacturers. This was a major tipping point for Lamont and his team: 'That was a real seminal moment for us because suddenly all the retailers said, "let's go" and consumers are suddenly talking about us and you can even see it in our rate of sale. It's all just clicked.'

Tony's have been one of the flagbearers of the power of changing consumer spending for the better. The way they have built their brand has also been a masterstroke in how a small player can challenge the market leaders and we'll look closely at some of the tactics they've used later in this book, such as the unequally divided chocolate bars and their highly controversial advent calendar. They've also taken market leading steps to embed their impact within the future of the

---

* https://fortune.com/europe/2024/03/30/tonys-chocolonely-fastest-growing-chocolatier-uk-ireland-cocoa-industry-europe/

company and help other chocolate companies follow them on their virtuous path with their Tony's Open Chain platform for sourcing cocoa (more on this later in Chapter 10).

The Accidental Change Brand

In 2008, Milda Mitkute had just moved to Vilnius, the capital of Lithuania. 'I had just moved from my native town to the capital to study. I had to move my whole closet and the new apartment had much less space than I had at my mum's house. I realized how many things I don't wear anymore. I had over 100 items that still had tags on, or I had worn them only once. Lots of stuff in my closet but nothing to wear,' Mitkute explains. 'A thought popped into my mind that I must not be the only girl in the world in this situation.'*

'A few days later I was at a house party and I met Justas Janauskas, who was a developer. I remember telling him my idea at about 2am and he said, "why not, we should try it",' Mitkute continues. They agreed to meet again in a few days to think about name and action planning. Within ten days Justas had built the site. 'I took pictures of my clothes and uploaded them on the weekend. We emailed friends asking them to add items so we could make the catalogue bigger for the launch. We didn't have a launch budget but a few of my friends worked in journalism so we managed to reach some media contacts and radio stations and newspapers started getting in touch.'

The site was an amateur effort initially that they even forgot to include a 'buy' button. But that original idea from Milda that she wouldn't be the only person with a few extra items in the wardrobe was proved right. The site grew quickly within Lithuania and beyond.

---

* Business Insider https://www.businessinsider.com/milda-mitkute-vinted-cofounder -lithuania-success-2024-2 Nordic Business Forum https://www.nbforum.com/ nbreport/vinted-founder-from-a-shy-and-insecure-girl-to-a-global-clothing-player/

'There was no macro analysis, no budgets, nothing. But we were booming. By 2011, we were in the Czech Republic and Germany, and growing 60 per cent or 70 per cent a month,' says Mitkute. 'Top companies in Lithuania started offering to buy us, but we rejected all of them – this platform was our passion and we didn't want to lose that opportunity. Then we thought, let's try and spread this movement all around the world.'

Mitkute continues, 'We thought that buying second-hand clothing was a post-Soviet Union concept and didn't expect that other markets might be interested as well.' But when they did research in other markets including France and the US the audience saw the chance to make a bit of extra cash and consume more sustainably as key drivers. 'For us, it was an eye opener. Our business could be successful across borders.'

An early Angel Investor, Mantas Mikuckas came on board in 2011. 'He said "Guys, do you understand what you have created?" And we said "Yes, it's a platform for girls to sell items",' Mitkute reminisces. 'He said, no, it's much bigger.'* How right he was.

In the 16 years since launch, the platform that Milda and Justas built has become Vinted, the leading global marketplace for second-hand clothing. It has tapped into an increasing backlash against fast fashion and attracted people looking to live more sustainable lifestyles, as well as those looking to make a bit of extra cash from the platform.

It's no wonder its gathered steam when you look at the numbers surrounding the disposable nature of fashion. There are enough clothes already in existence to clothe the next six generations.† That means dressing the entire world for the next one hundred

---

* https://www.theguardian.com/fashion/2024/jan/09/the-vinted-phenomenon-how -one-woman-sold-her-clothes-and-created-a-billion-dollar-company

† Generation ReWear Documentary: Vanish and The British Fashion Council

years. Every year, 32 billion garments are produced for the fashion industry and 64 per cent of those will end up in landfill. At this rate, there's a pile of clothing the height of Mount Everest going into landfill every seven minutes.[*]

Vinted has ridden this wave to perfection. As of June 2024, Vinted operates in 21 countries and has 65million registered users.[†] It reached a £3 billion valuation during its 2021 fundraising round and has continued to grow since then. It made a net profit of €18m with sales surging last year by 61 per cent to reach €596m.[‡] While the founder Milda Mitkute has stepped away from the day to day, she remains an investor, and it's clear the company is in good hands.

Vinted are reshaping people's behaviour across the world. A 2024 survey of 100,000 platform users showed that 65 per cent of people have a wardrobe with at least a quarter of the clothes being second hand, and 37 per cent said at least half is second hand.[§] Almost three quarters said they were buying fewer items than before and just under a third now buy second hand more often than new. 'Our impact report shows that second-hand has the potential to become the first choice across Europe,' Vinted Group CEO Thomas Plantenga explains. 'But despite this positive trend, second hand is still a small part of the fashion market so there is a lot of potential ahead of us.'

What started as a platform for people to swap clothes and make a bit of extra cash has become a sustainability juggernaut. More than one in three of the items bought on Vinted avoided a new purchase. That has saved 679 kilotonnes of CO_2 in 2023 alone, the

---

[*] https://fashion-responsibility.fiveofus.com/#/
[†] Vinted.com/about
[‡] https://www.retailgazette.co.uk/blog/2024/04/vinted-profit/
[§] Vinted Impact Report, 2023.

equivalent of over half a million flights from London to LA.* Vinted is changing consumer behaviour on a huge scale and giving millions of shirts, dresses shoes and jeans a second life, rather than ending up in landfill. The brand is truly a triple win for consumers. They save money and do the right thing for the planet, all while looking good at the same time.

Smells Like Change

Every single deodorant you've ever used is still in existence. That's right, that first can of Lynx Africa or Old Spice you got from your aunty when you were a slightly smelly teenager, along with every single spray can or roll-on you've used ever since, is still in a landfill somewhere. And they're all still going to be on this planet when you are long gone.

Every year, billions of single-use deodorants are sold globally. They're extremely difficult to recycle and more often than not, find their way into landfill. The personal care industry, as a whole, is a huge polluter, generating 120 billion different pieces of waste packaging every year.† These are predominantly made from plastic: shampoo bottles, shower gel, deodorant, moisturizer, hair styling products. Plastic is widely used because it's cheap, flexible and robust, but a large proportion of the packaging used in our bathrooms never finds its way downstairs to the recycling bin.

The average British adult uses 312 plastic bottles a year. That's 19,665 during their lifetime, which is equal to four times the height of the Burj Khalifa skyscraper in Dubai if piled up on top of each

---

* Vinted Impact Report 2023 - https://press-center- static.vinted.com/Impact_Report _EN_2023_d4e3d4399e.pdf
† Zero Waste Europe, 2024

other.* While six out of ten people want to live a more sustainable lifestyle, the vast majority don't know where to start.

Freddy Ward and Charlie Bowes-Lyon, co-founders of Wild Deodorant, spotted an opportunity to make a dent in the problem and create something that wasn't quite so throwaway. 'Plastic is a huge problem in so many people's minds and bathroom plastic is so visible,' says Ward. 'We looked at the kitchen and there were companies already doing a great job there. In the bathroom there wasn't really anyone in that space, coupled with the crazy high percentage of all plastic waste that comes from the bathroom, which tends to be single-use. After all, how many households have two rubbish bins, one for recycling, in their bathroom?'

'With deodorant, it felt like a really easy product to disrupt,' adds Bowes-Lyon. 'Historically, it's probably been the most boring product there is. We felt we could go and create something that was really vibrant, really colourful and fun that people would share on their Instagram and be happy to talk about. Whereas I think previously the idea of people talking about their deodorant was probably kind of a farcical idea.' With this in mind, Wild created a beautiful, refillable aluminium deodorant applicator and paired it with 100 per cent natural ingredients that would be kind on the skin and work effectively, as well as being fully biodegradable. The product also contained none of the potentially harmful chemicals in traditional anti-perspirant, such as aluminium salts that block sweat pores.

---

* https://www.independent.co.uk/climate-change/uk-bathrooms-plastic-bottles-recycling-b1931829.html

Wild's innovative packaging and compostable refills © Wild

Wild has clearly struck a chord. Since their launch in 2019, they have taken the market by storm. After just a year they had reached 150,000 customers and in 2023 were announced in *The Times* as the number one fastest-growing company in the UK. In 2022, they hit £26.2 million in sales and grew at 441 per cent year on year.[*] They now have listings in every major supermarket and have also launched in Germany, France, Italy, the Netherlands and the Nordics, with the US and Australia on the cards in the very near future. Also, they haven't limited themselves to just deodorant, broadening their impact in the bathroom with the launch of a compostable, refillable bodywash, shampoo and conditioner. As a result of this huge growth, their deodorant refills have meant 6 million fewer single-use deodorants have been bought and they've diverted over 150 tonnes of plastic from landfill.[†]

[*] https://www.thetimes.co.uk/article/uk-start-ups-to-watch-sunday-times-100-p8p2bstjp
[†] Wild Impact Report, Q4, 2022

It's 'Wild' how much of an impact they've had just by changing the deodorant people use.

Search and You Will Find

The impact described above can extend beyond just how you are spending your money. There's even a Change brand challenging one of the biggest tech companies on the planet in Google. A company so ubiquitous that they're not just a brand, they're a verb. If someone asks you a question that you don't know the answer to, you're very likely to Google it. Well, please allow me to suggest you Google a great German company called Ecosia.

Every time you search for something on Google, they make money from advertising revenue. Those first few results that pop up when you search are paid for as part of a bidding system that brands pay healthily for to ensure they're top of the pile. And with more than 2.4 million searches happening on Google every single minute of every single day, that's a lot of advertising revenue. About 80 per cent of Google's revenue comes from the ads it places next to search engine results, on sites across the internet and before YouTube videos. In 2023, Google's advertising revenue amounted to US$237.86 billion.[*] A very pretty penny indeed.

Alternative search engine Ecosia, on the other hand, is diverting all of its surplus profit into a more positive direction. The idea took shape when founder Christian Kroll was travelling through Nepal and South America, where he witnessed social inequality and massive deforestation. He returned to Berlin knowing that he wanted to start a business that would put its profits into ecological

---

* Statista, 2024. https://www.statista.com/statistics/266249/advertising-revenue-of
-google/#:~:text=In per cent202023 per cent2C per cent20Google's per cent20ad per
cent20revenue,and per cent20apps) per cent20to per cent20web per cent20users.

conservation. He settled on creating a profitable search engine business with a positive impact, focused on reforesting the planet, and Ecosia was born. It would still fulfil the familiar role of a search engine, but it would use the revenue generated from advertising results to fund tree planting projects.

An incredibly simple idea – like most good ideas – that started small and has snowballed into something huge.

Today, 20 million people are now using Ecosia as their search engine. It's now the fifth largest search engine in the US and at the time of writing, Ecosia have planted over 210 million trees in 35 countries across the world and diverted €85 million from advertising income to tree planting programmes. Over 25 million trees were planted in 2023 alone. This makes Ecosia the largest financier of tree restoration in the world and the search engine produces enough renewable energy from solar plants they've built themselves to power all searches made on Ecosia twice over.

It's not been easy to break the status quo in the search market as people are slow to change away from the default browsing options on their laptop or mobile device but new laws recently passed in Europe mean that it's now simpler to make Ecosia the default search engine and browser on your mobile phone and desktop rather than automatically being pushed to native Apple or Google browsers. The EU's Digital Markets Act is a once-in-a-decade piece of legislation that has the potential to really start to level out the digital playing field, which has been dominated by just a few incumbents for so long.

The company also now has their own browser for desktop, something that has been a long time coming but is a potential game changer for Ecosia, making it easier than ever to take climate action and plant trees as you browse. The great thing about this switch is that it is something you do once with no costs attached and then just go about your browsing as before without giving it a second thought. Carry on as you were, but with added tree planting impact.

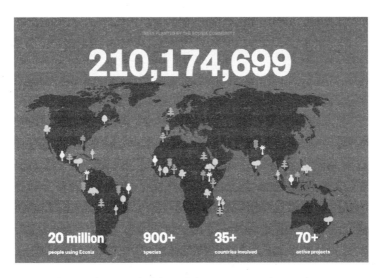

Ecosia's tree planting dashboard (correct at 3 July 2024) © Ecosia

Despite this incredible achievement, Christian Kroll's ambition remains undimmed. The importance of tree planting in the fight against climate change has been much talked about by numerous scientists and using humanity's unwavering thirst for knowledge (or cat videos) to fund restoration and green initiatives could be the way forward: 'We need to plant a trillion trees as quickly as possible. We're still far away from achieving that – by we, I mean not just Ecosia, but we as a global society – we have to scale up.'

It's a huge ambition but one that Ecosia has the potential to be the conduit for: 'We calculated that if everyone used us instead of Google, we could plant around 300 billion trees every year and we would get to that 1 trillion very quickly – it's not impossible but we need more users to do it.'*

---

* https://www.forbes.com/sites/mariannelehnis/2022/08/25/if-everyone-used-us-instead-of-google-we-could-plant-300-billion-trees-a-year-says-ecosia-founder-christian-kroll/?sh=7a51f730f0a3

The runaway success of Ecosia has given them the ability to broaden their impact beyond the original tree planting mission to support climate vulnerable communities and bring biodiversity back to degraded landscapes around the world to ensure the trees thrive for future generations. Ecosia has also moved towards contributing to a growing number of climate impact projects, including renewable energy, regenerative agriculture and supporting Europe's largest climate tech venture capital fund, the World Fund.

So, there you have it – change how you search the internet and you can change the world.

The Cost of Change

There are all sorts of Change Brands in all sorts of categories having major success with a business model that is not just commercially successful but also has a positive impact on the world but one thing we haven't talked about yet is price. One challenge faced by Change Brands is that they tend to operate at a price premium to the mainstream of the market. Let's call it a 'Purpose Premium'. The fact of the matter is that to do things differently in the manufacturing process, it often costs more than doing things in the same way as everybody else.

By their very nature Change Brands are also smaller than the established major players so they don't have anything close to the same economies of scale. When you're making things in smaller quantities, and you're looking to do it differently, it inevitably costs more. And when people's finances are under pressure as the global economy dances on the precipice of recession, this makes it harder for Change Brands to genuinely shift consumer behaviour on a large scale by going fully mainstream.

Slavery- and child labour-free chocolate costs more than chocolate sourced through the usual channels. The transparency of the supply chain required to eliminate slavery and child labour and the governance, checks and balances required to keep it that way means the chocolate has a higher cost. In the UK a Tony's bar currently costs around £3 and a bar of Cadbury's Dairy Milk is £2. Is a 50 per cent price premium worth paying for a chocolate bar that hasn't been created through child slavery?

The same is true for Oatly. A half-gallon carton is at present $5.23 in Walmart, compared to $3.57 for a gallon of regular whole milk. This represents a price premium of 46 per cent for the smaller, planet-friendly version and if you went for a full gallon of Oatly, it's almost three times as expensive.

But as Change Brands grow, they can narrow the gap and get closer to the prices people are paying for big-name brands. Change Please coffee costs exactly the same as any other coffee on the high street. In supermarkets, the brand currently retails for £4.50, just a tiny bit more than a bag of Taylors of Harrogate, the UK's leading coffee bean brand at £4.30 a bag. When the price is this close at a premium of under 5 per cent, it becomes a much easier decision for the consumer. If they're looking to make a positive impact with the brands they buy, picking Change Please instead of the branded competitor becomes almost a no-brainer.

The same is happening in other categories. A ten-pack of Nuud chewing gum currently sells for £1 compared to 80p for the plastic gum-based Wrigley's Extra. While still at a premium, it feels like a small one in this instance. Serious Tissues is currently selling at £6.50 for a nine-pack compared to around £6 for a comparable pack of Andrex, just 8 per cent more than the market leader. And that's at very small volumes in comparison.

Cano Water, a UK-made canned water brand (the clue is in the name) is at present £1 for a 500ml resealable can and is cheaper than the £1.10 you would pay for Evian in a 500ml plastic bottle. Refillable cleaning sprays work out much cheaper over time because you're not paying for the plastic bottle and the shipping of water with every single purchase. Brands like smol have even removed the barrier of switching by providing the refillable spray bottles in a free trial pack.

Being more expensive than the current brands in the category is not all bad. While it may be out of reach to certain demographics, a more expensive product with an audience keen to buy it is actually very attractive to a supermarket buyer. Many of the categories they operate in are fairly commoditized with a battle on price and promotion determining the products that succeed. What Change Brands offer when they sit at a higher price point is a chance to grow the size of the category in value terms. If they can get their customers to trade up to a more expensive product, they will be ultimately generating more revenue from the same shelf space and growing the category. While challenging in times of economic hardship, this 'Purpose Premiumization' of a category can be a really smart strategy on the part of the supermarket when consumers have a little more disposable income.

As Change Brands reach significant volume, they can really close the gap on the big-name brands. The tricky bit is how do you get to critical mass so that you can compete on price?

The picture of how Change Brands scale looks a little like how a new piece of technology or innovation enters the mainstream. The journey they go on can be seen in the Innovation Adoption Curve below.* When the iPhone first burst onto the scene in 2007, it would have first been picked up by those people who are really into their tech, the innovators and early adopters who relish all things new and exciting. It's a key part of their identity. They scour tech blogs to see the latest and greatest and are happy to pay a premium. These

---

* Rogers, Everett M. (2003), *Diffusion of Innovations*, 5th Edition, Simon & Schuster

are the people who formed those enormous queues outside Apple stores all over the world. In the case of successful innovations, they cross what's called 'the chasm' and tip over into the early majority and have soon reached critical mass where that innovation can take over from the previous way of doing things. Once the early majority is reached, costs come down and it becomes far easier to compete on price.

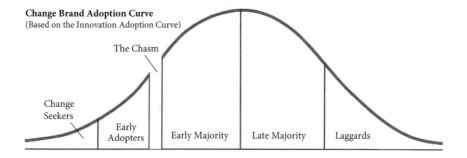

Change Brand Adoption Curve
(Based on the Innovation Adoption Curve)

The Chasm

Change Seekers

Early Adopters

Early Majority

Late Majority

Laggards

The same is true of Change Brands. The early buyers are often people who are very focused on the particular issue that the brand has set out to challenge, whether that is sustainability, health or a social issue such as homelessness. In the case of more sustainable behaviours, this group are likely to spend time looking for ways to live a more sustainable lifestyle and eliminate plastic from their weekly shop. This means they'll spend time on sustainability blogs or following sustainability influencers. They place a lot of importance on living more sustainably and so they are often willing to spend more, with a lot of them being in the fortunate position to be able to spend a little more to change their habits.

These people are vital to Change Brands. People who place a priority on impact and can afford to pay a little more will make changes more quickly and stick with that business along the way. They are also likely to become vocal advocates for the brands they love and support, helping to spread the word and adding an important layer of social proof. This group of early adopters help these brands cross the chasm and achieve widespread acceptance and adoption. It means they can secure a supermarket listing or two; they can also afford to spend a little more on advertising to take the brand to a wider audience than traditionally found digitally. And perhaps most importantly, it means they can access the economies of scale that come with extra volume that means that price can come down and be accessible to the entire population. In the early days of Serious Tissues, price was a major barrier with people being incredibly keen to support the mission and plant trees while they poo, but price proved a barrier for many. As we have grown, it has allowed our price to become more competitive and opened up a wider customer base, but there is still a long way to go.

Businesses can also play a big role in helping Change Brands to scale. Large B2B contracts for coffee supply for Change Please, including Virgin Atlantic, David Lloyd Clubs and Google, helped the brand reach the volumes that gave them greater buying power and helped bring their prices down for both the consumer and wholesale business.

Businesses spend a lot of money every year through their procurement channels on a wide range of other products, whether that is food and drink, cleaning, travel, uniform, software or banking. By changing how businesses spend that money to supporting Change Brands who are having a positive impact on the world, they can have a major impact with the hundreds of thousands spent every year. The same principle applies with businesses as it does with individuals. If we can change how businesses spend their money, we can change the world. One person might use 100 toilet rolls in a year, but a business uses thousands. Coffee is the fuel that large businesses operate on. If they're more thoughtful and creative with the brands they support, they can use that buying power to have a positive impact and help Change Brands to scale across their entire business.

The Great Purpose Debate is Over

Despite often operating at a slightly higher cost, it is clear that Change Brands are having a major positive impact on the world by changing how consumers spend their money. They're attracting more and more people into their respective movements and as they grow bigger and achieve greater scale, it will become even easier for them to steal even more share from the legacy brands.

These are brands that are clearly purpose-led, but their success is down to far more than just having a brand purpose. For the past decade conversation has raged in marketing circles about the importance of 'brand purpose'. I believe these brands are putting the debate to bed. It's not about purpose, what you say you're going to do. All too often this leads to meaningless manifestoes and empty pledges. Advertising agencies being thrown the proverbial turd and told to roll it in green glitter and make that brand seem more sustainable or mission-led with very little substance sitting behind it.

Impact eats purpose for breakfast every time. Change Brands have proved that it's not what you say, it's what you do. It's the actions you take that really matter. The impact you make on the world, both by reducing the negative impact of the product and increasing the positive impact a purchase with that business has. Tangible impact beats intangible purpose every time. Stories of people's lives being changed, calculations about the positive impact of that purchase, evidence of success… Prove that a dollar spent with you is better than a dollar spent somewhere else.

Change Brands have shown that we're living in a post-purpose world. The time for talking is over. We need to step beyond empty promises, greenwashing to paper over the cracks and just acting to maximize sales and profit margin. It's time for action. For brands that take a stand and make a difference to the major problems facing humanity. We're stepping into the age of impact now.

Do you want to come with me?

CHAPTER THREE

The Decade of Disruption

'The next thousand unicorns won't be search engines or social media companies, they'll be sustainable, scalable innovators – start-ups that help the world decarbonize and make the energy transition affordable for all consumers.'

Larry Fink, BlackRock CEO in his 2022 letter to CEOs

To say 'change is the only constant' in today's increasingly volatile world would be an understatement of epic proportions. While it's an idea that's been around since about 500 years before the birth of Christ, credited to the Greek philosopher Heraclitus, it certainly feels like things might have accelerated just a little bit since those days.

Social, political and economic volatility combined with the rise of disruptive technologies like artificial intelligence (AI) alongside the backdrop of the existential threat of climate breakdown means things rarely stand still – and this applies firmly in the business world.

One of the core principles in economics is the idea of 'creative destruction', introduced by the economist Joseph Schumpeter. This means new, successful companies and business models arise to dismantle and take the place of long-standing models that are no longer fit for purpose. It's a process of industrial mutation that revolutionizes the structure of a category or sector from within. The car replacing the horse and cart, digital photography replacing

film, the rise of streaming services, smartphones and the internet...
these are all examples of creative destruction. It's the idea at the
heart of the quote at the start of this book from Buckminster Fuller,
the famous American inventor, architect and futurist, that gave the
book its title:

'You never change things by fighting the existing reality.

*To change something, build a new model that makes the existing model
obsolete.'*

Creative destruction is accelerating. In 1965, the average tenure of
companies on the S&P 500 was 33 years. By 1990 it had dropped to
20 years and is forecast to shrink to 14 years by 2026. This means that
half of the S&P 500 companies will be replaced in the next decade.[*]
During economic downturns, with higher interest rates and capital
in short supply, creative destruction is at its most powerful.

We are now entering a decade of 'social disruption' where the
brands that have dominated for the past century are put under
pressure in a whole new way. We've seen entire categories being
changed by innovation, with the likes of Apple and Netflix rising
to dominance and leaving Nokia and Blockbuster in their wake.
We've seen the disruption caused to the grocery and airline markets
by discounters such as Aldi, Lidl, Southwest Airlines and easyJet.
We've seen customer experience-led disruption with fintech start-
ups like Monzo and Starling taking on the high-street banks or
Harry's and Dollar Shave Club going direct to the consumer to take
on the might of Gillette.

Social disruption is the next major market disruption. It will
form a key part of the next industrial revolution alongside other,
better publicized forces like AI and Blockchain. We're starting to

---

[*] Innosight Corporate Longevity Report, 2021

see its impact on categories across the board. Octopus Energy, a 100 per cent renewable energy supplier, has risen rapidly in the UK market to 6.5 million customers after acquiring Bulb in 2022 and Shell Energy in 2023. Method and Ecover, two eco-friendly cleaning brands from the same stable, have gained major market share and were acquired by SC Johnson in 2017. Wild, with their natural and refillable deodorant, have built a foothold in a category traditionally dominated by Unilever and grew at over 400 per cent in 2022 to hit £26 million in sales.

It hasn't come about by accident. Given recent developments, you might argue that the emergence of this rising tide of Change Brands was inevitable.

A Different World

As you would expect, Agent Change has an interesting point of view here. The rise of the FMCG giants came about because of the unique set of conditions that came together in the US and to a lesser extent, Europe, during the late 1960s and early '70s: 'It's important to understand the world where these companies were created. It was the time of cheap energy, subsidized agriculture and the creation of vast monocultures in the Midwest. The growth of the interstate highway system, with big trucks chugging along. Supermarkets where companies could dominate the shelves. The rise of television, but just a few channels so you could dominate the airwaves with your brand.'

A totally different world, it created a perfect set of conditions that they could use to their advantage: 'It was the most incredible environment for building huge brands within the US that could then go global through American culture and through the spread of this same way of operating the economy. And so that is the world big companies are optimized for.' But fast forward to the present day and things are fundamentally different. Adjusting to a different time presents a serious challenge to these companies: 'Energy is not cheap anymore and monocultures are a catastrophe. Plastic packaging was hailed as a miracle product in the 70s but now it is deeply unpopular and problematic. Supermarkets don't dominate like they used to so there's loads of different ways to buy things. We have many different TV channels and media, so monopolizing them as we did in the 70s is impossible. Regulation is getting tougher and consumers are getting more discerning.'

The fundamental conditions that enabled the rise of the big consumer goods companies have shifted. These changes have made life a lot harder and opened the door for Change Brands to come in and upset the status quo. Agent Change expresses the challenge they're all facing: 'The question all of us are grappling with is whether it is possible for a company built to thrive in one world to thrive in the next and we don't have the answer yet, because it's not been done. Nobody has done it yet. Or even got close.'

So while these huge companies that dominate what people currently buy have a lot of things in their favour – vast scale and manufacturing capability, universal distribution and deep pockets for marketing campaigns – they also were built for a different time. The world has shifted under their feet and just like the conditions that led to the rise of big FMCG in the 1960s and 70s, we are now seeing a similar shift in conditions that are working in the favour of Change Brands. Let's dive into the key macrotrends that have come together to create a perfect storm for social disruption:

I. A Major Shift in Attitudes

The brilliant book *Factfulness* by Hans Rosling et al. (2018) highlights what Rosling calls our 'negativity instinct'. In answer to the question 'do you think the world is getting better, getting worse or staying about the same?', more than 50 per cent of 18,000 people surveyed from 17 different countries answered that they believe it is getting worse. Turkey, Belgium and Mexico saw things through the bleakest lens, with close to 80 per cent answering in the negative and approximately two in three people in the US and UK believed things were on the decline.* This was from a YouGov survey conducted for the book in 2015 and numbers have been consistent since with a 2020 YouGov study showing 70 per cent of people believe the world is getting worse.[†]

This may not come as much of a surprise because you might sit in that negative majority. It certainly seems that way, doesn't it? War after war. Extreme weather events, poverty, crime, obesity. Financial crashes and pandemics. Escalating ocean plastic and an accelerated path beyond the 2°C mark. Heightened political rhetoric and highly charged protests... But when you look at the numbers, as Rosling actively encourages us to do, we're far better off on a lot of metrics. Life expectancy, crime, literacy levels and those living in poverty have all improved dramatically in the past few decades. But perception and fact are two very different things and perception is a far more powerful force in driving our behaviour.

We have built up a high sensitivity to potential threats because, ultimately, we wouldn't have survived very long if we hadn't. Fear kept us alive. But the world we live in today has fewer threats to our survival than ever before. We are living longer due to huge improvements in medicine and are far less likely to be a victim of conflict or violent crime. We are safer than we've ever been, but it's very easy to think that the complete opposite is true. Turn on the TV or open a newspaper and we are inundated with bad news and apparent danger – stories of war, murder, terrorism, knife crime, mass shootings, plane crashes and something else that will give us cancer.

---

* Rosling, H. (2018), *Factfulness: Ten Reasons We're Wrong About the World – And Why Things Are Better Than You Think*, Sceptre

† https://yougov.co.uk/topics/politics/survey-results/daily/2020/06/16/0c101/3

And the reason for this overwhelming tide of negativity and fear? Bad news captures our attention, but good news barely gets a reaction. Negativity and drama keeps us coming back for more to see how the situation is developing. We refresh the website to see if that threat has increased. At the end of the day, the news media is a business and it needs to keep us reading, watching and clicking to earn those advertising dollars. The social algorithm adds fuel to the fire by prioritizing content that people engage with, feeding our insatiable appetite for negative content. The always-on, 24-hour news cycle provides an almost constant stream of sensationalism and drama that plays to our evolutionary need to be highly aware of threats.

This hosepipe of negativity has certainly increased in intensity in the last 20 years. In the 1990s, someone might have read a single newspaper in the morning and watched the evening news, but now it's almost impossible to get away from. Access to multiple news outlets on your morning commute and breaking news notifications throughout the day direct to your pocket. Social media adds to the spread. Shocking footage travels rapidly and everyone has a voice, no matter how extreme their worldview. While in the past you might have been oblivious to many of the problems happening in the world, now it is almost impossible to bury your head in the sand and avoid them.

Now there are many drawbacks to this constant stream of negativity. It leads to increased anger and anxiety in society. It has a detrimental effect on our mental health and we find coping mechanisms to escape the stress. It creates threats where they don't exist and leads to calls to build walls or tighten immigration. It allows political campaigns to be won on fear, targeting our inner neuroses to win elections and harvest power, rather than setting out the best course of action for the future. But this greater awareness and concern also focuses the collective mind on finding solutions to problems that may have previously slipped under the radar. People who may have just continued going about their business and focusing on their own lives are looking to make positive changes that impact more than just themselves and they are advocating for positive change in society.

We have seen a generational shift in attitudes with Gen Z and Millennials (basically anyone born after 1980) being significantly more engaged in both sustainability and broader social issues. They are more likely to talk about the need for action on climate change and to have taken concrete action such as donating money, contacting officials, volunteering or attending protests than older generations. Pew Research found that 32 per cent of Gen Z and 28 per cent of millennials have taken a firm action, compared to 23 per cent of Gen X and 21 per cent of Baby Boomers.[*] This trend continues when it comes to social issues such as racial and gender equality, mental health and poverty. These groups have a stronger tendency towards action and change when it comes to the problems the world faces and this is in no small part driven by the rising tide of negativity we're faced with every day.

This shift in mindset extends to the brands they choose to buy as they look to make choices that align with their values. They look to put the health of the planet first, cutting down on consumption, reducing their carbon footprint, supporting circular solutions and buying previously owned clothes and electronics. Sustainability is more important than brand name when deciding which brand to buy according to 75 per cent of Gen Z.[†] They are also hugely influential over other generations, particularly their Gen X parents. Nearly 90 per cent of Gen X consumers said they would be willing

---

[*] https://www.pewresearch.org/science/2021/05/26/gen-z-millennials-stand-out-for-climate-change-activism-social-media-engagement-with-issue/

[†] 'The State of Consumer Spending: Gen Z Influencing All Generations to Make Sustainability-First Purchasing Decisions' (2022), First Insight and the Baker Retailing Center at The Wharton School of the University of Pennsylvania https://www.firstinsight.com/white-papers-posts/gen-z-influencing-all-generations-to-make-sustainability-first-purchasing-decisions

to spend 10 per cent extra or more for sustainable products. This figure has leapt from 34 per cent between 2019 and 2022, and the trend looks set to continue.

We're seeing a generational shift in mindset, with people increasingly driven to take action to address the world's biggest problems with sustainability considerations being a major driver of behaviour. This shift, in combination with the next trend is when things start to get interesting.

2. The Biggest Movement of Money in History

We stand on the cusp of the biggest wealth transfer in history. Baby Boomers and the preceding Silent Generation, who have benefited from rising house prices and growth in stock markets, are currently sitting on US$78 trillion of wealth in the US alone. The average house price of a US house has increased by 500 per cent since the mid-80s and the S&P 500 Index is up by 3,000 per cent since the start of the 80s.* To say timing has worked in their favour would be an understatement, but because of their good fortune, there is a lot of money set to be passed down to the next generation within the next 15–20 years. That $78 trillion will have passed almost entirely into the hands of Gen Z and Millennials by 2045.

So, if money is humanity's most powerful invention and suddenly a huge amount of that money is moving to a generation whose attitudes and values have shifted towards looking to address major problems, this is going to have a significant impact on society. This shift in purchasing power is likely to shift consumption patterns, investment behaviour and brand preference over the next decade.

The Bank of America goes as far as to predict that Gen Z will be the most disruptive generation ever, given the shift in attitudes and

---

* 'The Greatest Wealth Transfer in History is Here, With Familiar (Rich) Winners', *New York Times*, 14 May 2023 (retrieved 30 June 2023)

their growing spending power. Their income will reach $33 trillion by 2030 and surpass that of millennials by 2031. By the start of the next decade, Gen Z's income will then account for over a quarter of global income.* And these figures don't even consider the wealth transfer we'll see in the next two decades. The impact of Gen Z will also be seen in emerging markets such as India, Mexico and the Philippines with buying behaviours set to shift dramatically due to the high proportion of Gen Z in the population.

As Gen Z reach maturity and their spending power peaks, they have the potential to reimagine the world around them. While Gen Z is now a well-established term, I think there's an argument to rebrand this group as 'Gen Re' or 'The Regeneration'. They've grown up in an environment where the world's problems have been impossible to avoid and this has shaped their worldview. Their attitudes have been forged in this fire and they want to make a difference in the world with a bias towards action. They have the most to lose from climate change because they'll be in their 30s or 40s and having children of their own when the worst effects of climate change are predicted to kick in.

In the US, the Regeneration is the school shooting generation. They have grown up in a time where their lives have been repeatedly interrupted by news of deadly school shootings and can't remember a time when gun violence wasn't a major threat. Active-shooter drills in schools have become as routine as a fire alarm test. Is it any wonder that as they reach adulthood, they are using the tools at their disposal to change the conversation and vote against those politicians who resist gun control?

This determination, combined with the spending power they will soon inherit, means this group has a real opportunity to 'regenerate' the planet, navigate us back onto a better path and get past so many

---

* https://www.cnbc.com/2020/11/20/gen-z-incomes-predicted-to-beat-millennials-in-10-years.html

of the wicked problems facing humanity now. While it's a tall order for a single generation, I wouldn't put it past them.

We're already starting to see this shift in attitudes play out in financial markets. Impact Investing, which is simply defined as investing that looks to achieve positive measurable social and/ or environmental returns alongside financial returns, is growing rapidly. In 2022, the Global impact investing market currently exceeds US$1.16 trillion in assets under management and this has more than doubled since 2019, despite the challenges of Covid, when it was sized at $502 billion by the Global Impact Investing Network.* More and more investors are looking to put their money to work to address problems and this doesn't just mean individuals. Large institutional investors with serious funds under management are looking to change the way they invest. Pension funds, insurance companies and university endowments are being put under pressure by their customer base to align their investments with their values and the world they want to see. Pension funds have traditionally been major investors in fossil fuels, but this is becoming increasingly untenable.

The Climate Action 100+ is an investor-led initiative setup to ensure the world's largest corporate greenhouse gas emitters take necessary action on climate change. Target companies include the oil and gas sector, every major car company and FMCG companies such as Nestlé, Coca-Cola and Procter & Gamble. This is a collective of over 700 investors, including most of the world's largest banks and pensions funds, with over $68 trillion in assets under management. That amount of money buys you a seat at the table and they've actively engaged with 170 companies on their climate plans, putting pressure on boards to have firm plans in place and take appropriate action to accelerate the transition to net zero.

---

* https://thegiin.org/research/publication/impact-investing-market-size-2022/

The rise of impact investing and large investors taking a more activist role in driving companies to make changes faster is challenging the idea of shareholder primacy, coined by the economist Milton Friedman. This has been the dominant idea in business since the 1970s with the argument being that the primary responsibility of a company is to its shareholders. This results in a focus on maximizing shareholder value by prizing increasing stock price and delivering dividends to the detriment of all else. The principle of stakeholder primacy, where a company must consider its broader responsibilities, such as to the environment or local communities, as well as taking a longer-term view, rather than just thinking about the next quarterly results, is gathering momentum.

"Yes, the planet got destroyed. But for a beautiful moment in time we created a lot of value for shareholders."

© Tom Toro, *New Yorker*, 26th November 2012

Larry Fink, the highly influential CEO of Blackrock, one of the world's largest asset managers, identified this shift in his 2022 letter to company CEOs. He highlighted that money is shifting behind companies who are setting out to make a positive impact on the world: 'The next thousand unicorns won't be search engines or social media companies, they'll be sustainable, scalable innovators – start-ups that help the world decarbonize and make the energy transition affordable for all consumers.'

Money is moving behind the brands who are making a positive impact. Some of the Change Brands we've talked about so far have raised serious money from Venture Capital and Private Equity. Oatly was valued at $10 billion at IPO stage with Blackrock, Jay-Z and Oprah all taking a stake in the business. Liquid Death, a highly disruptive canned water brand that we'll talk about in detail later, have reached a valuation of $1.4 billion after multiple raises. smol, Wild, Tony's, Who Gives A Crap, Cheeky Panda and others have all raised significant capital to fuel their growth.

Attitudes are shifting to a focus on solving problems and the money is moving into the hands of people who want to use it to solve those problems.

3. The Rise of Political Disillusion

While society is faced with what feels like a constantly growing shopping list of problems to be solved, there is a major lack of belief that politics and politicians are capable of finding solutions. There is major dissatisfaction with the current political status quo, leaving people with few options when it comes to driving the change they want to see in the world.

More than eight in ten Americans (86 per cent) currently believe politics is more focused on inter-party fighting than solving problems and elected officials are often viewed as self-serving and ineffective.* In 2023, trust in government reached record lows over seven decades of polling, with just 16 per cent of people saying they trust the government to do the right thing always or most of the

---

* https://www.pewresearch.org/politics/2023/09/19/americans-dismal-views-of-the -nations-politics/#:~:text=More per cent20than per cent20eight, per centE2 per cent80 per cent9D

time.* It's a lot of hard work to keep up with the constant infighting and political point scoring. Indeed 65 per cent of Americans say they often feel exhausted when they think about politics.†

And it's not just the case in the US. Globally, across 17 advanced economies including UK, France, South Korea, Japan, Germany and Spain, an average of 56 per cent of people believed their political system needed major reform or a complete overhaul.‡ But while the desire for change is there, more than half of those polled have little or no faith that the system can be changed effectively.

One of the major issues is the complex web of vested interests and self-preservation that plays out constantly in politics. Once you're elected and have stepped into the 'career' of politician, the tendency to do all you can to be re-elected is simply human nature coming to the fore. You've achieved a position in the hierarchy that bestows power and influence on the individual and losing that seat would mean a step down in the hierarchy. This means that when weighing up decisions that will help you get re-elected at the next election vs longer-term decisions that won't payback in the short term, it's very easy to plump for the short-term option that maintains your seat. There is a strong argument for imposing a shelf life or time limit on political careers so that politicians don't see it as a lifelong career where they need to maintain their position of power and influence, more an opportunity to make a real positive difference to society in the time they're in office. If you're limited to a decade or so in politics, it focuses the mind on doing the right thing for the country

---

* https://www.pewresearch.org/politics/2023/09/19/public-trust-in-government-1958 -2023/

† https://www.pewresearch.org/politics/2023/09/19/views-of-the-u-s-political-system -the-federal-government-and-federal-state-relations/

‡ https://www.pewresearch.org/global/2021/12/07/global-public-opinion-in-an-era -of-democratic-anxiety/

and the future rather than what will get you re-elected or allow you to swell the campaign coffers with fundraising contributions.

This short-termism and self-interest is particularly true in the case of climate change, public health and education, where policies being put into place now may have a cost in the short term and may not pay off until years after that politician is out of office. This means health, the environment and education turn into political footballs, changing from government to government and allowing the can to be kicked down the road. On the most important issues, there's a strong argument to take these longer-term decisions that are so fundamental to society's future out of the hands of the politicians (who are so focused on keeping their seat in government) and allow them to be run by experts with a fixed budget in much the same way as the Bank of England or Federal Reserve have independence from central government to keep the economy on the straight and narrow.

Money is also seen to play a big role in politics and this contributes to the lack of belief in politicians. Eight in ten Americans believe politicians do a bad job of 'keeping their personal financial interests separate from their work in Congress', while 80 per cent of people believe campaign donors, lobbyists and special interest groups have far too much influence on the decisions made by members of Congress.[*]

If people don't trust their politicians, and don't believe politics is set up in the right way to change the world, where do they turn? Money plays such a powerful role in the world, including within politics, that if we move the money, politicians will have to follow. People are taking things into their own hands by building and

---

[*] https://www.pewresearch.org/politics/2023/09/19/americans-dismal-views-of-the-nations-politics/#:~:text=More per cent20than per cent20eight, per centE2 per cent80 per cent9D

supporting the businesses who are making the change happen as they see this as a stronger avenue for change.

4. The Changing Brand Landscape

Big brands used to be held in very high esteem. Brands like Kellogg's and Coca-Cola were seen as the benchmark in quality and had strong emotional resonance in people's lives. For example, Coca-Cola were the ones who changed Santa's outfit from green to red. They wanted to break down borders and 'buy the world a Coke'. Their Christmas advertising still holds a warm place in the heart for many with the famous 'Holidays Are Coming' song signalling the start of the festive season. Too many iconic posters to mention. But alongside these positive brand associations built up over decades with brilliant advertising campaigns, Coca-Cola are also seen as one of the biggest polluters on the planet. Single-use plastic bottles have quickly become a powerful shorthand for sustainability, or the lack of it. And as the world's biggest soft drink brand, ubiquitous in every chiller cabinet across the world, they've also become the poster child for ocean pollution. The bottle they've spent years building into an icon has become a lightning rod for environmental campaigners.

Brands that people used to love are increasingly under pressure to drive change but this is not a simple process. In the case of many major global brands, everything is optimized to within an inch of its life. A small change in the production process costs money and erodes margin. The impact a major brand can have by changing dwarfs anything that a Change Brand can achieve on its own, but it takes time and investment to make these changes. As a result of perceived slow progress where more sustainable options are entering the market, these big companies are perceived to be dragging their heels, which reflects poorly on their brand.

Alongside the changing perception of brands, the marketplace has also changed dramatically. First, let's look at supermarkets. Retailers' own label offering used to be seen as the inferior alternative to the branded options. Clearly it was a case of trading down. But years of investment from retailers across has seen own labels emerge as a highly viable alternative and a powerful competitor to brands. In almost every category from the chiller aisle to cereal to toilet paper, buying own label is no longer the compromise it was once viewed as. Private label share of market has reached 38.2 per cent across Europe* and this has eroded the advantage that branded products previously enjoyed, built up by years of investment in advertising. After 40 years of investment from retailers, 60 per cent of shoppers in Europe now believe that private label brands are as good as national brands.† This move in people's perceptions has basically opened the door for any new brand entering a market.

We have also seen a major rise in discount supermarkets. Aldi and Lidl have enjoyed massive success in Europe with a supermarket offering that doesn't rely on stocking the household brand names that you would see in major supermarkets. This shift towards the discounters was helped in no small way by pressure on the cost of living and the threat of recession and they've achieved a combined market share of almost 18 per cent.‡ Those who would previously have thought twice about setting foot in Aldi or Lidl were encouraged to look for savings and saw those savings for themselves on their receipt at the till. With more and more people flocking to Aldi and Lidl, and chatting to their friends about it, any social barriers that might have stopped them in the past disappeared.

---

* https://www.plmainternational.com/private-label-today#:~:text=The per cent20overall per cent20private per cent20label per cent20share,the per cent20first per cent20quarter per cent20of per cent202023.

† https://www.thegrocer.co.uk/talking-shop/the-growth-of-private-label-is-about-more-than-cost-savings/679257.article

‡ https://www.kantarworldpanel.com/grocery-market-share/great-britain

Aldi's long-running UK advertising campaign line 'Like Brands. Only Cheaper' was voted the campaign of the decade for the 2010s in a *Marketing Week* study.* By positioning their products as a much cheaper alternative to well-known brands in a funny and disruptive way, they further eroded the dominance of big brands. People have become far less tied to the giant brands that they used to buy and are far more willing to try new brands.

The rise of Amazon into one of the biggest companies on the planet has also had a major effect on consumer behaviour. As the world's biggest marketplace, the barrier to entry is almost non-existent and people are willing to buy any products that meet their need at that particular time and have them conveniently delivered to their home the very next day. This means the value of established brands is diminished and they don't need to go through the traditional gateway, retailers like Walmart, Tesco or Target, to meet their needs.

Another major shift in the marketplace in the last decade is the rise of Direct to Consumer products. A whole raft of new brands have emerged that have done their research and created a proposition they believed would resonate. Social media gave them a cost-effective way of finding the right customer and online ecommerce offerings like Shopify made it easier than ever to build a professional-looking and efficient website. They would then send the product straight to people's homes, cutting out the middleman of the supermarket and holding that relationship themselves, which would allow them to sell different products or be available on subscription.

The landscape has changed fundamentally and almost all the barriers to entry for new brands have been eroded to make it far easier to start a new brand and gain a foothold in markets that were previously out of reach.

---

* https://www.marketingweek.com/inside-ad-campaign-of-the-decade-aldi-like-brands
-only-cheaper/

A Perfect Storm

So, what's the result of all this? They all come together to create an almost perfect set of conditions for brands and businesses who are setting out to change the world.

People increasingly care about the problems the world is facing. This is in part due to a generational shift in attitudes and partly due to increased coverage and the ability of social media to spread bad news and shocking imagery quickly. But, despite increased protest and social activism, people have lost faith in politicians having the ability to solve these problems amidst a complicated web of vested interests, political ideologies and decision-making clouded by what's best for them, rather than what's the right thing to do.

At the same time as faith in politicians has fallen, attitudes towards the big brands have changed. Huge brands, such as Coca-Cola, that were celebrated and widely loved because of their advertising and brand positioning are now seen in a totally different light. 'Buying the world a coke' and announcing the arrival of Christmas with their festive trucks have been replaced by a position as one of the world's largest plastic polluters, seen by many not to be doing enough to move things forward and obscuring that inactivity with attempts at greenwashing.

Supermarkets have shifted the dial dramatically too and this has opened the door for Change Brands. People who would once have been highly brand loyal, buying only the leading brands because of the perception of better quality, have been persuaded that other options are just as good. First, private label options offered by the supermarket were seen as good enough to replace their favourite brands and then discounters like Aldi and Lidl came along and blew the doors off with their lookalike brands, aided by economic pressures driving consumers to give them a go to save a bit of cash. Amazon fundamentally changed the game with the ability to have almost any product you can imagine delivered to your house the next day. This hyper-convenience almost removed the function of brand as the algorithm just surfaced the product that would best meet your needs.

Direct to Consumer (D2C) brands then walked straight through the door that had been opened for them and have been one of the biggest success stories of the past decade. The barrier to entry for new brands of needing to be on supermarket shelves has been removed and with social media making it easy to reach the target audience, D2C brands have been able to build loyal followings without having to go through the traditional gatekeepers.

And finally, with the money shifting to people with the motivation to use that money to make the world a better place, whether that is through the brands they buy or going a step further and investing in companies making a difference, the opportunity for these brands to flourish is better than it's ever been. People are starting to realize their money holds power and they're using that power to build the future they want to see. This in turn has created a perfect storm for Change Brands. A window of opportunity for brands who have seen a problem in a category and created a product with the potential to make a positive impact.

CHAPTER FOUR

The Catalyst for Change

*'Change happens when the pain of staying the same is greater
than the pain of change.'*

Tony Robbins, bestselling author, life coach
and motivational speaker

This rising tide of Change Brands clearly has the established order worried. Brands like Vinted, Ecosia, Wild, Oatly and Tony's Chocolonely have proved they're not just a pesky fly in the ointment to be dismissed out of hand and squashed with their superior fire power but a threat to be taken seriously.

By taking market share these brands are really hitting where it hurts. Because if we move the money, things change pretty quickly. A 1 per cent shift in a category might not sound that significant on first pass but when you look at it in terms of cash, a single percentage point can be enormous. We're talking hundreds of millions in multi-billion-dollar categories.

Tesla's market share in the US and Canada has to date risen to 4 per cent of a car market that's worth over $100 billion. They have moved a long way beyond being merely an inconvenience to the established players. Now a clear and present danger to major car manufacturers, they have been the driving force behind the shift towards electric vehicles. US EV sales surpassed 1 million for the first time in 2023, outperforming forecasts to reach 1.2 million, almost five times that of the 250K sold nationwide in 2020.[*] It's the fastest-growing segment of the market and a key source of future growth.

As of Q3 2023, one in two EVs sold in the US was a Tesla. A 50 per cent share of the future of the sector is staggering but interestingly that proportion had dropped from 62 per cent at the start of the year.[†] A sure sign that the status-quo brands are working hard to compete and offer a decent proposition to car buyers. EVs have now reached 7.6 per cent of the US total vehicle market in 2023, up from 5.9 per cent in the previous year.[‡]

It's hard to think of Tesla as an insurgent Change Brand when they currently have a market cap of almost $700 billion and are in the top ten most valuable companies in the world, but there's no way the car industry would have moved so quickly towards electric vehicles without an outside player coming in, shaking up the sector and threatening their bottom line.

A lot has been written about the power of hindsight, but Tesla Motors CEO Elon Musk laid out this exact strategy back in 2006

---

[*] https://statzon.com/insights/us-ev-market#:~:text=EV per cent20Sales per cent20Share per cent20in per cent20the per cent20United per cent20States&text=Indeed per cent2C per cent20in per cent202023 per cent2C per cent20a per cent20remarkable,Book per cent2C per cent20a per cent20Cox per cent20Automotive per cent20company.

[†] Q3, 2023 – https://finance.yahoo.com/news/ev-sales-hit-new-record-in-q3-as-tesla-market-share-dips-194135842.html?guccounter=1&guce_referrer=aHR0cHM6Ly9jd3cuZ29vZ2xlLmNvbS8&guce_referrer_sig=AQAAANcQTJfRy38gXWZLYAPSuDIHaTzKNSNjH0HVWlTgwHG15DKSytQfEevY5nmJVWgo-6xsH6bcYqU7YuKRsII_oDOHXJvK_9D9gJ_ryzLU08AwjbJJk-hFTxEXrIJtP5rnNPtVGUsT92_qxoTzaGw8mdWNZJ5mXaVMiv3TNUR9-S1k

[‡] https://statzon.com/insights/us-ev-market#:~:text=EV per cent20Sales per cent20Share per cent20in per cent20the per cent20United per cent20States&text=Indeed per cent2C per cent20in per cent202023 per cent2C per cent20a per cent20remarkable,Book per cent2C per cent20a per cent20Cox per cent20Automotive per cent20company.

when he published a blog post on the Tesla site entitled 'The Secret Tesla Motors Master Plan (just between you and me)'.* In the first paragraph, he said, 'The overarching purpose of Tesla Motors (and the reason I am funding the company) is to help expedite the move from a mine-and-burn hydrocarbon economy towards a solar electric economy, which I believe to be the primary, but not exclusive, sustainable solution.'

The plan to do that was simple. They would start with a high-priced sports car, the Tesla Roadster, because new technology is expensive to bring to market. Musk continued, 'Almost any new technology initially has high unit cost before it can be optimized, and this is no less true for electric cars. The strategy of Tesla is to enter at the high end of the market, where customers are prepared to pay a premium, and then drive down market as fast as possible to higher unit volume and lower prices with each successive model.'

He finished by saying:

'So, in short, the masterplan is:

1. Build sports car
2. Use that money to build an affordable car
3. Use that money to build an even more affordable car
4. While doing above, also provide zero emission electric power generation options

Don't tell anyone.'

So, it was all part of the plan from the beginning. Not just to build a successful business, but also to force the other players to act and be a catalyst for a move away from fossil fuels. Musk continued in his follow-up 'Master Plan: Part Deux'† in 2016: 'The main reason

---

* https://www.tesla.com/blog/secret-tesla-motors-master-plan-just-between-you-and-me
† https://www.tesla.com/en_gb/blog/master-plan-part-deux

(for writing the initial master plan) was to explain how our actions fit into a larger picture, so that they would seem less random. The point of all this was, and remains, accelerating the advent of sustainable energy, so that we can imagine far into the future and life is still good. That's what "sustainable" means. It's not some silly, hippy thing – it matters for everyone. By definition, we must at some point achieve a sustainable energy economy or we will run out of fossil fuels to burn and civilization will collapse. Given that we must get off fossil fuels anyway and that virtually all scientists agree that dramatically increasing atmospheric and oceanic carbon levels is insane, the faster we achieve sustainability, the better.'

The impact of Tesla has driven established players to change their strategy. Volkswagen, the world's biggest car company, has committed in a big way to the shift to EV. The CEO, Herbert Diess even warned the troops 'we don't want to end up like Nokia.'* Saying, in effect, we don't want to become obsolete.

It's not just Tesla causing big companies a few sleepless nights. Change Brands are driving change across the world with their revolutionary business models. Tony's Chocolonely are the fourth-biggest chocolate bar in the UK market. In a category worth £7 billion,† that's millions in sales and votes for exploitation-free chocolate. And at a growth rate of 25 per cent per year, that's millions of pounds sliding away from the status-quo brands that continue to try and protect their share.

Liquid Death have grown rapidly from a standing start to turnover $263 million in 2023 through retail, more than doubling their sales year on year and proving to be a real thorn in the side of the traditional market leaders.

---

* https://www.bloomberg.com/news/articles/2020-11-06/vw-s-boss-warns-the-troops-we-don-t-want-to-end-up-like-nokia

† https://store.mintel.com/report/uk-chocolate-confectionery-market-report

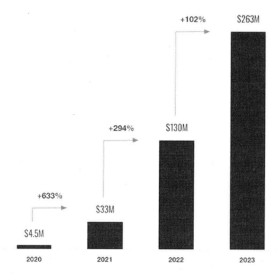

Liquid Death Retail Scanned Sales grew 102 per cent in 2023
© Mike Cessario via LinkedIn

Change Brands are not only vehicles of change existing in their own right and impacting the world in a positive way. Nothing exists in a vacuum and if they are taking market share and revenue away from the status-quo brands and occupy more of a place in the hearts and minds of consumers, these legacy businesses will need to react to what is happening to avoid becoming obsolete.

Change Brands are not just a catalyst for change in society, they are a catalyst for change among business. They highlight new paths, show that the 'impossible' is possible and move the needle so people expect more from the brands they buy. They keep big players on their toes, pushing them to achieve more and move faster, rather than resting on their laurels. This is perhaps one of the most important functions of Change Brands. While they can make a major impact on their own by shifting consumers to more sustainable or impactful purchases, their role as a noisy agitator should not be underestimated. If they can move major players like Coca-Cola or Nestlé to adopt better practices in their supply chain to compete, the positive impact on the world can be exponential. Better practices, combined with massive scale and reach, accelerates the pace of change.

Why are Big Companies Not Changing Faster?

This is the question on the lips of every environmentally minded individual. At a time when the need for more sustainable practices is extremely prominent, why aren't these major companies, with seemingly infinite resources, not moving faster?

I put the question to Agent Change and the answer was enlightening. There are two main reasons: scale and growth. These companies are scale businesses. The competitive advantage comes from delivering a brand and product that people know and love, across millions of touchpoints. Changing that at the scale required to make a difference is the challenge: 'You can't underestimate the difficulty of acting at scale. Big companies who have a plan and an engaged CEO are taking it seriously. And they're investing billions into it. The problem is that the solutions must be implemented at vast scale to make a difference. Introducing a new way of delivering your product, you can do that. The problem is how do you scale that up to a billion consumer interactions every day? Across many, many, many markets.'

In Agent Change's mind, this presents an opportunity for Change Brands to exploit. 'Small brands have the ability because they've grown from scratch, to start slow and start small with a new way of doing things.' They can work with manufacturers to produce their product in a different way, but this is harder for the major players. 'At a big company, you can do a million little pilots, but the trick is to do it at the scale that you're operating. That's the whole point of your business: you are a huge scale operation. That's where the value comes from – the massive ubiquitous brands where you're able to build the economies of scale.'

Scale is a huge advantage to these companies during business as usual. It allows them to optimize their supply chains to maximize margin but when the world is going through a period of change and people are expecting these brands to be leading the way and driving things forward, it becomes a major challenge. These major companies with brands people have loved for years are suddenly seen as part of the problem as opposed to the solution because they're not moving fast enough: 'Their incredible logistics expertise is the foundation of these companies. They are all based on the idea of scale. So, solutions have to be scalable and that's what's incredibly hard to do. When you've got something where there are distinct technical barriers, like new ways of doing packaging, at scale that becomes a gigantic barrier. Everything is hard even if you come up with a perfect solution. It's going to be more expensive, a lot more expensive, and building the systems around that to enable them to do it at massive scale.'

Despite rising consumer pressure, it becomes hard to justify the investment. 'The challenge for a big organization is where the sustainability transition involves significant upfront costs with long-term payoff and that is a real finance challenge that requires a shift in the way that finance teams think.' Massive upfront costs with the potential of a long-term payoff, but that is by no means guaranteed: 'Investing billions in retooling existing factories to meet these sorts of ethereal targets is a very difficult thing for an organization to digest and it's that kind of change that is going on in the background of big organizations that isn't necessarily visible, but which is actually quite fundamental.'

The challenge of scaling solutions is clearly not an easy one, especially when billions have already been spent on production lines and operations that are still fit for purpose. It's a huge cost with no guarantee of an upside, which makes it hard to justify. But this creates an opportunity for Change Brands. They can be nimbler and work with smaller manufacturers who also see the opportunity to grow; they can pick up customers with benefits that people are looking for. And done right, it can be very hard for the big players to follow without taking a hit to their bottom line.

One of the big questions asked by investors when faced with a new solution is 'why don't the market leaders just do this?' They clearly have a point. Surely it would be easy for the major players to make a small shift in their production to tread a little lighter on the planet and appeal to a growing consumer need? But as expressed above, the reality is very different. The change is likely to bring significant cost, the need for major upfront investment and a dismantling of the equilibrium they've built in their supply chain. Yes, big companies could follow Change Brands to quickly squash them, but the likelihood is they won't be able to move fast enough. Sign-off processes to justify the financial investment to change a production line don't happen overnight, so this creates a pretty sizeable window of opportunity for a Change Brand to reach the scale where they become an acquisition target.

The other point is that by changing their business practices, they are effectively admitting that what they've done in the past is no longer the best thing to do and that there is a better path available to consumers. If Mars Wrigley's suddenly launched a plant-based chewing gum, they would be admitting that most of their range contains plastic, which is hugely problematic for the brand. If toilet roll brands moved to recycled or other eco alternatives, they would almost be admitting that virgin pulp toilet roll that is made from trees is no longer the best available option. Change puts these brands in a tricky position and opens the door for Change Brands to walk through.

Alongside the necessity for scale in big organizations, the other fundamental challenge stopping these companies from making progress on sustainability that Agent Change talks about is the need for growth: 'So many of these companies are delivering much lower packaging use per unit and lower greenhouse gases per unit. The problem though, in terms of overall impact, is growth. If your growth is outpacing your unit impact reductions, then your overall impact is still going up and so even small increases in revenue can wipe out improvements that you've made over the year.'

When tasked with reducing the footprint of a business while the business is always getting bigger, you're fighting a losing battle. Reductions per unit need to outpace growth for it to make a dent and in a business world where growth is prized above all else, this makes it a major challenge: 'There's a fundamental tension there and yet it is impossible to imagine how you get out of that loop. Because the shareholders require it. The CEO that says we're going to stop growing the company will not be CEO anymore and somebody else will come in who isn't going to say something so stupid. The whole culture of the company is based on growth. It's muscle memory. Every instinct is about growth and winning and all these aggressive, hyper-capitalistic ideas. It's absolutely embedded in how the company works. If we're not killing it, somebody else is going to be killing it. It's kill or be killed.'

These two conflicting ideas of needing to grow while reducing overall impact are difficult for big companies to manage. It's like trying to plug the dam while the hole keeps getting bigger. Reassembling the rocket ship as it flies further and further into deep space. Growth will always take priority unless the business world changes fundamentally. 'So, within the failure, there is a huge amount of progress that is happening. And when it happens, it happens at vast scale. But the growth that the system requires can make hitting absolute reduction targets incredibly difficult.'

It's hard to see this unhelpful dichotomy changing any time soon. The only way for it to happen is for growth and lower impact to become aligned, rather than being in opposition. This means the brands that are growing the fastest and attracting more consumer spend are the ones that have the lowest footprint and do more good for society. This is why Change Brands need to grow because then these two almost diametrically opposed ideas become complementary and fall into alignment. Positive impact becomes a commercial advantage rather than a cost base. The brands that people are buying more often are the ones that are changing the world for the better. It changes the system, changes what's important and removes the sense of company-wide cognitive dissonance and conflict to get companies to focus on growing the right brands and changing consumer behaviour for the better.

A Cat(alyst) Among the Pigeons

It's interesting to hear about the internal challenges at big organizations. Understanding that they're not just delaying progress because they want to, but because of the way these companies were set up in the first place. There's a lot of great people in big companies who want to drive positive change, but it's incredibly difficult to do so inside the world they occupy.

This heavily conflicted inner monologue happening within the major players presents a major opportunity for emerging brands. Change Brands at their very best are the ultimate cat among the pigeons: they disturb the status quo, shake things up and make stuff happen. These major players might sit on their hands at first, slightly amused by the audacity of a new brand starting from scratch and attempting to take them on with tiny resources and armed with nothing more than a great idea and a belief that things could be done better. But as Change Brands start to get a foothold in the market, they need to sit up and take notice. Legacy brands that have been comfortable for years wake up to these outside agitators and realize that what has served them so well in the past might not help them in the future.

These brands are very happy not to change. Change means cost to them. It erodes margin and disrupts highly optimized supply chains. Change asks questions they don't want to ask. It questions brand strategy. It means they must invest in NPD. It means new hires, new skillsets. Unlike Change Brands, these big companies aren't setup to move quickly. Decision making takes entire months and sometimes years, needing to go through a complicated hierarchy and get signed off from every department who is a stakeholder. Decisions are researched to exhaustion. A costly process that could almost be out of date by the time the debrief happens. The ability to act on a hunch, take risks or try something different to see what happens has been managed out of these companies by process upon process.

Being able to think differently, take risks and start from a blank sheet of paper is an advantage to Change Brands. While they'll never have the firepower of a major multinational in terms of media spend or distribution, this ability to move faster and be unpredictable when the behaviour of legacy brands is largely predictable due to their slow-moving nature is an advantage that shouldn't be underestimated and goes a long way towards explaining the ability of these brands to steal share. And as these brands get bigger, that fleet-footedness is important to maintain.

Soon enough, hitting these big brands where it hurts as we've shown in the previous chapter is impossible to ignore. Less customers means less sales revenue, which in turn means less profit. It could mean targets missed and bonuses lost. A short-term blip might be able to be explained away, but after a while, the trend becomes impossible to ignore. The increasing brand power of Change Brands that comes from these brands being more distinctive in the category means they generate more future demand and the ability to sell at a higher price point.

So how does an incumbent brand try to turn things around? They might start to focus more of the budget on promotions to drive sales and prop up share. A new campaign? A celebrity partnership? Something with influencers? They might work but are only a sticking plaster rather than a long-term solution.

They might try and compete by trying to retrofit 'purpose' into the brand to respond to consumer demands. This could work for some brands where the product and an area of impact fit well together. Dove's Campaign for Real Beauty and their accompanying Self-Esteem project is a good example, as well as Lifebuoy soap's work in India to improve hygiene and health outcomes for millions of people. But for many brands it can be hugely counterproductive and an almost impossible task with the potential to backfire. Trying to force purpose into a legacy brand can be a bit like trying to fill Cinderella's glass slipper with an Ugly Sister's hairy size 14s. It can get very ugly indeed.

It might even descend into a spate of greenwashing. A brand making spurious sustainability claims to make themselves more attractive to the audience, but unless this is on a solid footing it is likely to backfire. There are numerous examples of brands attempting to bolster their green credentials but Coca-Cola, the biggest plastic polluter on the planet and a major user of fossil fuels to make that plastic, sponsoring COP27 was an example of greenwashing at its most cynical with minimal promises to improve their sustainability credentials.

So, do businesses stick with the current approach that's seeing them in decline? Look to find ways to protect the status quo, manage the decline and cling to as much revenue as possible? Or do they twist? Change the strategy fundamentally and invest in a big way to try and turn around that decline or slowing growth? This can be an expensive exercise with no guarantee of success. It's sometimes hard to know if you're throwing good money after bad and flogging a dead horse when the expectations of brands in the category have fundamentally moved past what this brand is known for. A tipping point will come when water sold in plastic bottles will be a thing of the past. Where single-use packaging will be replaced by refillable options. Where chocolate with slavery in the supply chain will leave more than a bad taste in the mouth.

Declining brands cause major problems for big companies. Their shareholders are hooked on a diet of growth above all else and if brands are losing share, then they become a stick with which to beat the CEO. If the decline continues across multiple brands, it can impact the share price and put company boards under pressure, leading to questions being asked about the strategy of the business.

If Change Brands continue their current trajectory, I believe we're going to see some major scalps in the next decade or so. Huge brands that have for decades been household names will lapse into irrelevance and ultimately become obsolete unless they fundamentally change the way they do things. At the very least, certain models and practices will become untenable and disappear.

The Kodak Moment

No one wants to be the next Blockbuster Video, Kodak or Nokia. Brands that led their categories for decades but were so slow to react to change and so invested in the status quo that by the time they tried to catch up, that ship had sailed. When all your revenue comes from bricks-and-mortar video stores or cameras with film rolls, investing heavily in a new route to market can seem like folly.

They've invested in the status quo and optimized it to within an inch of its life. They then act to reinforce it and do all they can to protect it, rather than react and change. In the case of Kodak, when millions of dollars were coming from a camera film-based model, they acted to protect it, rather than realize the opportunities that digital photography would bring, even though they invented the technology. The Kodak management's reaction when the first digital camera was invented in 1975 was 'that's cute, but don't tell anyone about it'. After all, it would jeopardize the film-based model that had been the driving force behind the company for decades.

In 1999, the new Kodak CEO, George Fisher, told *The New York Times* that Kodak 'regarded digital technology as the enemy, an evil juggernaut that would kill the chemical-based film and paper business that fuelled Kodak's sales and profits for decades'.* This is an example of the behavioural bias of Loss Aversion in full flow. Humans have evolved to prioritize behaving in a way that ensures our survival and that means guarding against losses rather than focusing on gains. In survival terms, a gain might have just made us a little bit more comfortable, whereas a loss, of food, shelter or water, could have been the difference between life and death. Landmark research in the late seventies, that would play a big part in Daniel Kahneman winning the Nobel Prize, showed that a loss is twice as psychologically powerful as an equivalent gain. Effectively, we would prefer to avoid losing £100 than to find £100, and when given the choice in various experiments, we almost always take the option that we thought would minimize losses rather than give the potential for gains.[†]

In the case of Kodak, this was loss aversion on a large scale, with the entire company focused on survival mode, protecting the millions in revenue that came from camera film. Kodak saw digital photography as an existential threat so they did all they could to protect themselves from the loss that would come their way as it reached mainstream adoption. They may have delayed its progress and banked a few more million along the way but when the inevitable happened, they were in no place to take advantage of all

---

* Forbes – 'How Kodak failed' – https://www.forbes.com/sites/chunkamui/2012/01 /18/how-kodak-failed/

† Kahneman, D. & Tversky, A. (1979), 'Prospect theory: An analysis of decision making under risk', *Econometrica*, 47, pp.263–91

the opportunities that could have come their way through taking a leadership position on digital photography.

There's an interesting parallel happening now in the world of sustainable cleaning products. A typical cleaning spray such as Flash, Cif or Clorox is 95 per cent water and shipped in a plastic bottle. Single-use plastic is a major and well-known problem. The cleaning spray sector in the US contributes millions of plastic bottles into the system every single year. The shipping of large quantities of water is also grossly inefficient when it is readily available in every household across America.

New Change Brands are emerging in this sector with a tablet or concentrated liquid-based solution that you simply drop into a reusable bottle and dilute with water. Brands such as smol, Homethings, Ocean Saver and Podsy offer a solution that you can have delivered directly to your home. Shipping tablets the size of a stack of quarters rather than a plastic bottle full of water are far more efficient in carbon terms. You can fit thousands more tablets in a truck than plastic bottles so the shipping footprint of refillables rather than single-use products is estimated to be 90 per cent lower per product.

In the words of Homethings co-founder Tim Keaveney, 'When I read that an average cleaning product is over 90 per cent water and packed in single-use plastic it just felt like a really bonkers way to consume. And that was the light-bulb moment for me. There is no need in terms of the product formulation to be shipping this product in this way and it's obviously creating a lot of downstream bad impacts. That's why we created Homethings.'

It clearly makes sense from a sustainability point of view to switch cleaning to refillable products. The technology is readily available with numerous brands popping up in this space and own label options starting to be seen on the shelves of supermarkets but something is holding back the massive legacy brands from bringing it to market. Keaveney continues, 'I think history has shown time and again that these big CPG conglomerates are not very good at starting up brands internally and getting them from zero to 50. You know, they're incredibly effective at taking a brand that's doing 50 million and taking it to half a billion through distribution. But I think there are massive challenges for them in terms of trying to retrofit the sort of sustainability expectations of a modern-day consumer onto those legacy powerhouse brands.'

One of the things holding back massive FMCG companies from running into refills is the size of the market. A key concept at the heart of the seminal *The Innovator's Dilemma: When New Technologies Cause Great Firms to Fail* by Clayton M. Christensen[*] is that emerging technologies and new markets don't meet the short-term growth needs of big companies. To move the needle inside a major corporation, a new opportunity needs to generate tens of millions in year one to make it worthwhile to pursue. This is often easier to achieve with a new flavour or variant of an established product than it would be to launch something genuinely disruptive. And this means they often miss opportunities until it's too late. P&G have tried to dip their toe into the water-free market with their brand EC30, which acts just like a Change Brand, operating via Direct to Consumer channels with almost no mention that it's part of P&G. At this stage, it's an experiment that is worth keeping a close eye on as this idea of innovating from within large FMCG and disrupting your own categories is one of the key recommendations of *The Innovator's Dilemma*.[†]

In the words of Agent Change, 'The overriding school of thought is that if it isn't making tens of millions in year one, we shouldn't do it. Big FMCG expectations simply aren't compatible with the reality of how sustainable innovations launch.' These companies

---

[*] Christensen, C.M. (1997), *The Innovator's Dilemma: When New Technologies Cause Great Firms to Fail*, Harvard Business School Press

[†] More on EC30 in Chapter 11

are so focused on growth and the need to demonstrate that to their shareholders, and sometimes the opportunities in these spaces are too small for them to bother with, at least in the first year. A couple of million extra in revenue almost isn't worth it, even if the longer-term opportunity is far bigger than that. That is barely a drop in the ocean for companies turning over tens of billions every year. For growth to move the needle it needs to be at a significant enough scale and this means they are destined to follow rather than lead when it comes to these sorts of opportunities.

Christensen concludes that big companies are great at 'sustaining innovations', those that might unlock some incremental growth such as a new flavour or variant on an existing brand or theme. But they fall down when it comes to 'disruptive innovations' – those that will transform a category, such as digital photography or refillable cleaning, are often found wanting.

This could well be a case of history repeating itself. As in the case of Kodak and digital photography, it threatens the business model of cleaning companies. Buying a refillable tablet is significantly cheaper than buying a bottle of cleaning spray. A normal cleaning spray is currently around $5 in Walmart but you can buy four refill pods from Podsy for $7.99. What would have been $20 for four sprays for the manufacturer shrinks to just $7.99. A 60 per cent decrease for the manufacturer to deal with. The same is true in the UK. For example, currently £4 for one bottle of Method Antibacterial spray compared to £6.50 for four refills of Ocean Saver. So, £16 for four bottles, down to £6.50. Almost £10 less and a 59 per cent drop in consumer outlay.

While it might be much better for the planet and better for the customer, it clearly is not ideal for the likes of P&G, Clorox, Reckitt Benckiser and Unilever. If the entire market moved to a refill model, you're wiping away 50 per cent of the value of the category. Billions of dollars with the vast majority of that currently sat with the above four companies. Another case of corporate loss aversion on a category-wide scale. The likelihood of them driving a change that is such a serious act of self-sabotage, especially in the eyes of their shareholders, is about as likely as a turkey being struck by lightning while voting for an early Thanksgiving.

Truman's cleaning was a trailblazer in this space, growing rapidly in the US. They raised $5 million in investment in 2019, just seven months after launching. In 2021 they were acquired by Henkel, a big European home and personal care business who own the likes of Schwarzkopf, Oust and Colour Catcher. Fast forward three years since the acquisition and the Truman's brand is nowhere to be seen and Henkel still don't have a refillable cleaning brand visible in their portfolio.

It's not just the big FMCG players standing in the way. Supermarkets are complicit as well. They take a cut of 30–40 per cent of everything sold on their shelves and 100 per cent of their own label range so if you cut the revenue from water-based cleaning sprays in half, it hits them hard as well. The only way they might smooth the path for these brands is if a compelling case can be made for them to be able to increase revenue by reutilizing the shelf real estate that is freed up by switching to smaller refillables rather than bulky, water-based sprays.

The numbers just don't add up for the status-quo businesses to do the right thing for people and the planet. The only way this is going to happen is if they vote with their wallets and the money moves to Change Brands. If people snap out of default mode and start making the smarter choice themselves and the planet by buying refillable options, large companies and retailers will have to act. It may take a while but surely it is only delaying the inevitable before the market moves to a cheaper and far more sustainable option.

In many ways, the resistance to change and protection of losses is short-sighted. There is a tremendous opportunity to be grasped if one of the bigger companies ran hard at this. Currently a brand may have a 20–30 per cent share in a market predominantly bought via supermarkets. It's a competitive environment and people tend to buy a range of brands based on promotions and marketing cycles. If they looked to move their customer base to refillables with a home subscription in place they could have 100 per cent of that person's spend on cleaning products each year and they wouldn't need to give 30–40 per cent of that revenue to retailers or invest heavily in in-store promotions to stand out on shelf. The opportunity is there to own the future of the category and drive a major change in behaviour, but it's far more likely to be a case of slow, managed decline that doesn't do anyone much good and merely delays the inevitable shift.

Shifting the Conversation

There's a concept in politics called the Overton Window. It relates to the window of political conversation and shows how viable a particular idea is at that time. The window is always shifting with what's happening in the world. At the very heart of that window is the status quo, ideas that are already policy. Either side of that are small incremental shifts that are likely to become policy soon because they are easy and popular among all parties.

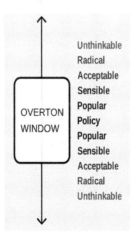

The Overton Window Developed by Joseph P. Overton and the Mackinac Center for Public Policy

As you move further to either end of the model, you start to see ideas that sit outside the accepted window of debate. Ideas that are seen as radical when they first come on the scene gradually gather support and move to the middle before becoming policy. This is the journey that ideas like the abolition of slavery and women's right to vote have been on and what we are seeing with the climate movement at the moment. They are driven by populist movements and often noisy protest before becoming the accepted way of doing things. Societal change comes from taking seemingly revolutionary ideas and proving that if they become reality, they can make the world a better place. This is known as the 'Radical Flank Effect'. A movement coming in at the radical end of the conversation, making a lot of noise and then shifting the window of what's possible quickly in their direction.

In many ways, Change Brands operate in a similar way to protests and social movements. They are protest brands that show there's a better way and that it's possible to take the path less travelled and build a successful business from it. The current status quo in a market, occupied by the legacy brands, sit at the heart of the Overton Window. Most people are buying a product that occupies that space, be it water in a plastic bottle, petrol cars or toilet paper made from trees. Change Brands come along and are the closest thing you can find to protest in a supermarket. They are the radical flank in the category, a social movement in a can.

Liquid Death is a brilliant example of this. The status quo is to buy water in plastic bottles. Billions of these single-use bottles are sold every year across the world and only a small proportion are recycled. Aluminium cans offer a more environmentally friendly option, requiring less energy to make and are simpler to recycle.

In 2018, Liquid Death saw an opportunity. CEO founder Mike Cessario was working at a music festival sponsored by energy drink brands like Monster and noticed the musicians had poured out the energy drink and replaced it with water they could drink while performing. He also noticed the enormous amounts of plastic bottles piling up across the festival site. This was a double lightbulb moment for him. He would create a water brand that would look cool and compete with energy drinks and beer brands, while also offering a more sustainable option in aluminium cans rather than plastic bottles.

Liquid Death was born. A brand that promised to 'Murder Your Thirst' and bring the punk rock spirit to a category that traditionally felt like it was targeted at yoga mums. The brand has grown rapidly through its highly distinctive branding, disruptive marketing activity and partnerships with music festivals all over the world to hit retail sales of $263 million in 2023, expanding to more than 100,000 shops across the US and UK.[*]

Liquid Death – The Best Way to Murder Your Thirst © Liquid Death

---

[*] https://www.thegrocer.co.uk/fundraising/liquid-death-hits-unicorn-14bn-valuation-as-it-raises-67m-for-npd-drive/689242.article#:~:text=Liquid per cent20Death per cent20 per centE2 per cent80 per cent93 per cent20which per cent20made per cent20its,across per cent20the per cent20US per cent20and per cent20UK.

This rapid growth has seen more and more people switch to drinking water from cans rather than plastic bottles. It's had such an impact in the US that Coca-Cola's Dasani brand is now available in cans, as is PepsiCo's Aquafina.

Liquid Death have created one of the most compelling Change Brands out there. They've carved out a hugely distinctive brand positioning while taking moral leadership of their category and done a lot of smart things along the way. We'll take a detailed look at them in Part Two of this book to understand the ingredients behind their success.

Something to Chew On

The conversation is also shifting in the chewing-gum category, driven by the Change Brand Nuud, founded in 2020 by Keir Carnie. If you look closely at the back of a packet of chewing gum, most likely bought from a brand like Wrigley's, you'll see that the main ingredient is something called 'Gum Base'. Now this seemingly innocent-sounding ingredient is actually a combination of resins, waxes, rubbers and elastomers that give it the chewy texture. These ingredients are basically different types of plastic. Ingredients include Polyethylene, also used in plastic bags, and one of the main microplastics in the oceans, Polyvinyl Acetate, a polymer used to make the PVA glue that you may remember from your school days and Butadiene-styrene rubber, which is also used to make car tyres.

This means chewing gum is basically another type of single-use plastic and one that is impossible to recycle. It ends up all over our streets and pavements and finds its way into rivers and oceans. Like all plastic, it's not biodegradable, taking thousands of years to break down, and is a hazard for birds and aquatic life. That explains why you're not supposed to swallow it.

Carnie describes the problem: 'Plastic gum is stuck to something like 90 per cent of urban pavements. It costs Mars Wrigley's less than a penny per piece to make but costs the taxpayer £1.50 to clean it up.' Gum also finds its way into the oceans. 'Scientists from the UK's National Oceanography Centre calculated there's over 12 million tonnes of microplastic floating in the Atlantic Ocean and the main plastic they found was polyethylene, a key part of bottles and chewing gum.' [*]

Around 374 billion pieces of chewing gum are chewed and then spat out every year.[†] This amounts to over 7.5 million tonnes of plastic. It's the second most littered item on the planet after cigarette butts and is likely to become number one soon as the number of smokers continues to fall. The market is also absolutely dominated by the major players. Wrigley's, the owners of multiple brands and part of Mars, has a close to 90 per cent market share in the UK and US so there is very little incentive to change.

People are basically chewing tiny bits of plastic and then spitting them out, all in the name of fresh breath. A regular one-gram piece of gum contains 0.4 grams of plastic. The same amount of plastic as a plastic straw, something that has been banned in large parts of the world, yet chewing gum continues to fly under the radar. Most people don't realize that gum is made of plastic. If they did, it might well change things. It's not exactly an appetizing thought to be chewing on a little bit of plastic. You wouldn't put a plastic bag, a car tyre or a dog toy in your mouth so it seems madness to chew plastic chewing gum, especially with the growing concerns about microplastics entering the food chain and the recent findings about a litre bottle of water containing nearly a quarter of a million pieces

---

[*] https://www.bbc.co.uk/news/science-environment-53786555

[†] Milliways website – https://www.milliwaysfood.com/pages/about-us

of tiny microplastics.* While yet to be proven, chewing on a piece of plastic for five to ten minutes is unlikely to be good for you.

But there is another way. Nuud Gum are starting the revolution. Carnie continues, 'Once people understand the massive environmental impact of chewing gum, not to mention the idea of chewing on a bit of plastic, they are really open to the alternative option that Nuud offers.' The natural alternative he refers to is a sustainably harvested tree sap called Chicle. Native to Central America and the Caribbean, it is harvested in a similar way to tapping trees for maple syrup so it doesn't involve cutting down any trees. And because it's natural, it's 100 per cent biodegradable. Also, chewing chicle is not a new thing, for years it was chewed in ancient Maya to stave off hunger and keep teeth clean. In fact, it was also the original base for chewing gum before plastic presented itself as a cheaper alternative that could be mass-produced in factories and pumped out across the world.

It seems like it's time for things to go full circle.

Nuud have created disruptive advertising that brings the truth about regular chewing gum into the cold light of day. They're looking to make chewing gum made from plastic as socially unacceptable as using a plastic straw, shifting the Overton Window of what people expect from their chewing gum. Carnie's initial appearance on BBC reality show *Dragons' Den* kickstarted the business and they've already had major traction getting into Waitrose. Other Change Brands are also looking to disrupt the dominance of the market leader including Milliways in the UK and Glee in the US.

It seems like the winds of change are starting to blow in this category.

---

* https://www.pbs.org/newshour/science/scientists-find-about-a-quarter-million -invisible-microplastic-particles-in-a-liter-of-bottled-water

Nuud Gum billboard © Nuud

The impact a shift in this space can make is there for all to see. 'For every pack of Nuud we sell, we're stopping the equivalent of nine plastic straws from entering the environment,' says Carnie. 'I firmly believe that when we look at chewing gum in 10 years' time, it will be plant-based and plastic-free. It has to go that way so the big players have to adapt if they want to future-proof their business. They're going to have to do something because awareness of hidden plastic in chewing gum is growing quickly and the desire to move away from single-use plastic is heightening. For them not to react is potentially commercial suicide.'

It might well be time to change what you chew to change the world. And at a tiny price premium currently of £1 compared to 80–90p for a plastic gum, it seems like a very easy choice to make, for your own health and for the planet.

Change Brands = Change Squared

It's clear that Change Brands don't just change the world through their own positive impact, they move things forward and change the behaviour of others. They shift the conversation in a way that challenges the status quo to be better. Thought leadership and the moral high ground is increasingly sitting with these emerging players. They acknowledge the elephant in the room in a category, whether that is toilet roll made from trees, chocolate made by slaves or chewing gum that is 90 per cent plastic and try and create a path to a better solution. They raise the bar in the categories they are in and accelerate progress when the incumbent might be sitting on their hands trying to protect the bottom line. The faster the money moves over to these brands, the faster change happens, and the sooner big companies are forced to act.

They change the behaviour and body language of entire categories. They make brands rethink the messages they're putting in the world for both better or for worse. Brands that previously hadn't communicated on sustainability are now briefing their marketing agencies to find a way to bolster their sustainability credentials. This is great when the brand treats it seriously and takes meaningful steps to lessen their negative impact or increase their positive impact. When big brands already selling millions of products make a change the potential impact is huge but it can also be a bad thing because it can manifest itself as meaningless and unwarranted sustainability claims. It puts an unfair onus on those in marketing roles and their creative agencies to come up with an answer to the brief that solves the problem when the messages being put into the world are the equivalent of putting lipstick on a pig when real change to the supply chain is needed. This has led to a spate of greenwashing claims, requiring people to be vigilant of what they believe and advertising claims to be monitored more seriously.

At their best, Change Brands drive these companies to not just change what they say, but to change what they do. This might be smaller shifts like packaging improvements, such as Coca-Cola and PepsiCo's water brands becoming available in cans, toilet paper wrapped in paper, not plastic or laundry brands moving away from large plastic jugs to cardboard boxes. It could be bigger things like brands offering refillable options and really accelerating their New Product Development (NPD) process to move faster and compete with disruptors.

In the case of the car category, the seismic shift driven by Tesla proving that it was possible to mass produce an electric vehicle at a (reasonably) affordable price point when they launched the Model S in 2012 got everyone else to accelerate their development of EV cars. All the other major car manufacturers have now made big commitments to the EV revolution as they've scrambled to be a part of the future of the category. Volkswagen, the biggest global car manufacturer in terms of revenue, have committed to have an electric version of all their 300 models by 2030 and expect 50 per cent of their global sales to be electric by 2030. *

This shift has also given governments the confidence to legislate for the move away from the Internal Combustion Engine. For instance, the UK, German and Dutch governments introduced legislation ending the sale of new petrol and diesel cars by 2030. Arguably without Tesla showing what was possible, the automotive industry and governments would have continued to drag their feet and the world would have been far slower in moving away from its reliance on petrol and diesel fuel. While there are still numerous challenges to overcome before going fully electric, the presence of a trailblazing Change Brand in this category has clearly been a genuine catalyst in driving progress.

The opportunity is there for other Change Brands to disrupt categories and give governments the confidence to legislate for positive change. If someone is out there doing it successfully and profitably, then the better resourced legacy brands really don't have

_____

* https://www.bloomberg.com/news/articles/2020-11-06/vw-s-boss-warns-the-troops -we-don-t-want-to-end-up-like-nokia

a leg to stand on when it comes to resisting change. We may well see the same in the case of plastic bottles, chewing gum, ultra-processed food, slavery produced chocolate and numerous other spaces if Change Brands continue to build critical mass and capture a bigger slice of the financial pie.

The Ripples of Change

It's clear that Change Brands accelerate change in all sorts of ways and that changing how people spend their money is a hugely powerful lever in addressing the most pressing problems in the world. It's like ripples on a pond, starting small but growing to have an effect far beyond that single transaction that spreads far and wide. There are five levels to the change brought about by Change Brands, as shown in the model below:

Catalyst for Change Model

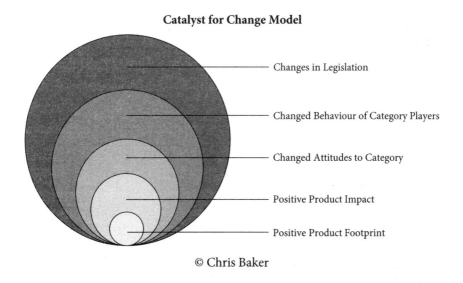

- Changes in Legislation
- Changed Behaviour of Category Players
- Changed Attitudes to Category
- Positive Product Impact
- Positive Product Footprint

© Chris Baker

First, because the Change Brand is generally an improvement on the default purchase in the category, it reduces the footprint of that purchase. These shifts could be anything from plastic-free packaging, refillable and recycled options to more sustainable manufacturing processes such as a change in materials used, removing of toxic chemicals or moving to an electric vehicle. Anything that is a positive move forward from the status quo is where the impact of Change Brands begins.

These brands also go a step further than just being an improvement on the default; they also have a positive impact on the world. This could be XO Bikes providing mechanic training to former offenders to help reduce reoffending. It could be Tony's Chocolonely tackling the issue of slavery in the supply chain and paying farmers a fair living wage to ensure it doesn't happen. It could be Serious Tissues tree planting programme that not only plants millions of trees to capture carbon and deforestation, but also provides employment in some of the poorest communities in the world. Change Brands don't just reduce their footprint, they have a positive forward impact.

The next significant shift is in changing attitudes towards the category. As Change Brands get their messages out into the world in increasingly noisy and fame-grabbing ways, people rethink their point of view on a category. They might decide never to buy water in a plastic bottle again because of Liquid Death. They could move away from pet food made from meat in favour of the lower footprint of insect-based options like Grub Club. They may realize that buying toilet paper made from trees rather than recycled paper or bamboo is becoming increasingly untenable at a time when we need trees more than ever to fight climate change. Tony's have forever changed the conversation around chocolate so it's impossible to ignore the fact that the supply chains of companies like Mars and Mondelez are rife with cases of exploitation and child labour. Anything for a cheap, sweet treat, right? And to protect that all-important margin.

Once attitudes have shifted and people's expectations of what they get from a particular product have changed irrevocably, the dominant behaviour of the brands in the category has to shift. It's merely a matter of time. Status-quo brands can try and compete by changing their messages and trying to dial up the impact they're having but if this isn't backed up by meaningful action, consumers are now more than savvy enough to see through it and call it out.

We've moved beyond a world of meaningless words. Companies trying to inject purpose into their ill-suited brands or indulge in a little bit of greenwashing without the claims to back it up. The most important word is 'Impact' and if there's not a robust roadmap towards major improvement then the money in people's pockets will shift.

The great thing is that when major companies change their behaviour in a big way, the impact of that shift can be huge and dwarf that of what Change Brands can achieve on their own. In the toilet paper category, brands like Serious Tissues, Who Gives A Crap and Cheeky Panda have taken significant share from major toilet roll manufacturers because of the improved footprint and impact of these brands. As a result, Essity and Kimberly-Clark, the leading paper manufacturers, have shifted to smaller cores in their rolls and they also offer double-length rolls. This means they can fit more product in a shipment, lessening the carbon impact of delivering toilet roll all over the world. The impact of this is huge and likely to have never come about without the pressure from more sustainable players eating away at their market share.

Progress is happening. And while they could potentially go faster, big companies are making significant strides forward. But one of the big problems is that when they do talk about a positive shift they've made, and one that will make a major difference when it's implemented at the sort of scale they operate at, it's rare they will get the positive returns from that. What happens is they put their head above the parapet and rather than receive a pat on the back for making a positive change, they get drawn over the coals for everything about the organization that isn't perfect yet.

This 'Virtue-Shaming' of companies for not being perfect in every single area of their business, while well-intentioned, is often counterproductive. It's not like they can flick a switch and suddenly morph into the greenest company on the planet, while still running a successful business. The shift towards more sustainable practices is a journey and can't happen overnight. If they're not getting credit and encouragement for positive shifts, will they even bother in the future?

This leads to the rise of something called 'Greenhushing' – companies deciding not to talk about their sustainability initiatives because of the risk of being slammed for something else they haven't done yet. Or even worse, deciding not to pursue the green agenda because of the reputational risk and making the decision that the cost isn't worth the aggravation.

Agent Change describes the conversation within big companies: 'It is really important that companies get the benefits from the positive steps that are taken. You know, greenwash and bullshit continues to be the enemy. But I agree with you that failing to recognize and celebrate when good things happen and always just saying "yes, but what about the other issue?" is counterproductive. I've experienced those conversations internally. We've done something progressive that hasn't necessarily been received positively. And the next time the proposal comes up, it doesn't make it through. There are other priorities and people will say it's not worth it, basically.'

While it's important to hold companies to account, they also need a bit of positive reinforcement and encouragement to continue down the track they're on. By celebrating progress rather than shouting about something else that is wrong within the company, you just stymie progress and stop good things happening rather than creating the conditions and incentives for them to accelerate the transition. By celebrating positive change and getting on board with better options, we speed up the transition. These companies are consumer-led after all, so if people change their behaviour, so will they.

Another thing we're also likely to see is big players buying up Change Brands to add to their own brand portfolio. This can be a shortcut for them to jump into the impact space and quickly make a difference at scale. It's difficult for existing brands that are so firmly established in people's minds to suddenly change tack and start pushing a different agenda. By adding a Change Brand to their portfolio, they can have a foot in both camps. They can have a brand that occupies the middle ground, but also have one that allows them to access a different (and growing) audience. They also bring the opportunity to tap into the price premium that Change Brands can command and add value sales to the category, getting people to trade up to a more expensive product and ultimately growing their revenue from that section of the supermarket.

While this might sound like a Change Brand selling out to the big boys, there are also major benefits when it comes to delivering on their original mission if they hold true to their values. It is even quite likely it will accelerate that mission if done right. For example, an acquisition is highly likely to unlock greater production efficiencies through access to factories, distribution and the economies of scale that these major companies enjoy. It would also mean being able to launch in numerous new markets much more quickly than a Change Brand could do on their own, which means that impact is accelerated and opened up to new audiences.

The key thing is locking in that mission so that it can't then be dispensed with by the new owner. Ben & Jerry's was a standard-bearer here in 2000 when they sold to Unilever with an independent board set up to have responsibility for their social mission and activism. Patagonia made 'Earth it's only shareholder' with a new structure* and Tony's Chocolonely implemented a 'Mission Lock'

---

* https://www.patagoniaworks.com/press/2022/9/14/patagonias-next-chapter-earth-is -now-our-only-shareholder

and governance structure which ensures the business cannot depart from their core missions.

The final ripple on the pond caused by Change Brands is the effect it can have on legislation. By demonstrating that there is a better way of doing things than the current status quo, it gives legislators the confidence to pass laws that accelerate the transition. This has already been seen in the case of Tesla and electric vehicles and legislation related to plastic packaging is highly likely to follow as more and more brands find a way to package their product without using plastic.

The progress of Change Brands like Liquid Death in the US has also put pressure on competitors who pollute far more than them and given legislators the confidence to act. On 15 November 2023, New York State announced that it was suing PepsiCo, accusing them of 'polluting the environment and endangering public health through its single-use plastic bottles, caps and wrappers'.* The lawsuit, filed in Erie County in upstate New York, is one of the first to target a major plastic producer and could set a transformational precedent leading to similar cases all over the world. Plastic pollution has become a major problem in the Buffalo River and PepsiCo contributed more than 17 per cent of the trash found in that river because it could be traced to their brands. PepsiCo are the owners of brands including Cheetos, Doritos, Gatorade, Lay's, Lipton, Mountain Dew, Quaker and Ruffles, alongside their Pepsi Masterbrand. The beauty of the millions invested in brand building and packaging design is that it's possible to see the source of the pollution and trace it back to its parent company to take action. This is something that unfortunately isn't the case with carbon emissions as they are ultimately invisible.

* https://www.reuters.com/legal/new-york-state-sues-pepsico-over-environmental -matter-court-records-2023-11-15/

New York Attorney General Letitia James said the company 'failed to warn consumers about the potential health and environmental risks of plastics in its more than 100 brands, and misled the public about its efforts to fight plastics pollution'. She highlighted the effect plastic can have on drinking water as it breaks down into microplastics. It can lead to health issues such as increased risk of cancer and altered reproductive functioning: 'All New Yorkers have a basic right to clean water, yet PepsiCo's irresponsible packaging and marketing endanger Buffalo's water supply, environment, and public health.'

While PepsiCo state they are 'serious about plastic reduction and effective recycling', the lawsuit states that 'PepsiCo has deceived consumers by announcing targets to reduce how much non-recycled plastic it uses in packaging, although it has actually increased its usage'. Fairly shocking given that context and the legal proceedings are probably long overdue against them and many other major plastic polluters. The lawsuit is seeking a ban on single-use plastic in the Buffalo region, without warnings like those seen on tobacco packaging that state 'the packaging could cause pollution and pose health and environmental risks'. They are also looking to get them to pay for damages and clean up contamination.

Major FMCG companies will be keeping a close eye on this case as it could be a landmark piece of legislation that becomes a template across the world in pushing back against single-use plastic. With refillable bottle brands such as Ocean Bottle becoming increasingly well-known and highly regarded, there might even be the opportunity to push for legislation for mandatory public water fountains in places that sell food to end the slightly ridiculous act of transporting bottled water around the planet, particularly in countries where good-quality drinking water is readily available in every premises. While this would have an impact on the bottom line of companies selling bottled water, it is clearly a step that needs to be taken for the good of the planet on both a local and global basis.

This dynamic is playing out more and more across the world. In 2023, when the UK government threatened to do a U-turn on mandatory reporting on food waste, a group of Change Brands that included Toast Brewing, Dash Water and Olio, the food sharing app, alongside celebrity chef and journalist Hugh Fearnley-Whittingstall campaigned and managed to get the government to stick to their original commitments. Similarly, WUKA, a disruptive femcare brand (the initials stand for Wake-Up Kick Ass), successfully campaigned for the UK government to drop VAT on their Period Pants product, reclassifying it from clothing to feminine hygiene products. This goes to show that Change Brands can also have a powerful influence on lawmakers. In demonstrating there is a better way of doing things and that changes are possible, this gives legislators the confidence to move forward.

The final step of enshrining these shifts in legislation is a vital one to ensure the progress is locked in and laggard brands can't look to undercut the new normal with cheaper options that use unsustainable practices.

Make Some Waves

It's fair to say that, for a Change Brand founder, what may initially feel like a lot of pushing water uphill and sunk effort is truly worthwhile. As the brand starts to reach critical mass, cut through with consumers and steal share from established brands, the ripples on the pond start to turn into waves and the difference that brand can make to the world grows exponentially. And they didn't even need to win an election or lead a march on Washington, they just had to change how people spend their money.

Change Brands change the behaviour of other brands and businesses. By growing and proving the commercial advantage of their model compared to legacy brands, they create the conditions for positive change to accelerate. Big companies see share slipping away, they see people changing how they spend their money and because they are consumer-led companies, they react to that change. And when big companies make changes, because of their scale, the impact is exponential.

There is no way huge multinationals like Nestlé, Mars, Unilever, P&G, PepsiCo and Coca-Cola are going to become obsolete. They have numerous brands with huge amounts of customers in multiple markets across the world. They have deep marketing, manufacturing and supply chain expertise and almost infinite resources. Where Change Brands can make a real difference is by accelerating change. By exploiting the limitations and challenges that come with operating inside a big company. This is what Part Two of this book explores in detail – how to build the brands that are going to change the world by having an eye on what makes them successful from the start.

When a Change Brand grows rapidly and steals market share, it creates the conditions whereby established companies need to change their behaviour and big brands must change to stay front and centre with consumers. This change in behaviour, whether an ingredient or packaging change or some sort of forward impact, makes a major positive difference in the world. There is also the potential that the combination of a Change Brand and a multinational could create the megabrands of the future by reimagining how things are done in entire categories. Brands that do billions in annual sales, while making a positive impact on the world and stealing a march on the competition.

Agent Change has an interesting point of view on the role Change Brands can play in driving positive change in the world: 'It can be very romantic to think about the sudden violent revolution, but they don't tend to end very well or in the way that they hoped. Gradual revolution, evolution tends to work better. And if you pull down the big Consumer Packaged Goods (CPG) companies, you pull down a huge part of economies and societies and communities. A lot of how we get goods we rely on. And so yes, Change Brands can create unbalanced conditions to help them move faster, encourage them to move faster, reward them for moving faster. We've got to change the incentives. And that's not enough of that.'

It's clear the world needs more Change Brands. Part Two of this book goes into the detail of how to go from the beginning of an idea to a brand with the potential to change the world.

How to Build a Change Brand in Six Steps

What shall we make Obsolete today?

CHAPTER FIVE

Start with Impact (and embrace the power of the blank page)

'The blank page is the great equalizer and the greatest opportunity.'

Unknown

So, you want to launch a Change Brand? Where do you start? Every category out there has a market leader and probably a handful of other key players who are already established in the audience's mind, have distribution in almost every supermarket and a war chest of resources that you can only imagine having access to. Each brand is a multimillion-dollar business in its own right, with deep pockets to spend on advertising, a team of people with a mix of useful skillsets and the backing of a large corporation. Not to mention an established product and supply chain where the numbers work.

You have a blank sheet of paper in front of you. And perhaps a dog sitting next to you or a window to help you daydream. But (as I've learned from writing this book) the blank page can be both intimidating and hugely liberating. True, it can feel daunting sat there, staring at nothingness. But you have the opportunity to create something that's never been made before. The blank page in business is extremely powerful and gives you an advantage over the big players that they will never have.

True, there are huge benefits to being sat in the comfortable offices of a major company on a comfortable salary with access to every resource you could ever need. But there are also problems and challenges that come with being part of a huge machine. Managing an established brand comes with baggage. These brands have been going for years. They have had good years and bad years and there is always pressure on them internally to grow and hit targets while maintaining margins. Bonuses rely on growth and hitting targets. Brands need to be growing significantly year on year to placate the higher ups and manage shareholders. And in multibillion-dollar organizations, growth needs to be properly substantial to move the needle in anyway.

Big brands have an established supply chain to manage. Any changes to the process of making the product, whether that's a packaging change or a new formulation, are planned a seriously long time in advance. Margins need to be maintained to ensure the brand is contributing to the overall business so any slight change to the production process needs to not negatively impact the margin and ideally needs to improve it. All of this makes it hard to react to changing consumer trends and needs because any product change, or even changing the wording on the packaging, could be at least 18 months away.

They have complicated relationships with multiple retailers to manage. This demanding group need a new plan every year to demonstrate how their brand will drive growth in their category and continue to feed supermarket margins. This is a full-time job for a couple of people at least.

Big companies are also complicated beasts. There is layer upon layer of hierarchy with juniors to manage and superiors to keep happy and bring along on the journey. Brand planning is an extensive process with forms to fill in, hoops to jump through and laborious internal sell-in to ensure everyone is on the same page. By the time you've got organization-wide buy-in, you're too drained to actually execute it. And it's hard to make late changes if you spot an opportunity because this could mean unravelling the whole thing.

When it comes to developing new advertising campaigns, this is a similarly lengthy and costly process. Working with expensive agencies to develop at least three routes for the campaign. (Agencies that may or may not get the brief with teams of varying levels of skill, experience and a potential bias towards a particular media output.) You then need to get buy-in from senior people on those routes to start moving forward and put the creative into research. It varies from company to company but there is often a level of pre-testing that creative ideas need to go through to ensure they meet the criteria of the organization. This invariably knocks off all the rough edges that made it interesting in the first place in the hunt for the elusive 'double green' score or to sit in the top-right box of a matrix that very few people even begin to understand. The cost of creating the stimulus for the research, whether it illustrated mood boards or more elaborate animatics (basically a rough version of the advert), often costs more than a lot of Change Brands would spend on content for a year.

If the concept passes the pre-testing first time around, something that maybe happens 50 per cent of the time if you're lucky, it is then onwards into further creative development and a bit more internal sell-in for good measure to give everyone a chance to add something into the ad, diluting even further what made it good in the first place. You then spend more time talking about the product shot than any other aspect of the ad that would make it actually cut through with the audience.

I've worked on major platforms for global brands and it can take such a long time to get to a new platform idea that once it's gone through the various levels of internal sign-off and jumped through the hoops of research, the world has moved on. Their more nimble competitors have executed against the same insight multiple times and that window of opportunity has passed.

Basically, it's really hard to create great advertising in huge companies. It takes a long time, involves a lot of people and costs a lot of money. And the above is just the process for a new campaign that's basically an evolution on what came before. If you need to take any more significant action, like a course correction, new strategy or brand platform, you're probably doubling the time and cost of the process and it could take a couple of years to get something out into the world. And that's if it doesn't get killed by one of the multiple stakeholders from different sides of the business along the way.

Managing a big brand is not all it's cracked up to be. OK, you have the resources, but you also have the baggage and complexity that comes with it and multiple people with a point of view on the brand who you need to keep on board. This is why big brands end up in a doom loop of mediocre creative work. They pump average, risk-adverse campaigns out into the world just to maintain their position in the market, to tread water and not lose share.

That blank sheet of paper and the chance to develop the strategy for a brand on your own doesn't sound quite so bad now, does it?

The Two Types of Strategy

Strategy can sometimes feel like a hugely complicated field and that's partly down to practitioners in the space making it seem more complicated to churn out enormous presentation decks and charge extortionate fees for something far too complex to execute. It's actually surprisingly simple. Sir Lawrence Freedman, the acclaimed historian, dove deep into the entire history of strategy across war, business and government and identified two fundamental areas of strategy. He defines strategy as 'the art of creating power' and states that there are two abiding ways to do this that have stood the test of time.[*]

---

[*] Freedman, L. (2013), *Strategy: A History*, Oxford University Press

The first is the 'application of superior force'. Think application of strength. More soldiers, better weapons, better technology. In business, this means greater resources, more money, more people, important relationships already in place, factories, supply chain, Research and Development budgets. This is the strategy used by the major multinationals with deep pockets and seemingly infinite resources. For them to succeed when launching a product, they often just outspend a competitor and leverage the relationships they already have in place. Freedman talks about the great warrior Achilles being an example of this with pure physical strength and power being the defining characteristics.

The second is the 'application of guile'. In other words, out-thinking and outsmarting your opponent, rather than simply overpowering them; using cunning and wisdom to win small victories. This means doing the unexpected and taking risks. If something doesn't work, move on to the next idea and give it a go. This strategic approach generally applies to the underdog and because underdogs are generally smaller, they can move faster and be nimbler than the behemoths they are up against. Speed of thought and execution are an advantage that should not be underestimated against slow-moving competitors. Freedman uses the example of Odysseus as an example of this with his wisdom and willingness to try things, best exemplified by the Trojan Horse that proved so decisive in the Trojan War. Application of guile was the strategy used by the Viet Cong, coming up with innovative ways to be a thorn in the side of the much more powerful and better resourced American forces. Be the Rebel Alliance and the Millennium Falcon to the Empire's Death Star.

Oatly Chief Creative Officer John Schoolcraft has an insight into the advantage Change Brands can have in this space with the brand and creative at the very heart of the business. 'After years of working with brands, I had some other issues in that I thought CMOs and marketing departments were terrible at buying creative ideas. Most of them were scared of losing their jobs. Others spent time with all kinds of market research, awareness studies and answering to KPIs, instead of creating brands that respected people and helped people improve their lives.'

He continues, 'After a couple of decades working in advertising, I have had some of my best ideas killed by incompetent marketing directors, so that was my only request to [Oatly CEO] Toni to join, that we could kill the marketing department, and he said, cool. We still don't have a marketing department to this day. Instead the creative department, now called "The Oatly Department of Mind Control", is looking for all kinds of ways to help consumers eat better and more nutritiously without taxing the planet, not just making ad campaigns.'

One of the things Schoolcraft is most proud of is 'I love that we proved that marketing departments are not needed. That corporate approaches are slow, boring, inflexible and filled with insecurity. And when you remove everything that gets in the way of creating great work, you can actually create great work.'

The success of Oatly and Liquid Death, among others, in baking the creative department into the heart of the organization and removing the barriers can be a huge business advantage over the legacy brands with numerous layers and sign-offs to negotiate. Through the application of guile, risk-taking and speed of thought, it is possible for the underdog to win, or at least be a real nuisance to the bigger brands and steal a big chunk of market share. You can do things differently. Be agile, take risks and experiment. If it doesn't work, you haven't lost anything anyway, so just move on and keep going.

The Power of the Blank Page

Most of the big brands in big categories have been around for a seriously long time. We're talking decades in lots of cases, if not longer. They're household names, well-known among large parts of the population. But this can be a double-edged sword. Yes, they have an advantage when it comes to awareness. When someone thinks about a category in a buying situation, they are highly likely to be among the first brands that spring to mind. This is called Mental Availability and is a key driving force behind the most successful brands in the world and their sustained growth* (more on how you can build this later). When you think of computers, Apple is the first that comes to mind. A pair of trainers? Nike. Thirsty? Coke or Pepsi. Hungry? Perhaps the Golden Arches are calling. But it also means they've built up a clear picture in people's minds of both the good and the bad. Some of the first associations with Coca-Cola are likely to be its high sugar content and the ubiquitous plastic bottles. McDonald's may offer affordable Happy Meals, but they also contribute to the obesity epidemic sweeping the world. Google may give you easy access to all the world's knowledge, but they also use the data they have on you to make a lot of money selling advertising.

Dove may have created the Campaign for Real Beauty that has done a great job of challenging perceptions around beauty and self-esteem, but they also sold 6.4 billion highly polluting single-use plastic sachets in 2023, a common format in the Global South, that led to Greenpeace interrupting their annual meeting. At a total Unilever level, they sold 53 billion sachets in 2023, the equivalent of 1,700 per second.

'Unilever really are pouring fuel on the fire of the plastic pollution crisis,' said Nina Schrank, Head of Plastics at Greenpeace UK. 'Their brands like Dove are famous for telling the world they're forces for good. But they're pumping out a staggering amount of plastic waste. It's poisoning our planet, you can't claim to be a "purposeful"

---

* Sharp, B. (2013), *How Brands Grow: What Marketers Don't Know*, Oxford University Press

company whilst bearing responsibility for such huge pollution. Unilever has to change."*

Volkswagen may make some great electric vehicles, but they are also remembered for the 'Dieselgate' emissions scandal that began in 2015, where the car's software detected when they were being tested and altered the performance to meet regulatory standards. But in real-world driving conditions, the cars emitted up to 40 times more nitrogen oxides than allowed. These brands are big and established, but they are by no means perfect and unassailable. We've also talked about how hard it is for them to adjust their positioning to be more purpose-led to adapt to changing attitudes and consumer demands when they've built up a positioning based on something entirely different.

The world has changed dramatically since these brands first came to market. The truth is that if you were launching a brand in 2025, there is almost no way you would do it in the same way as a brand that was launched in the eighties or even the early 2000s. Launching a brand now means you have a blank sheet of paper. You can come at a category or problem in an entirely new way, making links that have never been made before. You don't have a margin to protect or an established supply chain. You don't have shareholders to placate. You can do things differently. Start small and test and learn. Just because something has always been done in a certain way doesn't mean it always has to be done that way.

A lot of people who are far more creative than me see creativity as the art of connecting the previously unconnected. Making links between the familiar and the fresh to create something new. Bringing them together in interesting ways that have never been

---

* Greenpeace, November 2023. https://www.greenpeace.org/international/press -release/63892/unilever-sells-1700-highly-polluting-throwaway-plastic-sachets-per -second-greenpeace-reveals/

seen before. It's about seeing patterns and possibilities that others might not notice and combining them to create something original and disruptive. Creativity is the ability to see relationships where none currently exist.

This is how Apple's Steve Jobs described it: 'Creativity is just connecting things. When you ask creative people how they did something, they feel a little guilty because they didn't really do it, they just saw something. It seemed obvious to them after a while. That's because they were able to connect experiences they've had and synthesize new things.'*

It's not about starting with a completely blank slate. Everything you've ever read, heard, seen or used is an input when it comes to coming up with ideas. Things you've found interesting. Things that have shocked you or moved you emotionally. Things that just don't seem right. Things that you might know more about than most other people. This is all sitting in the back of your mind, or perhaps in a folder on your desktop, ready to be combined in a fresh way. Connecting the seemingly unconnected is when the magic happens.

Creating a Change Brand is an act of connection. The best Change Brands are born when you combine three things: a problem people care about, a category problem and a proven impact on that problem:

P x C x I

Problem   **Category**   **Proven**
People Care   **Problem**   **Impact**
About

The Change Brand formula © Chris Baker

---

* Steve Jobs interviewed for *Wired Magazine* in February 1995

First, you need to be setting out to tackle a problem people care about. The good news is there is no shortage of options at the moment. Think about where the 'heat' is in the world when it comes to issues. What is generating headlines and outrage? Where is the emotion? It becomes even better if you've got a personal reason to be tackling that problem.

The second thing you need is a category problem. No category is perfect, there is always room for improvement. By finding an issue with a category and then setting out to improve on the status quo, you have another tension to push against that will resonate with people. Solving category problems has been a key driver of business for years and the way to build competitive advantage. If you create disillusion with the status quo, you give people a reason to change what they buy. Virgin disrupted air travel as the customer-friendly, less stuffy competitor to British Airways. Nowadays, category problems are increasingly seen as social problems. High sugar content fuels obesity. Endless plastic packaging ends up in our oceans and enters the food chain as microplastics. Chocolate production exploits children. The Internal Combustion Engine pollutes air in our cities and contributes to climate change. When the problem people care about and the category problem fit seamlessly together, this is when you know you're onto something.

Finally, you need to deliver a proven impact on that problem. Impact is defined as the positive impact you aim to have on the world in an area people care about. This is the thing you are setting out to change. Whether that's tackling homelessness, climate change, reoffending, food waste, modern slavery or plastic pollution. It's the thing that gives Change Brands their tension. Their reason for being. And by picking an area people care about, you have a ready-made audience for your brand who are looking for solutions, but perhaps not currently finding them. The list of problems in today's world is almost endless so it shouldn't be too hard to find somewhere to make a difference.

Powerful things happen when you combine these three ingredients but if you've just got a societal problem you want to impact without a category problem, you're more in the realms of charity than Change Brand. And similarly, if you just have a category problem without a positive impact, you're simply playing within the realms of traditional business.

The best Change Brands come about when the combination of these three things is inarguable and intrinsically interlinked. That's why a multiplication symbol is at the heart of the formula. It creates a potent mix that gives Change Brands their unfair advantage. Finding a problem people care deeply about, a category problem and a way for your brand and product to make a positive impact on that problem is a powerful proposition.

It's important to match the product category with the problem to add resonance. There's a very clear link between climate change and toilet paper, a product currently responsible for cutting down a million trees a day at a time when we need trees more than ever to sequester carbon and fight climate change. The vast majority of household toilet roll is made from virgin pulp, trees that have grown for 20–30 years to be cut down for what is the ultimate single-use product. In a world where alternatives exist, such as recycled paper, the status quo seems pretty scandalous.

The idea for Change Please came about in a moment of connecting two things that were seemingly disconnected. Sitting in that coffee shop near Covent Garden in Central London, we saw numerous people walk past a homeless guy asking for a bit of spare change, saying they had no money or pretending to be on their phones, and then going straight into a coffee shop to spend £3 on a flat white. Coffee is a relatively high-margin product and is everywhere on high streets across the world. There is also a shortage of well-trained baristas. By training formerly homeless people as baristas and giving them a whole range of other support along the way, the coffee industry could be used as a way to give them a second chance and help them get back on their feet. Spending that money with a company who would use the profits to help someone get back on their feet, rather than giving it to a large corporation to bolster their profits even further, became a little bit of a no-brainer for people and businesses.

Upcircle Beauty Founder Anna Brightman had a very different idea of how to use coffee to tackle a problem. 'The penny drop moment was when we heard about the amount of coffee grounds disposed of each year in cafés, restaurants and bars. In the UK, we send 500,000 tonnes of coffee waste to landfill per year, and when it's disposed of at industrial-sized quantities, it rots and produces methane which is a greenhouse gas.' It's proven that coffee has a positive, energizing effect on the skin, so they set out to tackle this problem by collecting coffee grounds from local coffee shops and creating their first hero products, coffee face scrubs and energizing face serums and eye cream. They were also solving a problem for cafe owners, who were getting charged by councils to take their waste, just for it to end up in landfill.

Building the business has not been without its challenges, and it took a little while to persuade her friends and family they were on to something. 'This is beauty, right, we're talking about the least glamorous topics in terms of waste and we're trying to encourage people to apply it to their face!' But the brand has struck a major chord and built up a loyal following, perhaps by tapping into the issues inherent within the sector. 'The global beauty industry is responsible for 120 billion pieces of packaging each year, 95 per cent of which are thrown away. By collecting a wide range of different by-products from the food and drink industry with proven benefits, we've been able to grow our range and customer base,' Brightman continues. 'As the name Upcircle would suggest, the brand is based fully on circular economy principles. We're now upcycling over 50 different by-products into beauty products and have a full packaging return scheme. We're selling in over 50 countries and have a really loyal community."*

You can make connections that have never been made before. Toilet roll and climate change. Homelessness and coffee. Skincare and coffee. Slavery and chocolate. Deodorant and plastic pollution. Chewing gum and plastic pollution. There are infinite combinations out there and when you bring the two things together, you create a powerful force that is very difficult for legacy brands to resist. And as Change Brands grow, so too does the difference they make to the planet. Let's now dig a little deeper into a few more Change Brands that have created a powerful cocktail of impact.

Oiling the Wheels of Change

While volunteering in his local prison, Stef Jones came to a powerful realization: 'I'd bump into people that I waved off six months beforehand and ask them why they were back. By and large, it was because they couldn't get jobs and they'd got up to their old tricks through necessity and been nicked, ending up back inside.' Digging a little deeper, he discovered something called 'the cycle of reoffending', a problem that affects about half of those in prison. Once they had been to prison, it was hard to get out of the cycle and find a way to get back on their feet and make money without resorting to what landed them in prison in the first place.

Jones had already built a successful advertising agency but was looking to do something more meaningful that would help the

---

* Can Marketing Save The Planet podcast. Episode 75. February 2024.

people he was working with in prisons. 'So, I thought, why don't we create businesses specifically to train, employ and inspire these guys? Something that can tell a contradictory story to what you read in the *Daily Mail*.' He got together with another former ad man, Ian Priest, one of the founders of VCCP, and they set to work.

At the same time, they read an article about the shortage of bike mechanics in the UK. The Covid pandemic had driven a surge in people buying bikes, but there was now a shortage of around 8,000 bike mechanics across the country. The idea of training people leaving prison as mechanics was something that appealed to those he spoke to in Brixton Prison and an idea was born.

They developed a six-week course that would train former offenders as bike mechanics, with a view to employing them themselves or finding them a job with one of the big cycling chains. This approach of giving people a valuable skill helps them use that skill to get back on a good path. The self-esteem that came from learning an in-demand skill was transformational.

'The normal reoffending rate for people leaving prison is 48 per cent, but on our programme, it is just 3 per cent,' Jones says proudly. When £18 billion is spent each year on the prison service by the UK government, solutions like this that make such a seismic difference could save enormous amounts of the taxpayer's money.

The other stroke of genius was where they found the bikes. In almost every police station across the country there is a room at the back full of stolen bikes that have never been reclaimed by the owners. By building a relationship with New Scotland Yard and other London police stations, they suddenly had access to hundreds of free bikes that were just sitting there, taking up space. They take these donated bikes, give them a full service and a fresh lick of paint and turn them into XO Bikes in either Swag Black or Hot Orange. And at the same time, they're training someone in a much-needed skill, instilling a sense of pride and rebuilding their self-esteem. 'Our product is a bloke that never goes back to prison,' Priest says.

XO Bikes was born – 'We find a bloke with a past and a bike with a past and give them both a decent future.' The meaning behind XO is twofold, at the same time meaning 'ex-offender' and 'extraordinary' so it acknowledges the problem, but hints at the transformation.

'These guys are extraordinary individuals and I want to transition that meaning so that they look like anti-heroes,' Jones continues. 'There's a bit of edge to what we do, you can't avoid that. And we thought we'd call them fixers rather than mechanics. Again, it's a slightly moody expression but we're not trying to glamorize crime or prisons but keep the association because I think it's really important that people do know what they're buying and why they're buying it.'

The XO Bikes team © XO Bikes

XO Bikes are gathering momentum with more prison leavers going through their training programmes and more people buying the bikes. They've managed to get a place on the Government's Cycle to Work scheme, but as the first non-new bike brand which means one of their 'swagged' bikes, normally £500, would be only around £275 after the subsidy.

In Priest's words, 'It's a brilliant bike and a brilliant deal, with an amazing story behind it.' When you put it that way, it's impossible to argue with. A very cool bike brand making a real difference to a lot of people's lives and a self-sustaining business model with the potential to grow and grow.

A Period of Change

During a chat in the loos at London School of Economics, Susan Allen Augustin and Tara Chandra were hatching a plan. They had seen eco-friendly and organic brands growing rapidly in a range of categories, but they were frustrated that it was almost impossible to buy sustainable period products. Augustin elaborates: 'We knew that not everyone will adapt to a menstrual cup or a reusable alternative, so we set out to create a better alternative. As opposed to the standard period products, which are typically 90 per cent non-recyclable plastic materials, we pride ourselves in creating accessible options that are better for us and the planet.'

Chandra continues: 'We're challenging industries that have relied for too long on synthetic fibres, petroleum plastics and harsh chemical residues. So, we built a product range of tampons, pads and liners that uses either compostable, biodegradable or recyclable packaging, and we use no nasties like dyes, fragrances, allergens or harsh chemicals. Bye-bye chlorine bleach!'

A disruptive product needed a disruptive brand. 'We wanted something with a relatable tone of voice that would tackle the shame and stigma that defined the way periods were spoken about. We were looking for a relatable tone of voice, a bit like best mates having a shameless chat about their messiest moments,' says Augustin. The name, Here We Flo, felt a long way from established leaders like Always, Tampax, Kotex and Bodyform and the brand's distinctive bright pink was chosen to stand out and tackle stigma head on, rather than fade into the background.

They also set out to create a very different tone of voice. While period care advertising had moved on a long way from the days of women running along beaches and going windsurfing, there was still a gap that they identified. 'We believe humour is such a powerful tool for breaking the ice on the awkwardness we can feel about our messy bodily moments and create the opportunity to have open and honest conversations about them instead,' Augustin explains. 'There are many ways to smash the patriarchy, ours just happens to be humour.'

'Our strategy from the beginning has been to make people laugh,' Chandra says. 'We don't like anything where it's a hidden secret, no one talks about it and it's stigmatized. Any time we find one of those things, we make a joke about it. Everybody laughs about it and we start a conversation.'

Here We Flo have certainly lived this since launch and had a lot of fun while disrupting an established market with dominant market leaders. Their debut TV campaign, based on period dramas, tapped into a cultural wave as it broke around the same time as Netflix's Bridgerton while poking fun at the genre. (More on this later.) They even decided to have a little fun with their retail packaging. 'Tara always had massive cravings for ice cream during her period, despite being lactose intolerant. So, when we started talking about retail packaging, she had the idea to put them in an ice cream tub as a cheeky inside joke,' Augustin explains. But what started as an inside joke turned into a stroke of genius. 'It would actually make us really stand out on retail shelves, we thought. It will be a while before we can afford a billboard, let's turn our product into one.' The distinctive packaging has been a key part of their success in Boots, their first national retailer, with distribution quadrupling in early 2024 to over 1500 stores.

Here We Flo's iconic ice cream packaging © Here We Flo

The environmental disaster that is standard period products is hard to ignore and it has sparked a number of Change Brands to try and shake up the status quo in the sector. Ruby Raut, the founder of another brilliant period care brand, WUKA (standing for Wake Up, Kick Ass) digs a little deeper. 'Most supermarket menstrual products contain a significant amount of plastic, equivalent to five bags per pad. These products that are used for less than eight hours, end up in landfills and in the natural environment, with the average beach clean-up finding 4.8 pieces of menstrual waste per 100 metres.'

WUKA set out to tackle this massive problem with their period pants. 'We provide a sustainable, reusable alternative to single use pads and tampons. Our full carbon footprint analysis shows that we have five times less carbon footprint than traditional menstrual products,' Raut continues. 'And on top of that, switching to WUKA would mean a 50 per cent cost saving over two years compared to leading brands.'

So not only is switching better for the planet and your own health, it can also be a win for your wallet at the same time. Yet another category where Change Brands are emerging rapidly and making a really positive impact.

The Beyond Meat of Pet Food

When Alessandro Di Trapani heard the stat that 'dogs and cats consume 20 per cent of the world's meat and fish', he was blown away. In fact, 'if dogs and cats formed their own country, they'd be the fifth largest meat consumers in the world. It's basically USA, Brazil, Russia, China and then dogs and cats'. At a time when it's becoming increasingly clear that we need to cut down on the amount of meat we eat to reduce the effects on the climate, some of the biggest culprits are hiding in plain sight. While our furry friends might be cute, they eat a lot of meat, and that contributes a lot to climate change.

Armed with this insight, Di Trapani and his co-founder, Hugh Petit, set out to create 'the Beyond Meat of pet food'. There was clearly a big environmental issue with the status quo and they believed there had to be a better way: 'The question we set out to solve was how can we feed pets in a healthy and nutritious way without using traditional protein sources?' They started researching alternative sources of protein. 'The veterinary backing for plant based wasn't quite there and cats couldn't go vegetarian as they are obligate carnivores (meaning their diet is at least 70 per cent meat) so that would cut out half the market straight away.' The costs for lab-grown meat were prohibitive so that wasn't feasible from day one.

Their research took them into the world of insect protein, a fast-growing area with a lot of investment behind it: 'In terms of macronutrients, it has twice the protein of beef per 100 grams, all of the essential amino acids and is rich in omega-3s.' It also had huge sustainability benefits: 'One tonne of insects can be grown in 14 days using less than 30 litres of water and 20 square meters of land.' That's less than the size of a shipping container. 'And when you compare that to traditional livestock, it's quite compelling what you can do from a sustainability perspective.'

There was also one additional benefit that arose from using insect protein. 'A lot of people don't realize that dogs and cats develop allergies to traditional sources of protein, leading to skin and digestive issues. But because insect protein is a novel source of protein for them, it's really great for pets with dietary intolerances,' Di Trapani continued. 'The sustainability story was important, but we needed something beyond sustainability and the nutritional story was equally compelling, which is vital because people really love their pets and want to do what's right for them.'

The dual benefit of not only being the best thing for the planet, but also being great for your dog or cat, especially those with digestive issues or allergies, has been an important part of finding their first customers. By connecting a problem with the category and an area of impact, they've created a Change Brand that is gathering momentum and building loyalty among pet owners.

Di Trapani and Petit have carved out a compelling brand positioning in a nascent market. The benefits of insect protein for pets are there for all to see and it's only a matter of time before the bigger players who dominate the category like Mars and Nestlé come to the party. It feels like there's real parallels with digital photography here so it won't be long before we see this shift really gathering pace. The traditional supply chain for pet food from livestock requires hectares of land, lots of water and takes a long time. Insect protein offers a way to cut down on the land needed to become much more efficient in generating the amount of protein needed for pet food and without any of the ethical issues that come with raising animals for pet food.

After multiple rounds of testing with pet owners and working closely with an animal nutritionist to make sure they got the taste and texture right, in December 2021, Grub Club was born. The idea of a community of pet owners making a collective impact on a problem while still doing the right thing by their furry friends. For people who are concerned about climate change but don't want to stop eating meat themselves, it gives them a way to make a tangible difference without going fully plant-based. Getting us humans to eat a more planet-friendly diet is one of the most difficult behavioural switches for them to make because of our emotional relationship with food. Try telling a large proportion of the American population that they can't eat another burger or steak and you'll be met with serious resistance. So, for those who are motivated by sustainability, it's far easier to change what your dog or cat eats than to fundamentally alter your own diet and it's likely to be the right choice for them nutrition wise as well. An absolute win-win.

Raise a Glass

'There's a big debate about whether modern civilization formed around grains for food or grains for beer,' Louisa Ziane, Co-founder and COO of beer brand Toast, explains. 'There's a lot of evidence of the Mesopotamian people using grain to make beer, dating all the way back to around 3000 BC.' In fact, ancient civilizations used wild yeast to ferment the baked grains found in bread to create some of the earliest beers, and Toast decided to tap into this millennia-old innovation.

As Ziane explains, the relationship between bread and beer has always been closely intertwined, but modern production methods have moved on, and not for the better. 'There used to be a lot more symbiosis where you would have businesses like a brewery being located next to a bakery. The bakery would use the yeast from the brewery, and they'd work together. It was a much more circular economy because resources were scarce.' Ziane continues: 'That whole concept of "one man's trash is another man's treasure" was just how we really used to live. We've become this global society where a lot of businesses don't even know where the original supply of ingredients is coming from. They're focused on cost. "What's the price I'm paying? How do I get it as cheap as possible?"'

The Toast founders, Ziane and Tristram Stuart, a prominent food waste campaigner, saw an opportunity to solve a problem with something they loved. 'Nowadays, humans produce a lot of bread. This is an intensive process using land, water and energy, but 44 per cent of that bread is wasted. Food production is the biggest contributor to climate change, but one third of all food is wasted,' they explain.

Tristram met the brewers behind the Brussels Beer Project, who had just used bread in one of their beers in a nod to the origins of beer. Working in food waste, he joined the dots and dug a little deeper. Bread is one of the most wasted foods in the word, with the UK wasting 20 million slices of bread every single day.* Toast worked with local bakeries to collect surplus bread, particularly sandwich bread and heel end loaves that are usually discarded. The sugars in sandwich bread are easily accessible and it allowed them to put all this excess bread to good use, replacing a big part of the malted barley that goes into beer and requires a lot of land and water to grow.

'We pitched the idea into Jamie Oliver's team and he really loved it,' Ziane explains. 'So, we got the brewer over from Brussels to come over and it was all turned around pretty quickly. A month later and we were getting filmed for his show *Friday Night Feast* and Toast was born.'

Since then the brand has been on an impressive journey. 'If you stacked all of the slices of bread we've saved since launch in 2016, they'd be nearly five times the height of Mount Everest,' Ziane continues. The brand is now stocked in three major supermarkets,

---

* WRAP - https://www.wrap.ngo/sites/default/files/2020-11/Food-surplus-and-waste -in-the-UK-key-facts-Jan-2020.pdf

have won multiple awards along the way, including five Great Taste Awards, and they have their own bar in Central London. They've also had a big impact on the established beer brands and their supply chain. 'We've seen a real shift over the past three to four years. All the big brewers now have done something to improve their supply chain on the grain side, either working with us or starting their own trials.'

The creativity of taking a waste product hiding in plain sight in everyone's houses and turning it into something great should be celebrated. 'That's what I love about the circular economy. It's taking us back to people being super creative. How we set up the business it was seeing a problem, and then asking how do we solve it? A lot of businesses are setup because people just see an opportunity to make money. But I think that's the difference with purpose led brands. It's seeing a problem and then using the model of business to try to solve that, while creating a successful business at the same time.'

Let's raise a glass to Toast and the creative thinking that proves creating a Change Brand isn't all hard graft. As Ziane likes to say, 'If you want to change the world, you just have to throw a better party than those who are destroying it!'

From Little Acorns, Mighty Oaks Grow

In 2012, on a student exchange trip to the University of Hawaii, Canadians David Luba and Kalen Emsley spent a lot of time outside, enjoying the natural environment. While they were on a hike and, seeing as they had just graduated, they started talking about their future. They had an idea: 'We realized that there's nothing out there that gives back to the environment that the consumer has the option to buy.' Emsley and his brother Derrick had already been running a tree planting business and the three of them saw an opportunity to work together on a new venture.

Initially, they created a T-shirt that had 'One tonne' printed across the front to symbolize the one tonne of carbon captured through tree planting that its sale would fund. While it was positively received, it quickly became clear they needed a brand to hold everything together and Tentree was born.

'The fundamental concept was straightforward; we would plant 10 trees for every item sold,' Luba explains.

The simplicity of the idea was the secret to its success. It was in the name and front and centre in the branding and many of the original designs. One sale, ten trees planted.

'We set out to keep everything very simple,' Luba continues. 'At the time, there was a tonne of negativity and complexity surrounding the environment and restoring our planet and we wanted to be different. The simplicity of the Tentree model and in-built optimism really resonated. When we got this reaction, we knew we had something special as we started with a movement and brand first and product second. Most other businesses start the other way around.'

A selection of Tentree apparel © Tentree

Launching a fashion brand without any prior experience in the sector presented a challenge. While they knew tree planting from their previous experience, entering the clothing market proved a bit of a shock to the system.

'We didn't want to start an apparel company, we wanted to start a business that gave back to the planet. We picked apparel as buying T-shirts and screen printing on them was easy, inexpensive and fast to get started. Little did we know it is a very challenging and complex business,' Luba explains.

The rapid growth of the brand and the expansion beyond T-shirts into a full clothing range was a learning curve: 'Through experimentation, we honed our skills in sustainable product development alongside tree planting, embodying the motto progress over perfection.'

Fast forward to 2023 and it's fair to say this acorn of an idea has turned into a mighty oak. Tentree have planted over 100 million trees worldwide through selling their clothing. They have even gone a step further by setting up their own tree planting platform, which means they have full control of the regenerative side of the business and they can help other brands to meet their tree planting commitments. In many ways, the launch of the Veritree B2B proposition is a case of the brand coming full circle.

'For us, Tentree was never an apparel business that planted trees, it was a tree-planting company that sold apparel,' Derrick Emsley, now CEO of Tentree, said. Creating this platform is a way to accelerate the mission even further. 'We are big believers that businesses are going to be the most significant driver of change when it comes to climate, nature, preservation, biodiversity loss. Businesses have the ability to really be the catalyst and the driver of fixing some of these issues.'

Infinite Combinations, Infinite Possibilities

In a world plagued with a shopping list of problems, there is no shortage of areas where you can make an impact. There is room for improvement in almost every category. This means there is an almost infinite number of combinations. Infinite possibilities for how a Change Brand could make a real difference and keeping those two elements front of mind is vital.

Starting with impact gives you a North Star. A reason for being and something for people to care about. You can measure progress against that target and remind yourself of the difference you've made when times invariably get harder. It gives you something to constantly be aiming to address and a way to refocus if you need to evolve your proposition down the line. By starting with impact, it sits at the heart of the brand from day one, rather than other players who may try to retrofit purpose into the brand with spurious greenwashing claims or ill-thought-through partnerships to respond to consumer demands.

Addressing a category problem gives you another tension to push against and a way to build disillusion with the status quo. While at a top-line level this may sound easy, and there may be some easy wins to start with, there are often challenges and costs associated with moving the needle forward. A Change Brand needs to become an expert in the 'Art of the Possible', mastering what can and can't be done in each category to make a difference. This is something that the next chapter dives into in detail and its importance cannot be underestimated.

CHAPTER SIX

Take the High Ground

'When they go low, we go high.'

Michelle Obama

Leadership in different sectors of business can take many forms and isn't quite as clean-cut as you might initially think. This chapter will explore four different types of leadership and how Change Brands can think about each of those to set themselves up for success in the short and long term.

First, there is the obvious type of leadership. That of being the biggest player in the space. These are the true Goliaths of any category. Let's call it Category Leadership – the brand or business that sells the most product and has the biggest market share. More customers buy these brands than any other, in part due to being so well-known and having almost universal distribution, so they're very easy to buy. But history has shown that size isn't everything and that current success isn't necessarily a predictor of future success. The concept of creative destruction we discussed earlier in the book has shown that this type of category domination can be fleeting. Kodak, Nokia, BlackBerry, Blockbuster and many others have fallen by the wayside as new brands have emerged.

Success can breed complacency. Big businesses move slowly and have multiple layers of complexity. The traits that made them successful in the first place may be on the wane. We have seen that without a constant eye on the future and being fully plugged into audience trends and behaviours, these big brands have the potential to fade over time if they're not careful.

Big brands can become the victims of their own success. They are rarely unassailable and, with so many different routes to market and traditional gatekeepers no longer holding all the keys, it's now easier than ever to get your brand in front of their audience to start to eat away at their share. Change Brands don't need to take an enormous market share to be a serious thorn in their side.

In part, human nature fuels creative destruction. Brand loyalty is hugely over emphasized and the majority of people buy multiple brands in each category for a wide variety of reasons, changing their preference many times a year. This might be down to a hard-working promotion, an advert that caught the eye or their mood on a particular day. Humans are drawn to novelty, to the new and the interesting. We're hardwired to look for new options to meet our needs because they might be an improvement on the current preferred option. There might also be a little bit of something called 'Tall Poppy syndrome' at play. This is a cultural force that comes into play when people of high status or achievements are cut down to size because of their success. They become targets for criticism and we find new heroes to champion. We get bored when one sports team wins constantly and like seeing them come back to the norm after a period of success, having the same struggles as everyone else. In the words of the opening quote from Adam Morgan's original challenger brand book, *Eating the Big Fish*, 'everyone pulls for David, no one roots for Goliath'.

The second type of leadership in a space is Brand Leadership. You can be the preferred brand of the most people in a category, but still not have category leadership in terms of sales and share. This is likely a factor of current market dynamics, such as the leading brand being stocked in more places, and if that category leading brand has a weaker brand than another player, their leadership isn't likely to last for long.

Dom Boyd, Managing Director of Kantar Insights UK, would describe this as 'Brand Magic', the special sauce a brand needs for future success. Kantar have spent years studying this and their Brand Power methodology is the benchmark for measuring the equity of brands. Those with high Brand Power have the power to capture significantly more volume, can command a higher price point and have much greater potential to gain value share in the future. While these brands may not be leading the category now in terms of sales, they are certainly on the right track and are likely to take that leadership position in the future. A powerful brand also makes the business more resilient in times of crisis.

Strong Brand Power comes from three metrics. First, being meaningful. This means the brand meets people's needs functionally and they feel emotionally connected to it. The second is being seen as different; that the brand is perceived as a dynamic trendsetter for its category and is unique. The advantage of being a Change Brand when it comes to these two metrics is that by following the formula described in the previous chapter, you're highly likely to have identified a meaningfully different position in the market already.

The third metric is salience, being a brand that comes to mind quickly in a buying situation. This means the brand is highly recognizable and easy to recall. To an extent this is a result of time in market and media spend. It's really expensive to build salience in large markets. A brand that's been around for a long time and invested a lot in advertising and distribution is likely to be highly salient. It is created through a variety of different ingredients that help grow a brand's distinctiveness within a category. A highly salient brand can't be created overnight. It takes time, investment and careful thought to build, and we come onto how you can put the right ingredients in place in the next chapter.

After taking a look at the Kantar Brand Z data, it's clear that Change Brands have carved out an extremely differentiated position when compared to legacy brands. A cohort of brands that include Tesla, Oatly, Vinted, Method, Ecover, Patagonia, Beyond Meat and Tony's Chocolonely had an average difference index of 180, meaning they're almost twice as differentiated as the average brand. The data tells us what we expected to see, that Change Brands are seen as more unique and dynamic than the average brand.

Where Change Brands fall down currently is on salience. This is a direct factor of time in market, distribution and media investment. With these brands being relatively new kids on the block, they haven't had the time to build up the same memory associations in people's minds as brands who've been around for decades. The first brand you think of in a category is likely to be the massive player who is on every single shelf and you've seen their advertising for years. Compare Coca-Cola to Liquid Death. Liquid Death might be more differentiated and unique, but Coca-Cola is top of mind and therefore most salient.

A strong brand isn't just about sales today, it's about future sales as well. By building a brand in people's mind, you're also unlocking future sales so they think of you when they're next in a buying situation (and you're on the shelf). The Brand Z data looks at the future potential of a brand to grow and command a premium price. The Change Brands in the study are 16 per cent more likely than other brands to grow in the next 12 months and are 10 per cent more likely to be able to command a higher price in future than the average brand. People also see these brands as over 20 per cent more likely to gain importance in the future and standing for something unique than all the other brands in the study. So, a unique, differentiated brand unlocks future sales and the ability to charge more.

While Category Leadership is out of reach for Change Brands in the first few years, having a strong eye on Brand Leadership and making sure the right building blocks are put in place from day one stands you in good stead for the future and is a leading indicator of future success. The brand truly is everything, particularly in highly commoditized categories. While product is important when you're starting out, products can be copied and your advantage on that side can be short-lived. People can copy almost every element of your product, but they can't copy your brand. A strong brand can enter new categories and tap into new audiences. Ultimately, brand power beats product power over time.

Mind Over Matter

The third type of leadership in a category is Thought Leadership. This means that while you are not the market leader in terms of sales, you are driving the conversation in the category and doing things differently. One of the key credos from the original Challenger Brands playbook, this still holds true to this day. This is the brand that is the most talked about in a space because they're doing things differently and driving the category forward. The term 'Thought Leadership' might sound like it comes from technology, innovation and academia, but this is not the case. It's not about being seen as the cleverest brand or product in the category. OK, when Dyson first entered the market with their bagless vacuum cleaners or when the iPod disrupted how people listened to music, this put them at the vanguard of the category, but this sort of leadership is extremely rare, expensive to create in the first place because it comes from extensive NPD, and difficult to maintain as competitors catch up.

In practice it comes from doing things differently in a category, understanding the accepted way of doing things and then subverting them. Every category has a series of conventions. These are the things that people expect to see when shopping a category and they recognize them as a shortcut to help them make quick buying decisions. They could be the way a product is packaged (such as mineral water in clear plastic bottles), the colour pallet (chewing gums in 'fresh' colours like blue and green) or the way they advertise a product (toilet paper ads featuring puppies, bears and koalas in an effort to communicate softness). By playing with these conventions, a brand can establish standout and get talked about for pushing the envelope and having a bit of fun with the category.

Naming also has a big role to play in challenging conventions. When he first burst onto the scene among high-end London restaurants, celebrity chef Heston Blumenthal created a risotto dish called Snail Porridge that stood out like a sore thumb on menus that were typically a little more flowery in the language they used. This subversive naming that brought the conventions of a simple everyday breakfast into fine dining got picked up in the media, becoming a must-try dish that brought people into the restaurant in droves. Something that would never have happened if he'd just called it a 'fricassée of snails with an oat risotto.' The names Liquid Death and Who Gives A Crap use the same technique to really stand out in their category and create talkability. A water brand that offers 'death' and a brand entering the prim and proper toilet roll category, where no one mentions what it's actually used for, using a slang term for excrement, both created instant stand-out with just a few well-chosen letters.

The next chapter takes a detailed look at Category Conventions and how Change Brands have had real success by recognizing and playing with them to achieve real standout in their categories.

---

* Morgan, A. (2003), *Eating the Big Fish: How Challenger Brands Can Compete Against Brand Leaders*, Wiley

Take the High Ground

Now the final way a Change Brand can try to take control of a category is through Moral Leadership. As discussed in the previous chapter, no category is perfect in the way it does things. These imperfections, whether big or small, are becoming more visible to our audiences as the emphasis on sustainability and social issues gathers pace. In a world where the focus on the problems we face is at an all-time high, there is almost no place to hide for status-quo brands.

By talking about the problem in a compelling and credible manner, you can establish moral leadership of a category. Explaining the negative impact of the status quo in an impactful way and then positioning your brand as the solution is a tried-and-tested strategy. 'Problem-solution' marketing has been used to great effect to sell products like anti-ageing for decades. For each societal problem out there, it's highly likely they'll be compelling data and powerful stories you can leverage to establish the problem in people's minds.

Moral Leadership is a component of Thought Leadership that really zeroes in on what makes Change Brands special. Category problems create opportunity for Change Brands. Whether it is an issue with packaging, ingredients or the supply chain itself, it's almost impossible for a major consumer goods company to make quick changes to their established processes. They are operating at massive scale and shipping billions of units. Making a change to the supply chain costs serious money and takes a long time but a Change Brand can create an alternative because they're operating at a much smaller scale and starting from scratch in their production process.

It's a smart strategy for Change Brands to use their product to establish Moral Leadership of the category. A number of the brands we've talked about have done exactly that. For example,

Allbirds built a position as the most sustainable trainer on the planet. SURI toothbrushes have removed all the unnecessary features of electric toothbrushes to create something stripped back and stylish, while Oatly represented a major step forward in terms of carbon footprint.

SURI toothbrushes have done this very well. They've established a problem in the mind of the consumer and created a product that is the solution. They highlight that every year 23 billion toothbrushes are thrown away and that 'every toothbrush you've ever owned is still in existence'. They saw an opportunity to enter a market and make a real impact. 'There are only two big companies who have a 75 per cent market share so we felt like it was ripe for disruption. For someone to come along with a more sustainable, more design-led approach,' said Mark Rushmore, who co-founded SURI in May 2022 alongside Gyve Safavi.* Their simplified electric toothbrushes that strip away all the unnecessary features so they can be easily repaired, combined with recyclable plant-based heads made from cornflour, have been a real success with consumers looking for a more sustainable alternative.

In 2023, SURI sales hit £10 million and there remains ample opportunity for growth in an electric toothbrush market forecast to be worth £35 billion by 2031.

A smol Revolution

The laundry aisle has been a target of serious disruption in this way. Nick Green, former Unilever executive and co-founder of smol, had an interesting perspective on the sector: 'When we looked at the laundry market, put simply we believed there had to be a better option than the big multinational brands. We felt

---

* 'A Start-Up to Make You Smile', *City Am*, 7 May 2024

they had been lazy in their innovation; back then they were still in big plastic bottles and boxes, using chemicals and ingredients that weren't always necessary, selling via supermarkets in an aisle that just wasn't inspiring for anyone. We knew it was a category ripe for a revolution.'

Green, and his co-founder Paula Quazi, saw an opportunity. 'We felt the existing brands were focusing on profit ahead of the customer and the planet, and we knew we could offer something better. We also watched other brands with their "eco" propositions, but these are often premium priced and, disappointingly, currently can't match the performance that customers really need from a detergent. There is little point in being great for the planet if your product doesn't work and is prohibitively expensive – because the majority of people simply won't buy it.'

smol entered the market with their innovative, concentrated laundry capsules that, after a couple of iterations, were packaged entirely in cardboard. Every pack of 27 washes saves the equivalent of four plastic bottles and because of their smaller size, you can fit more of the product on trucks, reducing carbon emissions along the way and all at a very affordable price: 'By keeping prices as accessible as possible, we've grown our smol community to over half a million customers.'

A smol advertising campaign © smol

The plastic problem from laundry is a huge one: 'In 2022 over 70 million plastic packs of detergent went to landfill or incineration in the UK – that's huge. So, we placed a giant washing machine vomiting out plastic packs in the centre of Birmingham to draw attention to this and this really put us on the map with some major media coverage.'

A smol stunt in Birmingham, UK © smol

Since then, the 400 million washes that smol have powered since launch have saved 1.757 tonnes of plastic and reduced the amount of water shipped by over 2 million litres.* These changes have allowed smol to establish moral leadership in a category that was resting on its laurels and dominated by single-use plastic. Alongside laundry, they've also entered the refillable cleaning spray market, with tablets you mix with water at home to cut down on the needless shipping of water. They hit £25 million in sales in 2023 and grew at 131 per cent year on year, with distribution increasing across major retailers as

---

* smol website

well as strong online momentum.* The revolution may have started 'smol', but it's growing at pace now.

They've also had a big impact on the wider sector, with big legacy brands looking to reduce their reliance on plastic packaging. Green continues: 'As a disruptor brand, we're also really well placed to inspire change from the bigger brands. We moved to plastic-free packaging on our laundry and dishwasher products in 2020 and in 2023 we saw the big brands follow suit. It's brilliant when we can have an impact not only via our customers but also via bigger brands who collectively have an enormous footprint.' More proof that when Change Brands gain traction, they act as a catalyst for bigger brands to change their own behaviour.

The Race to the Top

Rather than joining the race to the bottom that we see in most categories, it's time for Change Brands to spark a 'race to the top' and drag other brands with them in the way smol have with the laundry category. By establishing Moral Leadership of a category, Change Brands effectively take the high ground in the space. There are multiple brands doing this and it's proving to be a powerful strategy. As consumers look for better alternatives that allow them to spend their money to live a more sustainable lifestyle, or make a positive impact, brands that occupy the high ground are well placed.

Agent Change believes one of the biggest fears of consumer goods companies is 'getting market share eaten away at from both below and above'. Private label and discounter brands steal share by being the cheaper option to an established brand. They eat away at leading brands market share from below, dragging them into a battle over price. Change Brands eat away share from above, not necessarily

---

* https://www.thetimes.co.uk/article/uk-start-ups-to-watch-sunday-times-100-p8p2bstjp

by being more expensive (although often they do come at a bit of a premium) but by doing the things consumers want and offering a positive alternative. By taking the high ground in a category and offering solutions to category problems, they give people the option to trade up and make a better choice.

One thing to bear in mind is not to be overly worthy or righteous. Trying to place a moral obligation on someone to change their behaviour is unlikely to cut through with large quantities of people. It can sound preachy and have the opposite effect of switching people off, rather than onto your cause. Where Change Brands have had the most success is when they get the message across with charm, humour and a lightness of touch. They are often pushing at an open door anyway and laying on the guilt trip is overly heavy-handed. You can start to sound more like a charity than a Change Brand.

Many of the problems facing the world already feel insurmountable. Turn on the news and you're inundated with a barrage of the things that are wrong with the world and very little in the way of positivity or progress. People are exhausted by this wall of negativity and if they believe there is no way of solving a problem, they are unlikely to engage. They bury their heads in the sand and do nothing. Charity fatigue has become a big thing in the past decade as people are subjected to more and more shocking imagery to try and elicit a donation, but it often has the opposite effect and leads to inertia and apathy. If a Change Brand becomes too negative and overly focused on the problem, it can add to this sense of charity fatigue. Be the ray of hope among the doom scrolling, offering a potential solution rather than adding more fuel to the problem.

By creating a brand that does the right thing in terms of its production and impact and communicating about it in a positive way, you position yourself as part of the solution. The constant value exchange offered by a Change Brand compared to a charity is also very different. People are likely to already be buying something in the category that brand operates in anyway as they go about their lives, so offering support is as simple as picking up one brand rather than a competitor. It's easy to keep 'supporting' those brands because you need the product anyway and get something you need back in return. The charity value exchange is often slightly more one-way, which makes it harder to maintain engagement. Charities can make a real stir with powerful, emotional campaigns that drive an uplift in donations, but it can be difficult to maintain support over the longer term, even with regular updates and new information. Change Brands, on the other hand, particularly those offering a subscription, keep customers for the long term if the customer service is – and remains – up to scratch.

Now of course I'm not saying don't donate to charity. That would be ridiculous. There are so many incredible organizations doing exceptional and vital work across so many sectors and I've been fortunate enough to have worked closely with a lot of them to see this crucial work close up but the point is that it is difficult for people to support every single issue they care about and maintain that support over time, particularly with pressure on household budgets. That direct debit might get cancelled. We're likely to see pressure on household finances for the foreseeable future and this creates extra competition between charities battling for a smaller pool of charitable donations. One thing that is encouraging to see is more charities are looking to explore enterprise style solutions to keep people engaged and increase income.

There is a huge opportunity for charities to launch their own Change Brands around the fringes of their core efforts. They have big and established supporter bases; they have serious trust and credibility in the space they operate in and understand how that money can be best used to make a difference. It helps them to diversify their sources of income and be less susceptible to economic headwinds. They are starting from a much stronger position than many Change Brand founders. I appreciate it can be tricky to make a case to divert funds away from core charitable operations in an already cash-strapped organization where every cent is allocated many times over but the potential upside and powerful precedent demonstrated by brands that are already gaining real traction makes a compelling case and the initial outlay required to test the water is small in the grand scheme of things, given the potential reward and resilience it offers.

I would absolutely love to see a whole raft of Change Brands launched by charities with the proceeds supporting their work. Serious Tissues could just as easily have come out of an environmental charity such as Greenpeace or the Arbor Day Foundation. Change Please could have been an idea launched by Shelter or Covenant House. Toast Ale or Dash Water could have come from the Waste and Resources Action Programme (WRAP) or another charity focused on tackling food waste and creating a circular economy. Dave's Killer Bread and XO Bikes could have come from a charity aiming to break the cycle of reoffending. Almost any charity could step into this space. There are numerous opportunities across adjacent categories where charities could take advantage and add significant income to their bottom line.

By positioning yourself as part of the solution and offering a product people both like and need to buy on a regular basis, you create a gravitational pull that draws people in and keeps them there. Taking the high ground is a powerful strategy as consumer demands continue to shift towards making a positive impact with their money and one that is resilient in times of economic downturns.

Frame the Problem

Wherever you turn nowadays, it's impossible to avoid bad news. It's easy to believe there's so much more going wrong with the world than going right. Political issues, conflict, environmental breakdown, social problems, culture wars... the list is endless. It's enough to make any sane person turn off the TV, throw their phone out the window and bury their head in the nearest plant pot.

So how can you make yourself heard and cut through the noise when people are running for cover and think the world's problems are increasingly insurmountable? Simplicity and clarity are crucial here. To paraphrase Jay-Z, 'I've got 99 problems. Pitch me one.'

Find a single killer stat that makes people care and illustrates the magnitude of the problem. On your journey of researching the problem, you will have become an expert. You will have countless stats and stories at your fingertips that come together to create a powerful impact. Sat down at a dinner party, you can make a hugely compelling case for your product. You have the time and space to communicate but when you're trying to talk to thousands of people, less is most certainly more.

That single killer stat, communicated clearly and consistently, gives you more chance to cut through. If I threw five tennis balls at you, how many do you think you would catch? Anything better than one is a great effort. Think in terms of a single tennis ball. If they catch it, you've done your job. There will be time for greater detail on your website or on social media, but that one killer stat that sticks in people's head is crucial. And do make sure that killer stat will stand up to scrutiny and that the sources are robust. You will need solid evidence to be able to put it out into the world as rightly regulators clamp down on unsubstantiated greenwashing claims.

Some of the killer stats that have landed well for Change Brands include:

- one million trees are cut down every day for toilet roll;
- over 70million laundry packs end up as waste every year;
- one in two people leaving jail end up reoffending;

- a piece of chewing gum contains the same amount of plastic as a plastic straw;
- dogs and cats consume 20 per cent of the world's meat and fish.

The beauty of these stats is that they make it simple for people. They illustrate the scale of the problem to create an urgent need for action and to get them to think differently about their behaviour. Many of them make it tangible. For example, Nuud could have talked about billions of pieces of chewing gum made of plastic that find their way into the world, but by linking it to a plastic straw, it becomes tangible. They also borrow from the negative emotion directed at plastic straws. People know plastic straws are bad, but they don't think the same about chewing gum. Borrowing that negative emotion is a powerful shortcut. Think about the way you talk about numbers too. One in two people reoffending after leaving jail is more powerful than 48 per cent. It's similar to a stat like 'one in two of us will get cancer in our lifetime'. It's impossible not to have our thoughts drawn instantly to the people we love. Will it be you or your wife? Which one of your kids? Now that's a pretty difficult thought to get out of your head.

But a stat alone isn't enough. There's a saying in fundraising circles that I love: you need to think in terms of 'the itch and the scratch'. While that sounds pretty gnarly, triggering thoughts of flaky skin, there's some sound logic here. You need to instigate 'the itch' for people, the problem that they need to act upon. No one can leave an itch unscratched for too long. A killer stat can do this. This then creates the space for 'the scratch' to come in. How your brand and product scratches that itch. A recent advert we created for Serious Tissues did this elegantly and with a touch of humour.

Our stat about 'one million trees' being cut down for loo roll creates the itch, and the panicked reaction of our tree character saying 'I don't want to be loo roll' introduces some emotion into the equation. Then comes the scratch: 'But Serious Tissues don't cut down trees. In fact, they plant trees. Trees like you and me...'. This tried-and-tested problem/solution structure gives you a simple and elegant way of landing why people should buy your product to address a problem they care about. Creating a powerful itch and offering a simple scratch, all in just 30 seconds.

Feeling a little itchy now? Me too. Time to move on and talk about the product.

Minimum Footprint, Maximum Impact

The main objective when it comes to the product is to be an improvement on the current status quo. This breaks down into two elements: minimum footprint and maximum impact.

The first consideration is the footprint it takes to make the product. This falls into a range of areas depending on the product and could mean things like carbon emissions, plastic packaging, harmful or unhealthy ingredients, the circularity of the packaging and what it requires to ship that product to the end user. For example, 90 per cent of what's in a cleaning spray is water, so if you remove the need for that water to be shipped all over the world and remove the unnecessary carbon emissions, the category takes a quantum leap forward in terms of reducing its footprint.

Toast Brewing have changed their source material for their beer to use bread, reducing food waste along the way. Allbirds have done this brilliantly in the shoe category with an innovative and highly sustainable merino wool upper and SweetFoam sole, derived from sugar cane, making the shoe far more sustainable than its synthetic counterparts without sacrificing on comfort. And all at the same price as an equivalent pair of Nikes or Adidas. Even just by shifting mineral water from a plastic bottle to an aluminium can, the footprint of that product is being reduced and you can claim superiority. The more you can minimize this footprint, the more you can position yourself as an improvement on the status quo and the size of these big companies means they'll struggle to match you anytime soon.

The second element is the forward impact of the Change Brand. What difference can a brand make in the world when it starts to reach scale? The options are almost infinite. You could look to make impact with every sale. Warby Parker have donated 15 million pairs of glasses to those in need through their one-for-one model. Tom's Shoes were a trailblazer in this space, first donating shoes and now giving one-third of profits to projects creating equality. It could mean partnering with a charity doing great work in an adjacent area to the brand. For example, Belu Water have donated £5.5 million to Water Aid and this partnership has improved the access to clean water for 330,000 people across the world. Serious Tissues plants trees with every sale and have planted over 1 million trees to date and created employment in some of the world's poorest areas through their partnerships.

You could also change your supply chain, so impact is baked intrinsically into that so just by operating, you create a positive impact. This is a core part of the Tony's Chocolonely offer, working with partners to ensure exploitation-free chocolate by paying a living wage. Change Please employ formerly homeless people as baristas so the impact is also baked into the business model. XO Bikes training model with people leaving jail also makes the impact a fundamental part of how the business operates. The bigger each of these business gets, the bigger the impact. Thinking about how you can maximize that forward impact makes it hard for the competition to compete and cuts through with the audience.

The truth is, it isn't as hard as you think to improve on the status quo. Often, you're looking at a pretty low base because of established practices and the fact big companies' supply chains are highly embedded and difficult for them to change. The key is finding the right mix to make it compelling enough to cut through to potential customers and change their behaviour. Thinking in terms of 'minimum footprint and maximum impact' gives you a powerful proposition that can cut through.

Perfection is the Enemy of Progress

Getting to the right product is a journey, not a destination. Beat the current default option and then keep going and keep improving: minimum footprint, maximum impact. As you get bigger, this will become easier as your scale will open up different supplier options and strengthen your negotiating position. You'll also learn a lot along the way and your offering will change to reflect your customers' preferences. Something that may have seemed key on day one could turn out to be a hygiene factor by the time you've been running for a couple of years. You may not be able to solve everything in one go or be perfect first time but you can get there over time.

Don't let the quest for perfection get in the way of progress. If your brand is an improvement on the status quo, every time someone buys your brand rather than that of a competitor, you have made a positive difference in the world. Change Brand leaders need to become masters of the art of the possible. Whichever category you are setting out to enter, there are already likely to be a lot of manufacturers operating in the space and, depending on their size, they are likely to be open to a conversation.

An important thing to note is that on day one, the really big manufacturers are very unlikely to want to talk to you. They have massive relationships with huge companies that take up most of their production lines and generate most of their revenue so as a new brand with almost non-existent volumes, you're going to struggle to cut through. But don't be disheartened, scroll down a little further and find those people on page two of Google. Always ask for recommendations and introductions if you get a knock back from one manufacturer and you'll find someone to speak to. The beauty of smaller suppliers is they're more likely to be open to a more creative conversation about how you make your product and that is exactly what Change Brands need.

When you enter a category as a new brand, you're likely to be met with some resistance and barriers are very likely to be put up by different manufacturers you might speak to. 'You can't do that' they might say. Or 'that'll never work'. Or even 'so and so is already doing that'. When Surreal were developing their offering, they were faced with resistance from traditional manufacturers. Cereal is a high-volume category and they had 50–60 different conversations with manufacturers before they eventually started working with an American university to develop the product. This gave them the chance to develop something unique that they could then take to different manufacturers as they hit scale.

Remember that someone new entering their category can be either an opportunity or a threat. They have business to protect and existing relationships to manage. Their jobs and commission might rely on a particular client. As a new brand, the immediate return for them is likely to be small in the short term and not a lot of salespeople think beyond the end of the current year. It's your job to get them excited about your brand and the potential for the future, while still offering them a way to make money in the short term.

Doing things differently can also add complexity to the manufacturing process. In the case of Serious Tissues, eliminating plastic from the supply chain has been a difficult process. The machines can run far more quickly when they're wrapping the product in plastic than using paper or cardboard boxes. We've had to think differently on multiple occasions and have been met with the chance to take the path of least resistance repeatedly along the way. It's important to hold true to your principles.

Asking questions and thinking creatively about the manufacturing process is vital. Just because something has always been done in a certain way doesn't mean it always will be. Homethings set out to create an effervescent cleaning tablet that would work in the same way as a vitamin supplement such as Berocca: you drop it in water and it fizzes to create your cleaning product. This was a challenge initially because most of the companies doing this used their machines for food grade products and were reluctant to use cleaning ingredients. By persisting, they found a supplier that could do it and Homethings was born.

SURI had a similar challenge when trying to find a factory to make their product and prove that perseverance is key. 'Twenty-four factories, I think, told us that it was impossible to make a toothbrush head with cornstarch [cornflour] and castor oil bristles, and I'll be honest, after about 22 of them I said to Gyve, maybe it's just not possible,' says Mark Rushmore when explaining the process they went through to produce their product. 'But Gyve just said, "nah, it is…" and finally we found one.'*

Improving your product is a journey, not a destination. It takes time and you'll always be striving to push it forward. The important thing is to make sure your initial offer is better than the status quo in the category and then continue to go from there and push for more and more improvements. The end result of a well-constructed product proposition is that it gives you moral leadership of the category but it is absolutely vital to be able to back up your claims and be as transparent as possible because if you don't, you undermine the efforts of every brand out there who is trying to move in the right direction. You're unlikely to be perfect from day one so it's important to share where you're not perfect and what you're looking to do to improve on that.

---

* *City Am*, May 2024

When Tony's Chocolonely identified in their Impact Report[*] that there were still some children working on their farms it caused a bit of uproar in some areas of the media. After all, weren't they supposed to be slavery-free? But the point was that through their monitoring, that they published themselves in their own report, they had shown that their Five Principles methodology, alongside International Labour Organization best practice,[†] had reduced child labour rates from the typical 46 per cent in any given farm down to 4 per cent over three years. So not only was that 90 per cent of the problem of child labour dealt with in just three years through their model of living income payments, long-term relationships and traceability, but they had also identified the 4 per cent and reported it so they could work on those final steps to achieve their goal.

The fact that Tony's were called out on this in the media is no surprise, but it was hardly a great piece of investigative journalism on the ground in West Africa. It was on the Tony's website and the journalist then made a headline of it. While at a high level it might reflect badly on Tony's, the fact they've identified it and been transparent continues to draw attention to the mission and the fact that the average cocoa farm is still operating at 46 per cent child labour rates, as opposed to a 4.4 per cent child labour rate at Tony's long-term partner cooperatives.

A similar thing happened in the world of toilet roll in early 2024. Three UK-based bamboo brands were found by a *Which?* magazine exposé, which conducted extensive testing of toilet roll fibres, to have 'astonishingly low levels of bamboo' and it sent shockwaves through the sector. The brands tested had just 2.7 per cent, 4 per cent and 26 per cent bamboo in the product that they were marketing as

---

[*] Tony's Annual FAIR Report - https://tonyschocolonely.com/uk/en/annual-fair-reports
[†] International Labour Organization (ILO) - Child Labor Monitoring and Remediation System (CLMRS)

100 per cent bamboo – and 100 per cent tree-free. This meant that rather than selling a more eco alternative to consumers, they were basically selling the worst of all worlds – a toilet roll made from virgin pulp trees like eucalyptus and acacia (linked to deforestation in Asia) and then shipped 20,000 kilometres to the UK to be sold at a premium price during a cost-of-living crisis.

It really didn't look great and if any of these companies knew what they were selling, it is one of the worst examples of greenwashing that we've seen. But whether they knew what they were selling or they were duped by an unscrupulous manufacturer somewhere in the supply chain, the key take out here is taking responsibility for ensuring that the product you're selling is what you say it is. The one good thing to come out of it is more scrutiny on the sector and more radical transparency can only be a good thing.

If this moral leadership is constructed well and you can be certain to the veracity of your claims, it is something that is almost impossible for big brands to follow quickly so gives Change Brands an advantage that can last. Agent Change eloquently explained the reasons for this: 'Scale is vital in large Consumer Packaged Goods [CPG] companies and the thing that gives them their advantage. They need to apply changes to the production line to billions of units, rather than a few thousand, for it to make a material difference to their business. It's possible for smaller brands to do it, but it's hard to generate the appetite to pour billions into changing production lines that are already highly optimized and generating lots of revenue. Yes, it's happening, but it takes years, not months, to see change come to fruition.'

This ability to experiment with product at a small scale to carve out a point of difference is a huge advantage to a Change Brand that can't be copied by big CPG players. Embrace the agility and use your product to carve out a competitive advantage that gives you the moral leadership of a category that consumers will find attractive.

This also has the effect of giving you a meaningful positioning in their mind, which strengthens the brand itself.

Sweat the Small Stuff

One final thing before we move on to the next chapter. There are some really important practical things you need to consider when it comes to your product and the underlying health of the business in both the short and long term. By getting into the detail and sweating the small stuff early, you identify problems sooner and know where to focus your efforts. A lot of the below is from lived experience, both good and bad, and things I would have done differently or earlier if I could turn back the clock.

1. Low Minimum Order Quantities – Starting small at the beginning is a sensible move. This allows you to test the product with the audience and start to build a following without overstretching. Yes, you will get better deals as volume grows, but starting with smaller orders is smart. Certain products will also have lower Minimum Order Quantities than others (MOQs) which gives you an easier entry point. Once you have product market fit and a growing customer base, you can then expand the volumes that you order at.

2. Postage Size and Cost – As a new brand needing to establish a customer base, operating as a Direct to Consumer business, at least initially, is likely to be a key part of your go-to-market strategy. This allows you to show that people are buying your brand. With this in mind, thinking about the size of your product and how much it will cost to get into people's hands is important. Unsurprisingly, smaller products cost less to post than a large box of 36 toilet rolls. Keep delivery costs down at the start while developing your customer base.

3. Unit Economics – Get as close to the unit economics as possible from day one. This means really understanding all the costs associated

with getting your product to the customer so you can have an eye on building a profitable business from day one. A good way to look at this is by calculating your Contribution Margin (CM).

There are three levels to this. CM1 is basically your gross profit (GP), calculated by taking your Sale price and deducting Cost of Goods Sold (COGS). This will give you a number and a percentage and calculating this on a per unit basis at the start makes sense before you get an idea of volumes. For example, if you sell your product for £30 and your COGS is £10, you have a GP of £20 or 66.7 per cent.

CM2 includes logistics costs such as delivery, fulfilment and storage. Let's say this costs £8 per unit, you then deduct this from CM1 to give you a CM2 of £12 or 40 per cent. Finally, you need to factor in marketing costs and this happens in CM3. How much will it cost you to land each customer? Now while this is tricky to pin down from day one, you will have an early indicator from online tools such as Google and Meta.

Working through this example, if your initial cost of acquisition is below £12 you would be profitable on first purchase, whereas if you're above that, you'd be slightly behind. Knowing this from day one gives you an idea of what you can afford to spend on getting customers for your model to work. Let's say you have a Cost Per Acquisition (CPA) of £7, you then deduct this from CM2 to give you a CM3 of £5 (£12–£7). This would mean you're making £5 per sale or 16.7 per cent.

As you grow and potentially add new products, calculating each CM with the volume of each product baked in is important because you will see products that are making you more money and those that might be losing you money. You do this by multiplying the sale price and cost of goods in CM1 by the units sold. If we sold 3,000 units a month, this would look like this:

CM1 – (3,000 x £30) – (3,000 x £10). £90K – £30K = £60,000 (66.7 per cent)

CM2 – £60,000 – (3,000 x £8). £60K–£24K = £36,000 (40 per cent)

CM3 – £36,000 – (3,000 x £7). £36K–£21K = £15,000 (16.7 per cent)

So, with this example, if you sell 3,000 units and keep costs as per the model, you would be £15K in front each month, but if your CPA suddenly doubles, your margin becomes very thin. This model also allows you to more finely calibrate what your sale price should be and any discount you offer upfront to make it affordable and attractive in the first place. Going through this process gives you a deeper understanding of where you need improvements along the way. Are your COGS too high? Is there a cheaper way to do fulfilment? How can you reduce your CPA? If you have customers on subscription, then after the first purchase, the contribution margin for each sale is the CM2 number because you don't need to pay again for acquisition as long as you retain customers. If your fixed costs are higher than what you're making each month, it gives you a target number of units you need to sell to hit break even. All of these insights help the business focus on what will make it successful in the long run.

4. Embrace Feedback – Listen to your customers from day one. Your early customers can potentially become your biggest advocates and if you can establish a two-way dialogue early on, it can be really valuable. They can give you an important steer on how the product needs to improve when compared to the competition. If you're contemplating a change to the branding or packaging, test it with your audience. Not only will they provide valuable insight, they will also appreciate being asked and it deepens the relationship. If you're thinking about a product extension, ask them what it is they'd like to see from you. When they then see it come to market, they're already primed to buy it.

Thinking of how you can build feedback loops into your brand which then go on to influence your product is a smart way to keep your growing customer base engaged and interested. Certain brands are incredible at cultivating their community and making it two-way. Lego are probably the gold standard in this with all sorts of initiatives to keep their community engaged, such as Lego Ideas, a programme where fans can create their own Lego sets, and if they get enough votes from the community, they go into production.

5. Future Extendability – While you might start with just one product, it's important to think of where the brand can go in the future. This shows you are more than a one-trick pony and a brand going places, rather than a single product. Liquid Death started as canned water but now offer a fast-growing Iced Tea range and electrolytes. Oatly now offer yoghurt and ice cream. Wild do a body wash, Allbirds produce clothing. They've done all the hard work of getting people to love their brand so extending the product range means leveraging your brand to increase the ways they can get on board. This also has the effect of increasing your revenue and therefore the impact you're having on the world.

    It's also important to look at different routes to market as well. Change Please started out as coffee carts on the street but are now stocked in retailers and have had major success in being the coffee supplier of choice in a range of major corporates, from Virgin Atlantic to Google.

You can't come into a category and dominate from day one but by putting the right things in place at the start, you can set yourself up for success. Creating your brand with an eye on the elements that will stand it apart in the long term is an important first step. A strong brand isn't a frivolous indulgence, it sets you up for future sales and it's firmly established that stronger brands are more resilient in tough times. Think in terms of those three dimensions of Brand Power to ensure you're meaningful, different and salient from as early in the journey as possible.

One of the first things you can do when you enter a category is to take the high ground. Establish moral leadership by demonstrating the scale of the problem and show how you offer a better solution to the status quo. Early on, this is a case of becoming a master of the art of the possible. Understanding what manufacturers can do and asking naive questions to get them to think differently can unlock new opportunities and help you to differentiate your product from day one. This gets easier over time because as your volume grows, you have more options from a production point of view and you are a more attractive client. This gives you an incentive to grow to take your product and business to the next level.

Finally, don't forget to dive into the detail from early on. Yes, it's important to have a compelling vision of how the world is going to be better with your brand in it and the difference you will make, but you won't survive long without sweating the small stuff, particularly the unit economics. You might be setting out to change the world, but you won't be able to do that if the numbers don't add up.

CHAPTER SEVEN

Smash Category Conventions

'Why fit in when you were born to stand out?'

Dr Seuss

It's a seriously hot day. The city is dry and dusty, and it feels like there's no respite. Shade is in short supply. You step into the welcome air-conditioned comfort of the nearest supermarket, feeling the relief as that first blast of cool air hits you.

You're properly thirsty. It's the kind of thirst where only an ice-cold water will do the job. You walk up to the chiller and you've found what you're looking for: those clear plastic bottles with condensation dripping down the outside. The purity of the liquid. Imagery of mountains. A smattering of different shades of blue. Meaningless names vaguely relating to the origin of the liquid. They all look exactly the same. You pick up the closest one. Walk to the counter and buy it. Job done. But do you remember which brand you bought? And does it matter?

Of course it matters. Marketing teams spend millions of dollars each year to get you to pick up their brand. But the bottled water category is a wall of sameness; full of what's called category conventions, the established thing to do in each category. The problem is, if you're a brand that wants to stand out, following category conventions means you become lost in a sea of sameness.

The water category. Same same, but different

The category conventions in bottled water are there for all to see. Clear plastic bottles, imagery of mountains, the colour blue and a name that alludes to where the water comes from. Promises of health, cleanliness and purity. Category conventions do provide an element of strength in numbers, ensuring instant recognition, but they also mean your brand just blends in and stands for nothing in the grand scheme of things. How do you stand out when everyone is wearing the same uniform?

But in 2019, a new brand entered the market that decided to do things differently. And they didn't just tweak things a tiny bit to stay within the world of water, they decided to go fully off the reservation and set fire to every single possible category convention in the process. Mike Cessario, an advertising creative, saw an opportunity:

'Why aren't healthy brands marketed in the same fun way that unhealthy brands are marketed? Why is it that big companies invest billions to have people associate their products with fun, but healthy brands don't do that? It doesn't make any sense.'*

Cessario saw big benefits in being an outsider in the category: 'Sometimes it's better to not know the rules than to just come in and be told you can't do that. My question was always, why can't you do that?'

It started with the name. Rather than something relating to purity or health, they went the other way and in their launch advert talked about the darker side of water, how water is deadly and even had their spokesperson 'waterboarding' a victim. The name 'Liquid Death' was born. Perhaps the most ridiculous name for a water brand ever, but that's kind of the point. Cessario elaborates: 'What's the opposite of what the water industry is doing? What would that look like? What's the dumbest, worst name anyone could imagine being on a water? That's when you start getting to something truly innovative.'

The highly distinctive Liquid Death brand © Liquid Death

---

* Uncensored CMO podcast, March 2024

Rather than a logo featuring mountains or flowers, their logo borrows from the world of rock music with a terrifying skull emerging from water. And instead of a tagline relating to purity or origin, Liquid Death promised to 'Murder Your Thirst'. Even the typeface used dispensed with the usual clean, minimal font to borrow from the world of rock music with a more gothic-looking font.

The black colour used in their brand, either in the typeface or as the can colour for their sparkling variant, was something that you just never saw in a water category dominated by blues, whites and the odd splash of green.

Everything about the brand was different. It was using the category conventions of different categories, bringing what people were used to seeing from energy drinks or beer brands to the far healthier water category. Now people could look like they were drinking something else when they were simply staying hydrated. It also tapped into a growing shift away from alcoholic drinks with younger generations choosing to drink less, or not drink at all. It gave a whole new audience permission to drink water in a wide range of social settings rather than being the boring one in the corner, holding the bottle of water. Perhaps that was years of marketing and brand building backfiring.

Perhaps the biggest move away from category convention was getting rid of the plastic bottle. Liquid Death is served in tallboy cans, much like a beer or energy drink that they were borrowing from. There was a belief that they needed to see the water inside the bottle to reinforce notions of purity and health but it's probably fair to say that people know what water looks like!

The cans also gave them a major point of difference. It is far easier to recycle aluminium cans than plastic bottles and aluminium is infinitely recyclable. People are wide awake to the problem of single-use plastic and its impact on the environment and Liquid Death gave them a more sustainable alternative and one that was far cooler at the same time.

While the line 'Death to Plastic' is something they've used over the years, the sustainability benefits of the brand come secondary to the enormously entertaining brand world they've created and the army of fans who have got on board. In throwing every single category convention out of the window, they've created something so massively distinctive that you can't help but notice it. Whether it's sat in the chiller alongside other water brands or being drunk at a music festival through their partnership with Live Nation, it stands out. Love or hate the brand, you just can't ignore it. They've built up a cult following with 4.7 million followers on TikTok and 2.7 m Instagram followers. In fact, over 200 fans love it so much that they've had the brand's logo tattooed onto their bodies.[*]

In 2023, just four years after launch, they were doing $263 million in sales and reached a valuation of $1.4 billion. There was nothing particularly revolutionary about the product. There are probably at least 50 other water brands on sale in the United States. All that value has been created by the brand itself, the different elements that have made it so distinctive and the way it has carved out a huge following through entertaining, fame-driving content (more on that later).

The rise of Liquid Death is a case study that will be taught on marketing courses for decades. Experts have long talked about the importance of distinctiveness in crowded, samey categories. Having distinctive brand assets that stand your brand apart and are instantly recognizable as a mental shortcut for people to bring all those positive brand associations to the surface is a big

---

[*] https://www.forbes.com/sites/chloesorvino/2023/04/14/even-with-a-700-million -valuation-liquid-death-may-need-a-lot-of-luck-to-become-liquid-gold/?sh =186606ae6ea3

advantage but until Liquid Death, no one has gone quite so far in eschewing absolutely everything about the category they're in to create something genuinely unique. And it's impossible to argue with the results.

The Change Brand Advantage

The quest for distinctive brand assets in established brands tends to revolve around a search through the archives, pulling out colours they've used in the past, their logo or maybe an old character or jingle. This need to look back and find something they've used in the past to be distinctive is limiting and actually places established brands at a disadvantage. They can't just rip everything up and start again. Any move forward in the brand looks more like evolution than revolution so they're not seen to be dispensing with everything from their successful past but this leads only to incremental nudges forward that barely register for the audience.

There is also safety in sameness. For these big brands, they don't want change. The status quo works very nicely for them so why would they reinvent themselves if they don't have to? They have a tendency to become overly focused on aligning with norms and this limits their ability to respond to changing consumer preferences of market conditions.

They follow the rules of the category, but aren't rules made to be broken? This is where Change Brands have a major advantage when creating and establishing their brands in a category. They can take a look at every single brand that exists, identify the common category conventions and choose to do what they want with them. They can walk the supermarket aisle and collect up a few years' worth of advertising content to see what stands out. They can identify all the rules that have been created over the years and decide what to do with them. While legacy brands are hamstrung by the past, Change

Brands have the liberation of a blank slate to create something with genuine standout. Having a wall in your office full of all the usual clichés is a good way to remind yourself of the need to stand out and always prompts new ideas or fresh angles to push back against.

A good question to ask yourself when entering a new category and trying to shake up the status quo is what would Liquid Death do? While that may sound a little scary given the lengths they've gone to in order to stand out in the category, the end surely justifies the means. Even if you only go 50 per cent as far, it's still a great start.

Another important thing to consider is that a brand very rarely exists in the isolation you might see it in when you just see the logo: just the brand on a piece of plain paper in an office setting. There is always the context of when it would be seen that grounds it in the category, so people know what the product is. Whether that is the chiller cabinet, a coffee cup or the toilet roll aisle of the supermarket. It's a bit like the presents sitting under the tree at Christmas – people will have a good idea what's inside the wrapper from the shape of the box or the context they see it in.

When creating Serious Tissues, we looked hard at the conventions in the category. Names that alluded to softness such as Cushelle, Charmin, Angel Soft and Andrex. Soft, fluffy brand characters such as puppies, bears, koalas and babies. Soft, pastel colours.

This is a category where almost every product on the aisle is made out of virgin pulp. We wanted our name to stand out and actually mean something. We believe this is a category that has serious issues, so we created Serious Tissues. This would also land well in the wider context of the permacrisis we're living in, with more and more issues talked about on the news every single day.

The other thing notable about the category was that despite the total reliance on trees as the source material, they were conspicuously absent from the brands that dominated the shelf. Unlike the water category, where everyone talks about where the product comes from with imagery of mountains and beautiful tropical gardens, no one talks about the fact that toilet paper comes from trees. It is the proverbial elephant in the room. So, we decided to bring our own trees to the toilet paper aisle to illustrate the fact that we were the tree-friendly version. We created two tree characters, Connie and Oakie, that would sit front and centre on our packaging and be our spokespeople in advertising. Sat in the context of a world of fluffy animals, bringing trees into a category that is so intent on destroying them, is seriously disruptive.

The other thing that is surprisingly absent from the category given its source material is the colour green. Something absolutely synonymous with trees and the sustainability movement. In a world of pastels alluding to softness, we would introduce green into the category. While there is still room to go further with the brand as we look to disrupt the category, these three ingredients give us a much needed point of difference and one that addresses the elephant in the room. One point to note is that we did keep a dusty pink secondary colour in the brand to make sure we still landed the important softness cues that drove the category so we didn't throw every category convention out of the window.

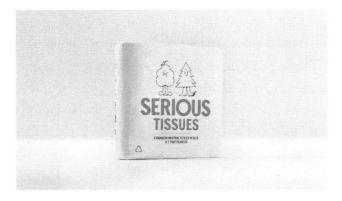

Addressing the elephant in the room with Serious Tissues packaging
© Serious Tissues

We're definitely not the only distinctive Change Brand in the toilet paper category. Who Gives A Crap, the bamboo brand, have done an incredible job of disrupting the status quo and started a long time before us in Australia in 2012. The tone of voice that starts with the name itself runs through the entire brand personality and they have a lot of fun with toilet humour. Introducing levity to a category that perhaps people were a little embarrassed to talk openly about until recently did a great job of helping the brand to stand apart from their 'dry' competition. Their promise to 'Uncrap the world' in their recent brand campaign has also struck a chord with people who are looking for solutions around sustainability.

Alongside the name, the one master stroke they've made to really dial up the distinctiveness of the brand is the way they individually wrap the product. Bright colours and beautiful designs adorn each roll, as well as a little bit of that sense of humour they've become famous for. I'd go so far as to say these rolls have become iconic. They sit proudly next to any toilet and a product that might previously have sat tucked away in the cupboard under the stairs now takes pride of place in the bathroom. They even have an 'Emergency Roll' to inject a bit more fun and trigger people to order again once they're down to their last roll. The packaging does a great job of dialling up the status of the buyer. Not only do they look good, they are also a powerful shortcut to knowing your host takes sustainability seriously (and pays a little more for their loo roll). Who would have thought toilet paper could become a status symbol? But that's the power of great branding.

The wraps also do a great marketing job for the brand when they're in a public location like a café, restaurant or office. The branding stands out in the bathroom and gives people the chance to try before they buy. It's actually worked so well that they might even have become a victim of their own success in both the home and outside, with some people proudly displaying their Who Gives

A Crap roll on the shelf for the world to see, while substituting in a cheaper and less sustainable alternative for day-to-day use.

Who Gives a Crap's iconic paper wraps © Who Gives A Crap

The Importance of Distinctiveness

We talked earlier about the importance of mental availability. The likelihood that someone will recall your brand over the other options out there when they're in a buying situation. This is one of the key reasons why it's vital to be distinctive in your space. Particularly in crowded marketplaces with numerous competing brands, you need to stand apart. Being highly distinctive is a key tool in building mental availability.

By dialling up the distinctiveness of your brand it becomes more easily recognizable and memorable. This helps it to carve out a unique identity that differentiates it from the competitors. It's vital in places like the supermarket shelf, where numerous similar looking brands compete to be the one that's picked up and with people only spending a few seconds making a decision in each category, being instantly recognizable and liked is a huge advantage. The virtual supermarket shelf is no different, with the lead image needing to speak volumes. A brand that looks new, interesting and different gives me a reason to click or pick up the box and find out more.

You can build distinctiveness in a wide range of ways. Your name should sound and mean something unlike anything else in the category and perhaps even start the ball rolling on brand personality. Who Gives A Crap and Serious Tissues both did this in the bathroom aisle. Method, Ecover and Homethings sounded nothing like the established players in the cleaning sector. Allbirds instantly stood out in the footwear market. Who's ever heard of a chocolate brand called Tony's? And what exactly is 'chocolonely'? Grub Club is hugely distinctive when compared to Pedigree or Purina.

Design has a major role to play with the logo and the colours you choose. When developing your brand identity, having all the other brands in the category up on the wall allows you to see if the logo and colour palette you're leaning towards genuinely stands out. If there's a colour that's absent from a category, that could be an opportunity for your brand. Could you bring something interesting from another completely unconnected category into your space in a similar way to Liquid Death bringing beer and energy drink cues into bottled water?

Distinctiveness is about more than just appearance. Brand personality also plays an important role. In a world that feels like it's getting more and more serious every day, a brand that entertains at the same time as meeting an active goal is definitely attractive and gives people a reason to buy, then buy it again and talk to their friends about your product. A Change Brand can talk about the world's problems in a very different way than a charity or government would never be able to. They can make positive change fun, tackling serious problems like climate change, ocean plastic or child exploitation with a lightness of touch that a more serious organization could never go near without getting into a bit of trouble.

If you think about the most memorable people in your life, probably not your very best friends or family, but the ones who've really stood out, it's not solely about looks, they've had something unique about their personality that stops them blending in. It could be the unbelievably optimistic ball of energy, the slightly left-field girl from work who was always coming up with something unexpectedly brilliant, or the posh boy who embraced every single cliché and almost became a caricature of themselves. Be the brand that is impossible to forget, the one you want to hang out with and see what they do next.

One of my least favourite jobs when working on a brand is to define its 'brand personality' or 'tone of voice'. It basically ends up with three to five loosely connected adjectives that give a vague idea of how that brand might communicate in the world. With 'optimistic' being perhaps the most overused word in branding. Andy Pearson at Liquid Death had a similar experience: 'I was like, we probably should put a brand book together because it didn't exist and then I would always go to try to write it. And I was like, man, as soon as I get on the page, this sucks and I don't like it and I feel like I'm just regurgitating dead, inert ideas. And so very quickly I just abandoned the idea of a brand book altogether.'

The breakthrough came when they started thinking more like TV writers than advertisers: 'We're not building a brand, we're building a character and it's really fun. And people like characters, people sometimes like brands, but they always love characters. And the reason why people love characters is because they're messy and they're organic and they're living and they're interesting." This approach liberated the brand from meaningless words on a slide to a living, breathing and evolving character that makes it unique and distinctive. Pearson described working on the brand as 'like being

---

* https://www.gale.agency/blog-posts/is-this-thing-on-ep-11-with-liquid-death -mountain-water-vp-of-creative-andy-pearson

in a TV comedy writers room, developing content for a character, rather than advertising for a brand'.

Distinctiveness cuts through and keeps you top of mind. It fosters loyalty and means people develop a preference for your brand. It means they talk about you because you have a great story to tell. If they're in a hurry, they'll reach for your brand over a competitor. Ultimately it means that more people think of you more often when they're in a buying situation, which will go a long way to driving more sales and a bigger market share.

Distinctiveness and differentiation are often used interchangeably, but in fact mean two different things. Differentiation on the grounds of a meaningful product feature or service is very different to a brand that is instantly recognizable through brand assets. If you see the red of Coke or the yellow of McDonald's, you instantly recall those brands.

People often obsess about the need to differentiate in a category. Spending lengthy workshops agonizing over trying to find a non-existent Unique Selling Point (USP). Differentiation is often overrated as a marketing tool. Do you think the audience really care that much? Be the brand that's liked and memorable, rather than the one that tries to differentiate on a meaningless feature. Differentiation is short-lived, whereas a well created brand can last for decades.

The combination of both is the ideal world. Someone like Apple is still differentiated on their products in some categories but the distinctive brand and the way they present in the world keeps that brand front and centre in people's minds. By following the Change Brand formula in Chapter 5 and combining an area of impact with a problem in a category, you have carved out a differentiated position for the time being. But what happens if that category problem goes away and the competitors catch up? The brand you have created in the meantime could well be what stands the test of time. Liquid Death isn't really differentiated in terms of product, competitors already have canned options in the market, but the unique brand, the character they've created, is what sets them apart for the long term.

Hey, Good-looking!

Walk down the dog-food aisle of any store and highly likely you'll be met with a wall of beautiful, pedigree dogs. Pristine smiling Labradors, shiny-coated working cockers, a snuggly shih tzu. You might be forgiven for thinking you're trying to get your dog ready for Crufts. Grub Club set out to change this. They know that the average dog isn't perfect. Just like humans, they've got flaws and quirks. The things that make them loveable and uniquely ours.

So, when casting for their latest film in 2023, Grub Club decided to search for a unique dog: 'We were looking for what in South Africa we call a "pavement dog", said Co-Founder Alessandro Di Trapani. 'We wanted someone unique, a dog you just couldn't miss.' Their search was over when they found 'Steven', a dog who has a face only his owner could love. You're not going to forget Steven and that only adds to the distinctiveness of the brand. Like Steve Buscemi standing in a line-up of the usual suspects of handsome Hollywood frontmen, he's the one who sticks in the memory.

The amazing 'Steven' from Grub Club's TV commercial © Grub Club

It paves the way for an approach a little bit like the Dove Campaign for Real Beauty, one of the standout campaigns by a brand from the last two decades. Before Dove came along, the women you would see in beauty ads were limited to models and celebrities, and this created an unrealistic and unhealthy view of beauty across society. Dove's campaign has been celebrating every aspect of beauty in whatever shape or form for a long time. When it first started in 2004, simply by featuring real women instead of the unattainable picture of beauty that other brands showed, they were incredibly distinctive in the category. Since launch, they've continued to challenge unhealthy attitudes with a wide range of different impactful activations that have carved out a perpetually powerful positioning for the brand and one that is doing a great thing for society. And while Grub Club might not be setting out to tackle unrealistic attitudes to beauty among dogs, it will certainly give their brand an injection of distinctiveness and dogs like Steven will walk a little taller next time they meet a pristine poodle in the park.

Here We Flo – No More Period Drama

The eco tampon brand Here We Flo created a stir in polite society with their first advert for TV in 2022. It played with the established conventions of 'Period Dramas' and the femcare category to create something that was simultaneously hilarious, informative and genre busting. The convention in the category for a long time was to avoid talking about what the product does and to show women doing a range of activities while on their period. Brands like Bodyform had started to bust taboos in recent years and done some incredible creative work, but humour was something that brands just didn't go near in this category.

Cue Here We Flo and their #NoMorePeriodDrama campaign. We open on a classic scene from a period drama. Stiff-looking British people in fancy outfits and opulent surrounds. Our heroine opens with the line, 'My dears, I'm in a bloody mess.' The assorted characters question what she means. 'Manor costing too much to run? Servant problems?' 'No… a bloody mess… down there', leading to all sorts of awkward reactions from the men in attendance. This opens the door for one of the other ladies to introduce Here We Flo and land some important product points: 'One hundred per cent organic cotton, no synthetic dyes or fragrances… and they're compostable so the gardener can bury them in your rose bush.'

'As an American who had lived in the UK for a decade, I'd always loved period dramas and we saw the opportunity to subvert the genre,' founder Chandra explains. 'We could create a funny contrast between the "posh" nature of the drama and a conversation about periods at the dinner table. It also meant we could talk about sustainability in a way that wasn't preachy.'

Using humour worked really well to land the product messages and threw the conventions of the category out of the window. The campaign also came to market at the same time as Netflix's cultural sensation, *Bridgerton*, tapping into a rich cultural wave and boosting the fame of the brand at the same time.

Here We Flo causing a stir in polite society with their Period Drama commercial
© Here We Flo

From Invisible to Icon

When Oatly brought in their new CEO – Toni Petersson – in 2012, their packaging looked like any other milk alternative on the market and was firmly in the world of health food. It was the kind of branding you might expect, given it had been created by a group of academics in the 1990s and scientists trying to find a better alternative to dairy. In the words of John Schoolcraft, the chief creative officer who was brought in by his friend Toni shortly after he joined, 'It looked like a Dutch multinational, just indistinguishable from anything else on the shelves.'

Oatly's packaging before the rebrand © Oatly

The category conventions in alternative milk packaging are largely the same now as they were then. You would see liquid being poured into a bowl over healthy-looking ingredients, normally from the right-hand side of the pack. The ranges were colour coded into something the designer understood but meant nothing to the average customer. There might be a hint to the ingredients. If it was almond milk, you might see an almond on the packaging. Same with coconut or soya. You might see a leaf to indicate the product is plant based. Oatly had been in existence for 20 years. They had a good product, but were still firmly trapped in the health food aisle and needed to do things differently to tip into the mainstream.

And so they set out to challenge these conventions and threw almost every single one of them out the window: 'The aim was to get customers to pick it up out of curiosity, so we intentionally made these look like we'd just made them in the basement at home,' Schoolcraft said. They also took the opportunity to bring the brand's messaging onto the box. It was their biggest communication channel, so it was the perfect place to communicate how the brand was changing and what they believed: 'We thought that on every side of the packaging there should be something interesting to read. The legal side on the back we refer to as the boring side. We know that once we're in people's hands, they read the copy, try us and tend, in great numbers, to like the taste.'*

Oatly's distinctive packaging after the rebrand © Oatly

Not everyone in the company liked it at first. Oatly had been operating for almost 20 years before this dramatic shift and it was a major change in direction.

'I remember Toni called the whole company together for a meeting and we unveiled the new packaging,' Schoolcraft continues.

---

* https://thechallengerproject.com/blog/2016/oatly

'Someone stood up and said this was the worst, most childish packaging they had ever seen and asked me why I was ruining this company. People can react quite negatively to change and for some of them, this just threatened their entire existence. The funny thing is those were sketches projected onto the wall. When we got things printed and people were sitting holding the packs, those same people told me how excited and proud they were.'

As they say, the rest is history. Redesigning the packaging to create something that, at the time, was unique and distinctive in the category was the first major step Oatly took before their exponential growth.

Schoolcraft takes up the story again: 'The packaging changed things straight away. It was almost overnight. Toni said to me when we change the packaging that our sales will drop by 15 per cent due to existing product recognition, but the exact opposite happened. We doubled our sales quickly, within the first 18 months, if not sooner.'

There have been copycat brands that have come along since, but the packaging has been a driving force behind the brand and so much of everything else they've done stems from that. It's fair to say it's become one of the most iconic brands in the world.

The packaging was also a key factor in their go-to-market strategy as Oatly entered the US market in 2016. Schoolcraft talks about the thinking behind the launch: 'How do we launch an oat milk in the US when no one knows what it is or how it tastes, and the supermarkets are packed with hundreds and thousands of other brands? Through baristas and coffee shops where people go to hang out with their friends and are open to try new things.'

They entered the market by focusing on baristas first and foremost. But not just any barista. Only those who worked at the cafés that had built up a niche following and were seen as the best places to get a coffee in each city. That distinctive light blue pack stood out on the counter. It started a conversation with their pointed messaging on the pack and when combined with a delicious coffee in the hands of a skilled barista, it was the perfect place for product sampling. Their trusted barista encouraging them to change their milk choices from almond or dairy to oat milk made a big impact when it came to widespread adoption of the brand across the country. An Oat flat white became the drink of choice for the aspirational coffee drinker.

Not All Distinctiveness is Created Equal

The way you create your product can also deliver distinctiveness. Tony's Chocolonely have pushed category conventions already with their branding, introducing a rainbow-like colour palette that stands out on the shelf. The original bar actually came in red, because red has connotations of 'alarm' that matched the severity of the situation Tony's wanted to highlight, and red wasn't often seen in the category. But there's one particular masterstroke that does a distinctiveness job, as well as communicating the mission of the business.

The majority of chocolate bars are uniform once you unwrap them. They're divided into equal segments to make them easy to share. Tony's saw an opportunity. The chocolate industry is not equally divided; it's rife with inequality, with certain parties doing far better than others. With that in mind, they created a bar that was split into all sorts of different shapes. Uneven chunks act as a reminder that the profits in the industry are not split fairly and don't really benefit the workers themselves. The shapes are also intended to be a nod to the nations of West Africa, where over 70 per cent of the world's cocoa is produced. The bottom of the bar represents the equator and then different shapes represent the Ivory Coast, Ghana, Togo and Benin, Nigeria and part of Cameroon.*

---

* https://www.delish.com/uk/food-news/a42667623/why-is-it-called-tonys-chocolonely/

While they still get a fair few complaints that this unusual break from the normal conventions of a chocolate bar is annoying for consumers, it is well worth it for the opportunity to continue to spread the message. This does a great job of communicating the core mission right through to the very end of the brand experience but it also creates a unique and distinctive eating experience. People have their favourite parts of the bar, creating a bit of conversation along the way. My wife has been known to get a bit angry if I eat her favourite part! It's the round 'button' shaped piece on the left-hand side of the image below, which is the logo of Tony's Open Chain. You wouldn't get that with a run-of-the-mill chocolate bar.

Tony's Chocolonely illustrate the inequality of the chocolate industry with their bars © Tony's Chocolonely

A Reason to Break the Rules

Category conventions should be seen as a big opportunity to spark creativity, rather than a set of rules to abide by. Just because something has always been done in a certain way doesn't mean it always has to be done in the exact same way. These rules are made to be broken and by breaking them in smart, interesting and relevant ways, you create an instant point of difference for your brand.

We've spoken about the power of the blank sheet of paper in earlier chapters. One of the great things about creating a brand from scratch is that you can see what everyone else in the category is doing already. You can collect up all their packaging and marketing materials. Surround yourself with it and immerse yourself. Quite quickly you will see ways to carve out a unique brand with different and distinctive assets. Look at what the category is doing and find ways to do things differently.

It's not just about doing things differently for the sake of it though. There needs to be a reason behind it. Oatly's move from packaging that faded into the background within the health food sector to packaging with so much personality it was impossible to ignore made a huge difference to the brand. This meant it managed to move from the health food part of the supermarket to the chiller cabinet and not be missed. And when you saw it in the hands of the uber-cool barista making your morning coffee, the brand lodged in your brain and made positive change aspirational.

By all means bring some madness to the category and shake things up. Smash those conventions and do things differently but don't just be different for the sake of it. There needs to be method in the madness. If it's well thought through, it only adds to the brand story and gives people more to talk about. It sticks in the mind, creating more reasons for them to remember you, and to keep buying your brand time and time again.

CHAPTER EIGHT

Play to the Brain

'The future, as always, will not be like the past.
But it will be better understood through the lens
of behavioral economics.'

Dan Ariely, renowned professor and author specializing
in human irrationality

Have you ever stopped to wonder why so many bad things happen in the world when most of the people you meet are fundamentally good?

Good people with good intentions. Good people who care deeply about their families and work unbelievably hard day after day to provide everything they need to live a good life. People who do the right thing more often than not and treat others as they would wish to be treated themselves.

People who laugh at the same jokes, cry at the same movies and sing the same songs. People who make wonderful friendships that last a lifetime. People who fall deeply in love and bring mini versions of themselves into the world. People who want those they love to be happy above all else and genuinely want the world to be a better place.

People who, regardless of where they were born, the colour of their skin, their religion, gender or sexuality, have more in common than we could possibly imagine.

Out of the eight billion plus people on the planet, it's a fairly safe bet to say that there are more 'good' people than 'bad'. But despite the scales being tipped in the right direction, something is clearly going wrong.

It seems that every time we turn on a TV or open a newspaper there is a new problem to worry about or an existing situation that is getting worse. News anchors and journalists discuss these problems at great length. Experts come on to share their wisdom. Politicians of every colour of the rainbow express their views. The problem is always someone else's fault.

We live our lives in an endless circle of blame that can only be counterproductive. We're always pointing the finger at someone else. It's the fault of the elites, the uneducated, the racists, sexists and homophobes; immigrants, drug addicts and criminals. It's the fault of the right, the left, the nationalists and populists. Big corporations, big technology and big banks. The media. China, Russia, North Korea and the United States. Trump, Biden, Putin, Macron, Starmer and Xi Jinping. Muslims, Christians, Jews. Scientists and environmental activists blame politicians and CEOs. Student groups clash with the NRA. Doctors blame food manufacturers.

No matter the problem, it's always somebody else's fault. We find it almost impossible to see things from the other side so that we might understand why someone might be doing the things they do. This endless blame game is only making things worse. We find ourselves saying, 'They need to do something' or 'They need to sort it out.' But in the case of some of the world's biggest problems this is far from helpful: it stops progress dead in its tracks.

The world is not walking in the wrong direction, it's broken into a jog. Perhaps instead of trying to find someone else to blame, we need to look in the mirror. While our hearts are most certainly in the right place, what's going on inside our heads is clearly far more complicated. If we were the well-intentioned, highly intelligent beings we clearly think of ourselves to be, surely we would be making more progress against the major problems we're faced with rather than endlessly squabbling among ourselves? Why do positions on either side of a debate become so highly charged and deeply embedded they show no sign of shifting and it becomes impossible to achieve even an iota of movement towards a common ground?

Yes, we have made huge progress in certain areas that we should be proud of. We've eradicated numerous diseases, improved equality, elevated living standards, increased life expectancy across the world and lifted millions of people out of poverty. But still problems persist, problems that we really should be able to solve.

It's not like we're unable to solve problems. We're a species of problem solvers and we're great at identifying solutions. We have brilliant scientists, innovators, entrepreneurs and visionaries putting their everything into solving problems. Nothing gets us more motivated and gives us a reason to get out of bed in the morning than a problem to solve. Nothing gets us talking or evokes our passion like an interesting conundrum.

While we're born to find these solutions, we're terrible at implementing them. The tangled web of social, cultural and economic forces often gets in the way of genuine and sustainable progress against the biggest problems facing humanity. In academic circles, these are known as 'wicked problems' because of the difficulty of finding a solution. They are hard to define, made up of complex interdependencies and solutions are never clear-cut or able to be tested. To muddy the waters even further, every interested party has a radically different point of view and set of beliefs that contradict each other, depending on the frame through which they see the problem.

This is brilliantly summed up by Gus Speth, a leading American environmental lawyer and advocate who has been wrestling with environmental issues since the 1970s: 'I used to think the top environmental problems were biodiversity loss, ecosystem collapse and climate change. I thought that with 30 years of good science, we could address those problems... But I was wrong... The top environmental problems are selfishness, greed and apathy... and to deal with those we need a spiritual and cultural transformation. And we scientists don't know how to do that.' *

On the surface, many of the most persistent problems that we face should have remarkably simple solutions. To end homelessness, we just need to put a roof over their heads. Poverty is not a lack of character, it's a lack of cash. We can stop global warming by stopping burning fossil fuels. Want to end gun violence? Ban guns. Need to fight fake news? Tell people the truth. Eager to end gang violence on the streets? More police with more powers. Fix obesity? Healthier food.

Unfortunately, it's not that simple. Imagine an unbelievably complex game of poker with billions of individual players at the table, all playing the hand they see in front of them. It's a high-stakes game with people reacting emotionally and acting without much thought. People try and play the hand to the best of their ability so they and their families are better off at the end but there are rarely any winners. Solutions lose their way amidst a fog of self-interest, apathy and distraction. Too hard, too complicated, too boring. All too often, we find ourselves deadlocked, trapped in an impasse with little prospect of progress – the ultimate Mexican standoff where our very survival is at stake. Tarantino would be proud.

To understand why we don't make progress, and to achieve the spiritual and cultural transformation that Gus Speth describes above, we need to look at what's happening inside our heads. We need to understand the psychology underpinning our behaviour because only then can we plot a path forward. As we build our understanding of this, we will come to terms with the fact that

---

* Gus Speth is founder of the Natural Resources Defence Council and World Resources Institute, Administrator of the U.N. Development Program and served in Jimmy Carter's administration as chairman of the Environmental Council

what's going on inside our heads is the overriding cause of the biggest problems we face. But we can also use our knowledge of our internal workings to move things forward, to present simple solutions to the challenges we face in a way that goes with the flow of human motivation, rather than trying to fight the tide.

The beauty of using psychology as part of your problem-solving toolkit is that it is totally neutral. It allows you to step back from the melee surrounding any problem and see things with a clear head. Psychology is politically neutral. It is ideologically agnostic, it doesn't have a favourite news website or social platform. Our irrational behaviour has formed over millennia. It was around before capitalism, socialism, neo-liberalism and feminism. It existed before Fox News, the *New York Times*, the *Guardian* and the *Daily Mail*. Before presidents and prime ministers. Benevolent billionaires and environmental activists. Psychology elevates us above name-calling and finger pointing; above vested interests and hidden agendas; to really understand what's going on in the mind of your audience.

This powerful toolkit is already being used to get us to behave in a certain way. Advertisers, tech developers, politicians and the media understand what makes us tick and they use this knowledge base to get us to buy, click and vote as they desire. Some of the world's smartest people are getting paid a lot of money to exploit our evolution and get us to do exactly what they want. Numerous behavioural science and psychology books focus on how this information can be used to sell stuff and consume attention. We can and must use this knowledge base to create brands that make the world a better place. Not to do so would place us at a major disadvantage.

Predictably Irrational

So where do you start when it comes to building a brand in a competitive category? Is it picking a logo? Choosing colours or a clever tagline? Thinking about a celebrity or influencer who could help get the ball rolling? Coming up with an idea for a launch stunt? While all of these have a role to play, it's important to first take a step back and understand why people do the things they do in life. Why they make certain decisions and ultimately why they are motivated to buy certain products and brands over others.

Think for a moment about your own behaviour. How do you make the big decisions in your life? The house, the job, the car? Your current partner? The person you choose to marry? The names for your children? What about the things you've done today? How did you choose what you're wearing? What you had for lunch? What you clicked on? And how did you come to be reading this book?

We may like to think that everything we do, we do for a reason. That we are highly rational and considered with everything we do; that we make the best possible choice for us as an individual. Every. Single. Time. But how could that possibly be the case when we're making thousands of individual decisions every single day?

For a long time, this was accepted as the way the human brain worked. Economists believed that humans are primarily rational, that we review every single bit of information available to us, evaluate the probability of different events, weigh up the costs and benefits and then make the decision that would give us the best return (we would act to maximize the utility we receive, known to economists as Expected Utility Theory). There was the belief that we would go through this laborious process every time we made a decision and be consistent in choosing the self-determined best course of action. This way of thinking has been the foundation of the economic models we have used for more than 200 years.

However, when this theory steps out of a textbook or economic model and comes into contact with reality it starts to crumble. It may be possible to go through something approaching this complicated process when trying to buy a new car. It is possible to gather all the information you need about each different model, compare miles per gallon, engine output and prices and look at how each car might meet your needs before making the optimal decision. But that doesn't take into account things like the brand of the car, the opinion you have of people you've seen driving similar models, the ambience of the dealership and even the salesman's overpowering aftershave. It's highly likely that before we even start that process, we've got some idea of the car we're after and, at most, only consider a couple of brands rather than every option available to us.

Now try applying this way of thinking to something more complicated. Buying a house? How many times do you hear people say things like 'it just felt right' or 'we knew the second we walked through the door'? That doesn't sound like the hyper-rational process outlined above.

What about trying to identify who to vote for? It's close to impossible to gather all the available information, evaluate the probability of every possible event and then calculate the pros and cons without the combination of a crystal ball and a supercomputer. We're far more likely to vote on personality than policy, on historical party preference, or because something makes us angry or afraid.

It may be OK for economic models to paint us as hyper-rational, decision-making robots capable of processing huge quantities of data and predicting the future, but the reality is very different. More often than not, we make decisions with emotion and then post-rationalize.

In the past few decades, the science surrounding the inner workings of our brain has gone through a quantum leap in understanding. The combination of behavioural economists and psychology scholars means we've learned more about how the brain works in the past 50 years than we have in the whole of human history. As the 'softer' subject of psychology has combined with the traditionally harder disciplines of economics and neuroscience, it has attained a level of credibility and buy-in outside of academic circles that has seen its impact on the real world grow.

This (relatively) new field of study has shown that while we like to think we are rational beings who make good decisions most of the time, almost the complete opposite is true. Evolution has created an autopilot that sits within all of us, based on hundreds of thousands of years of previous experience. We act on habit and instinct. We are highly irrational and emotional. We have over 200 behavioural biases and make decisions based on flawed 'rules of thumb'. These biases help us make decisions quickly and had big survival advantages in the past when we were faced with threats on a daily basis. But nowadays, when we're unlikely to be attacked by a sabre-tooth tiger on the way to Sainsbury's, the automatic choice isn't necessarily the right one. These biases are increasingly gremlins in the machine that lead to decision making not necessarily in our best interests in the long term.

We are hypersensitive to fear, easily distracted, focused on short-term rewards and crave social validation to make us feel like part of the group. We're drawn to high fat foods because, in the past, our propensity to eat more calories than we needed was an ingenious feature designed to make sure we survived tough times. But in the world in which we live today, with millions of dollars spent globally advertising junk food and sugary drinks, a fast food or takeaway outlet on every street corner and high calorie options everywhere we look, it's now easier and cheaper than ever before to consume more and more calories than we could possibly need. Our evolution, that has served us so well for years, has become a potentially lethal design flaw.*

These biases underpinning our behaviour are not bad things, they have been instrumental in our survival to this point and are

---

* Lewis, J. (2018), *The Science of Sin: Why We Do the Things We Know...* Bloomsbury

still very useful today. For example, when we are overloaded with information and can't possibly process all the stimulus coming our way, we have mental shortcuts that help us quickly get to a good decision that is maybe correct nine times out of ten. We have biases that lead us to behave in the same way as the group, such as Social Proof, Norming and the Bystander Effect, searching for the survival benefit that comes with safety in numbers. We resist changing our opinions (Confirmation Bias) and act to protect the known quantity of the status quo. There are biases that place greater value on things we own (Endowment Effect) or help us complete jobs we have started (Goal Gradient & Sunk Cost Fallacy) to make sure we look after our possessions and get things done. We are biased towards the present day, focusing on living in the now. We value a reward today over the potential of a bigger one in the future (Hyperbolic Discounting), something that comes in very handy when riding out a failed harvest but means we're less likely to save for a rainy day. We have biases that give us confidence and protect us from worrying about all the bad things in the world – the Optimism Bias and Ostrich Effect.

It's fair to say we're a little bit complicated. To use the term popularized by Dan Ariely in his great book of the same name, we are 'predictably irrational'. Up to 95 per cent of our thinking takes place in the unconscious mind.* We are 90 per cent Homer Simpson and only 10 per cent Mr Spock. The important thing to take out of this when creating a brand is that, most of the time, we are not going to choose a brand for purely rational reasons. There's a lot more going on under the surface than the rational argument you might make for someone to buy your brand.

---

* Zaltman, G. (2003), *How Customers Think: Essential Insights into the Mind of the Market*, Harvard Business Review Press

We're not going to have time to dive deep into behavioural science to understand every bias that might influence our behaviour, but this chapter will give us an insight into the inner workings of our brains and some important things for Change Brands to consider.

The Inner Conflict

Every new brand seems to kick off proceedings with an earnest video of the founder talking to camera, explaining the problem with the category and then explaining in detail while their product offers a solution to that problem. Films like these are plastered all over your social media feed. They're honest and earnest; they explain the reason why people should change their behaviour and give a glimpse into the founder's motivations. People are rational, so let's give them a rational argument. Surely that will be enough to get them to change, right?

Wrong.

While this kind of story is a useful exercise to go through as a founder trying to explain eloquently and succinctly why they're doing what they're doing, it's basically table stakes as any new brand. It'll be useful when it comes to speaking to partners, trying to get investors on board or land a new supermarket deal, but when it comes to getting real people to change their behaviour, don't be surprised if it hardly makes a dent.

The fact of the matter is that your potential audience aren't anywhere near as invested in the problem and your solution as you are. While it might generate a bit of traction with the part of the audience who are highly engaged with the issue in question, it's unlikely to tip beyond that.

People are lazy. They make the majority of their decisions on autopilot in an effort to save energy and streamline decision making. In his Nobel Prize-winning book, *Thinking, Fast and Slow*, Daniel Kahneman suggests that our brains employ a 'dual-process' model with two radically different modes of thought: System 1 and System 2.*

System 2 is slow. It is the mode of thinking we use when we need to give something serious thought. It is logical and considered. It is the process we go through when we are aware that we are thinking about something complex, like buying a house or a car, or trying to make sense of a complicated news story. We are conscious that we are using it, so it requires a lot more effort to use than System 1. We require System 2 to make decisions that are more difficult and require complex thought, but System 2 is lazy and is happy to default to the more intuitive System 1.

On the other hand, System 1 is fast, instinctive and emotional. It is automatic, operates on an unconscious level and can't be switched off. It is intuitive and impressionable. We use System 1 to make decisions quickly and with the minimum of effort. But System 1 is where the biases and heuristics outlined above exist. It loves to jump to conclusions and is too quick to simplify. This means System 1 is error prone, highly flawed and likely to make frequent mistakes because of the biases and heuristics it employs to shortcut more considered thought.

While System 2 might prioritize sustainable choices and be all too happy to talk about and advocate for them, System 1 just wants the easy solution to their immediate need. Let's take the growing problem of single-use plastic. You'd have to have been hiding under a rock for the last couple of years not to be aware that this represents a major environmental hazard and is a threat to marine life across the world. But when you walk into a place to buy a drink, you're thirsty and the wise words and dulcet tones of Sir David Attenborough are unlikely to be top of your mind so you take the easy option and buy the first thing that will quench your thirst – a

---

* Kahneman, D. (2011). *Thinking, Fast and Slow*, Farrar, Straus and Giroux

bottle of water perhaps. You may remember the latest advertising campaign from the likes of Coke or Pepsi promising happiness or energy so you buy something in recognizable packaging filled with sugar. Or you choose something with tenuous health benefits in the subconscious hope that what you drink says something about you as a person. If you remembered your reusable bottle, you could ask for a refill but that is very rarely the easy thing to do – the tap water is warm and there's a certain social barrier when everyone else is buying a drink so you go with the crowd and grab something off the shelf.

Societal attitudes to single-use plastic have changed fundamentally after Attenborough's intervention through the wildly popular TV series *Blue Planet II*, but that doesn't mean behaviour has changed. It's still too much effort for most people to carry a reusable bottle everywhere they go and it doesn't carry the level of social kudos as the numerous highly polished brands competing to quench our thirst. We may want to do the right thing and be part of the solution, but it's not that simple.

These conflicting motivations create a sense of what's known as 'cognitive dissonance'. It leads to a situation where conflicting attitudes, beliefs and behaviours create mental discomfort so that the individual is then forced to alter one of their attitudes or behaviours to make themselves feel better. Cognitive dissonance leaves us torn and feeling uncomfortable. When this plays out in numerous situations as we go about our lives, from what we drink to what we drive, this discomfort is magnified. The sense of turmoil that comes from feeling constantly conflicted plays havoc with our mental health.

Take our ancient ancestor as an example. Life was pretty straightforward. They had to make sure they had enough food and water to survive tough times. They had to ensure they had shelter that would keep them safe and secure and protect them from danger. They had to see off any threats to their position, either within the community or from the outside. This was all self-contained to a relatively small known world around where they were based. They certainly didn't need to worry about whether their agricultural practices or regular lighting of fires were contributing to global warming. Or burnt meat potentially giving them cancer. Today, when everything we do and think is constantly called into question, is it any wonder we doubt ourselves and feel conflicted? We're far more conflicted about far more things than we've ever been before.

In the case of single-use plastic, people may promise themselves that they'll bring their own bottle next time, or say they just need a sugar hit to get through the afternoon. Or that they can't live without their Diet Coke today. But the next time they go in search of a drink, little has changed.

For many food outlets, to stop selling drinks in single-use plastic is not an option without damaging their profits and threatening their business. For the huge companies who make the drinks and distribute globally, a change to packaging would have a major impact on their bottom line immediately and would add to logistics costs in what is a highly streamlined process refined over a number of years. Companies take decisions that protect their bottom line and defend against losses of any sort.

What is the motivation for them to change? They have an almost exclusive status quo on an enormous market that is showing very slow signs of change. The only way to force companies like Coca-Cola to change is to shift consumer behaviour on a massive scale so people stop buying single-use plastic but for the reasons outlined above, this is far easier said than done. Humans have evolved to love and stick to the path of least resistance.

Think Big and Small at the Same Time

The rational argument for why someone should buy your brand is important for System 2, but when our irrational and emotional

System 1 is the one in charge of most decisions, how do we get people to change their behaviour? The key thing to remember is that while we might think we're rational, our autopilot drives what we buy and they are dominated by emotion. You can create as compelling a rational case as to why someone should buy your brand as you like, but if there's zero emotion, it will never be as powerful.

Our tendency when diving into solving some of the biggest problems facing humanity is to talk in big numbers. It's so tempting to demonstrate the magnitude of these problems by showing just how big they are. But speaking in large numbers can be a double-edged sword. Yes, speaking in millions of trees, billions of plastic bottles, tonnes of carbon, thousands of people affected and so on goes a long way towards communicating that this is a big problem worthy of attention. But it can also make things feel too big, both in terms of being intangible – it's hard to get your head round just what that means – and making them feel insurmountable – it's just impossible to make a difference. If there are billions of plastic bottles going into the ocean anyway, what difference will it make if I buy one now? What's one more bottle among billions?

There's a psychological bias known as Scope Insensitivity* that suggests that someone's willingness to help does not increase in proportion with the number of victims in need, where logic would suggest that the more people in need of help, the more crucial it is that we act. The other side of the coin here is another cognitive bias called the Identifiable Victim Effect. This suggests that people are more likely to act or show empathy when presented with the story of a single individual rather than a large anonymous mass. Big

---

* Chang, Hannah H. & Tuan Pham, Michel (August 2018), 'Affective Boundaries of Scope Insensitivity', *Journal of Consumer Research*, Volume 45, Issue 2, pp.403–28

numbers create distance, whereas individual stories are powerful. There's a quote often attributed to Mother Teresa that explains this well: 'Show me the many and I will never act, show me the one and I will.' This allows you to put a face to a problem, to get specific about the circumstances, and it builds empathy by getting people to put themselves in their shoes. This is the reason imagery of large numbers of refugees in camps or on boats barely register with the public, but the image of a small boy washed up on a beach sent shockwaves around the world.

When a Change Brand is looking to persuade people to join the cause, it's important to find a way to make it more relevant and personal to them. Individual stories can be a powerful tool here. XO Bikes does this really well. Each bike has a unique serial number on the crossbar that shows the fixer's number and the number of the bike that they have refurbished. Visit the XO website and you can see a short film of Tray's story, creating an emotional connection between the bike and the customer and giving them a story to tell at the same time. In the words of Founder Stef Jones: 'There might be 5,000 blue Cannondales in London but there's only one XO1-003. And then when you look on the website, you can see Tray talking about his life and his aspirations for the future and what he loves about life now. So the idea is that you become an advocate and that's how we change society.'

XO Bikes embrace the human story behind each bike © XO Bikes

We saw evidence of this effect with the launch of Change Please. It wasn't the statistics about the number of homeless people that made the story cut through. Almost everyone could relate to having walked past a homeless person asking for change and then going straight into a coffee shop to spend £3 on a skinny latte, so the idea of training them as baristas cut through and made it feel close to home. It was also the ability to see formerly homeless people like Liam, Jay, Thomas and Lucy working as baristas and trying to turn their life around that really struck a chord and opened doors for the organization. Finding a way to tell the personal stories of the people you're helping makes a big difference.

Thomas, an early Change Please barista, described the impact on his life: 'I've made a lot of mistakes in my life, I never thought I'd make it past 30. Now I'm 34, I have my own flat and best of all, I can have a chance to have a nice productive, successful life with all the support anyone could ever ask for. Change Please means "LIFE" for me, I wouldn't be here now without them, I know this for sure.'

Founder Cemal Ezel and the early Change Please team © Change Please

Harness the Power of the Crowd

One of our biggest behavioural biases is the tendency to follow what everyone else is doing. We follow established social norms to avoid rocking the boat and we are also drawn to what everyone else is doing because it offers safety in numbers. While Change Brands start small, if they can create the feeling that they are bigger than they are, and more people are buying the product, this can become a self-fulfilling prophecy.

Reviews are an important first step in creating what's called 'social proof' for a brand. If people can see that other people like them had a positive experience with the product, then they become more likely to buy it themselves. Engagement with lots of people on social media also builds an element of social proof so it's important to look to build a community of early advocates for the brand. Your community can become really important when it comes to vital early feedback and in making decisions in the future such as testing new advertising, packaging designs or looking at introducing new products. The feedback and insight you get from your audience should definitely not be sniffed at and it can become a powerful tool in the toolbox.

But brands can go further in creating norms. Their branding and where the brand appears can help build momentum behind the brand. Who Gives A Crap's colourful wrapping of their rolls was a really powerful way of creating the illusion that the brand was everywhere. For a while, it seemed like every trendy café and cool office had Who Gives A Crap on the bathroom shelf. Then they started popping up in people's bathrooms at home. This created huge visibility for the brand and it became an emerging norm for people to think differently about their toilet roll choices. The same thing happened when Oatly started targeting baristas. Suddenly the brand was everywhere and Oatly became the default choice.

Liquid Death's partnership with Live Nation served a similar purpose and it made it feel like the brand was everywhere despite still being a lot smaller than the leading water brands. In the words of Creative VP Andy Pearson: 'People are walking around with water bottles all the time. It's just, it's like air. You just never notice it because we're so ingrained and there's no branding, it's just sort of like a bottle of water. But when you walk around with a can of Liquid Death, it's just instantly noticeable and it grabs your attention and it's a conversation piece. And I think that's why people also like it, it's something beyond water."* The brand being so visible in such a high-profile location can only help them tip over into the mainstream.

While these brands are still smaller than the bigger players, by showing up in a disproportionately big way in certain important and relevant environments it made them seem a whole lot bigger than they were and this fuelled the momentum behind the brand. Is there a way your brand can carve out a disproportionate share of the norm in a particular environment so you appear a lot bigger than you are?

Go for Goals

One important thing to consider is the motivation of your potential buyer. Why do people buy the brands and products that they choose? A useful way to look at this is to understand the psychology of motivation. Humans are goal orientated, which means that at any given time, we have both active and inactive goals. People act to meet the needs of their active goals and then move on to the next goal.

Our goals operate on two levels: the explicit and the implicit. Explicit goals are those that spring quickly to mind when thinking about a specific circumstance or decision. Thirsty? Your explicit goal is to quench that thirst as quickly as possible. Your explicit goals for a meal might be finding something quick, indulgent or healthy.

---

* https://www.gale.agency/blog-posts/is-this-thing-on-ep-11-with-liquid-death -mountain-water-vp-of-creative-andy-pearson

A pair of shoes may be chosen because of comfort or aesthetics. Choice of coffee brand might come down to convenience, price and a quick caffeine hit. If you're buying a car, your explicit goals could relate to price, miles per gallon, reliability and range on an electric vehicle. When thinking about a career, the explicit goals might include a good salary, flexible working hours and the ability to work from home. Explicit goals live on the surface and are easy to identify. They are very specific to the set of choices you find yourself considering when making any decision.

Implicit goals operate at a much deeper level. They are more generally related to your life as a whole and operate at an underlying psychological level. Products are designed to meet the explicit goals in your life but the brand that adorns the packaging is designed to appeal at a more implicit level and say things about you as an individual. Lots of shoe brands offer comfort and decent aesthetics at a similar price point, so how do you choose between those on offer? Nike offer associations of victory and links to the world's leading sporting talent. Allbirds is the most sustainable shoe brand on the market. Converse have built an intrinsic link to creativity. How you identify as an individual is likely to influence the shoes you buy, choosing the brand that best aligns with your implicit goals.

The same applies to the food we eat, the drinks we buy and the car we drive. Craft beer and speciality coffee have the same alcohol or caffeine content as their more mainstream competitors but by aligning yourself with brands like BrewDog or Monmouth Coffee rather than Carlsberg and Costa you position yourself as a more discerning individual and it may say something about your status. Walking down the street in an 'athleisure' brand like lululemon while drinking a Kombucha may appeal to your implicit goal to be healthy, even if you haven't seen the inside of a gym in years.

The science suggests there is a 'Big Three' when it comes to our goals. They have evolved from our fight or flight response, operating deep within us, based on physiological processes and universal in nature.* They provide a useful way to look at the world and cut through the endless complexity.

1. Security – The goal to ensure our safety and avoid danger.
2. Autonomy – The goal to raise our status in the hierarchy and be superior to others.
3. Excitement – The goal to seek stimulation, innovation and change.

If we look at the car category through this lens it helps us pull the brands apart and it can do a similar job in almost any category. When the explicit goals such as miles per gallon and cost are all broadly equal because of affordable-looking financing options, our implicit goals come in to play. If you have a young family, finding the safest possible option is likely to be a key factor so a Volvo may offer the best way of meeting the Security goal. If you are more driven by your status, then you may choose a car brand like a Mercedes that aligns with the Autonomy implicit goal. If sustainability and innovation is important to you, then a brand like Tesla will meet the Excitement goal.

The Excitement goal is designed to find new and innovative options that can create positive change in someone's life and overcome challenges. Also known as the 'Seeking System', it is the part of our brain that drives us to find everything we need to survive and thrive, from food and water to knowledge and new ideas. This goal has been crucial in solving the problems fundamental to our survival and driving humanity forward. It is motivated both by looking for little wins in life and the sense of achievement (and dopamine hit) that comes when it finds them.[†] It is the driving

* Barden, P. (2013), *Decoded: The Science Behind Why We Buy*, Wiley

† Heckhausen, Jutta & Heckhausen, Heinz (Eds) (2018), *Motivation and Action*, Springer

force behind the creation of the brands we've been talking about in this book. Change Brands by their very nature are looking to solve problems for people and society so they should straight away be meeting this goal.

The Security goal is almost the complete opposite. Stemming from the flight response, it is there to keep us safe and avoid potential threats. It looks to minimize wasted energy and means we behave in the same way as the crowd, seeking safety in numbers. This goal is where biases such as loss aversion, social proof and the tendency to follow social norms stem from. We act to maintain the status quo, taking the path of least resistance, and when faced with big problems, we bury our head in the sand and leave it to someone else to fix. This sense of apathy and inertia is one of the most difficult things to break for a Change Brand. Generally, you can get around it by removing as many barriers as possible to purchase by being available in as many places as possible and by bringing the price as close to parity with the competition as you can. The behaviour driven by this goal is what you might see during a recession, with people limiting their spending to navigate tough times. It is also the behaviour you'd see in the latter half of the innovation adoption curve, waiting for the relative safety of the mainstream, where more people are buying it and costs have come down. The social proof of showing people like them buying your brand, as discussed earlier, is vital when it comes to breaking down this barrier.

The Importance of Status for Change Brands

The final goal is one that Change Brands really need to consider and is easily put to one side when the focus is on the solution it is providing. The Autonomy goal is driven by status. We buy things to meet this goal that will improve our standing in the hierarchy and make us superior to others. While premium car brands and luxury items meet this goal, so too do products that have an interesting story behind them and we've seen a number of Change Brands harness this to great effect.

OK, Tesla is serving the excitement goal by providing a solution to a problem people care about, but it also became firmly established as a status play when it first came to market, with celebrities and business leaders queueing up to drive the car. In part, this was down to the higher price point but it was created in a way that would make it feel futuristic and premium that stood it apart from other early electric cars and elevated it far beyond the Toyota Prius hybrid that had been an early leader in this space. It also helped in the early days when supply was lower than demand and you had to go on a waiting list to get one, manufacturing a little scarcity into the experience.

The same is true of Allbirds and Patagonia. Market leading products when it comes to sustainability with a great story, but also something that became part of the uniform for Silicon Valley and the Venture Capital industry. When Method entered the cleaning category in 2001, not only were its sustainability credentials on point, it also looked beautiful on the kitchen counter and elevated the functional into a status play. Even the humble toilet roll became a source of bragging rights and status when it was beautifully wrapped to provide a point of interest and conversation in the downstairs loo.

The tendency when developing a Change Brand so focused on the problem it is looking to solve is to go a little bit 'too charity' in terms of appearance. But this is a mistake that is important to avoid. People buy brands because of what the brand says about themselves. If done right, a brand can simultaneously communicate that someone cares about doing the right thing and finding solutions to problems, while also enhancing their status to others around them.

Eco brands tend to fall into the category conventions that have been created for them. Tapping into a brown, almost craft paper, aesthetic with writing in green and imagery of leaves. This is common in the sector and limits the future potential of the brand, keeping it in a narrow space with a limited audience. The early Oatly packaging made this mistake, sticking to the conventions of the health food aisle rather than the lifestyle brand it became that massively boosted its appeal and potential audience. Compare the average eco brand to Method and you'll see they're in a totally different ballpark, while ostensibly playing the same game.

Early versions of the Change Please branding brought in cues from the streets, including textures, colours and graffiti. They leaned into homelessness and perhaps looked more like the conventions you would see in the charity sector from brands such as Shelter. For early iterations we even toyed with the idea of calling it 'Street Coffee'. But this didn't feel particularly premium in a sector where the coffee cup you were holding was a statement in itself. The idea of creating something that was basically 'homeless coffee' didn't really trigger great thoughts in terms of taste when compared to the competition. With this in mind, we created a brand that would sit comfortably shoulder to shoulder with high-end coffee brands, borrowing the cues of speciality coffee. When we first launched, we even made the social mission of the brand secondary to the quality of the coffee, hoping people would come for the great cup of coffee and then stay when they heard of the purpose of the brand.

'Virtue signalling' is an often derided term but is an important element of designing a Change Brand. People buy brands because of what it says about them. And if a brand says something positive about the end buyer, while looking great at the same time, you're on to a winner. Just because these brands are being created to address problems doesn't mean the normal rules of branding don't apply. It still needs to look great, be distinctive in the category and have a great story; it still needs to elicit joy just by interacting with the brand. Aesthetic is important.

Ocean Bottle is a prime example of this. When they set out to tackle the problem of ocean plastic by collecting 1,000 bottles of ocean-bound plastic with every sale, they might have been forgiven for creating a standard-looking reusable bottle and believing their environmental impact story would be enough to stand it apart in a crowded sector. But they went above and beyond. Ocean Bottle have created the most beautiful reusable bottle in the market. It uses high-quality, insulated materials in a brushed metal finish and is genuinely a thing of beauty. They've won numerous awards for the design.

'We discovered that ocean plastic was set to quadruple by 2040 and wanted to create an easy way for people to make a difference at a global scale. This isn't a future most people want to live in,' Founder and co-CEO Will Pearson explains. 'We started with two core propositions, leading impact and leading design, because we believed that combining the two would make for a great recipe.'

'We focused in particular on functionality, sustainability and aesthetics, making sure the product was timeless, built to last and had the potential to become a symbol of something bigger,' Pearson continues. On the website, they treat the product in the same way Apple would, deconstructing the various elements and benefits that come from choosing an Ocean Bottle over the normal refillable bottle. Every single bit of photography looks high-end. They've even resisted the temptation to put the impact of the purchase – the 1,000 bottles collected – on the bottle, choosing only a beautifully elegant logo that hints at the bigger story that sits behind it. They're making refilling your water bottle a high-status activity. Yes, it comes at a premium price point, but it's the only water bottle you'll ever need. The normal plastic bottle, even with all the expensive branding polish of an Evian, looks positively low-rent in comparison. 'To date, we've collected over 1 billion plastic bottles in weight and supported collection projects in over 300 coastal communities around the world. We still have a long way to go, but hopefully are just getting started.' So not only is it a highly desirable, high-status product, it's also making a massive difference to the problem of ocean plastic and providing employment in some of the poorest communities around the world.

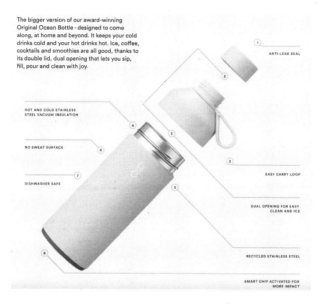

The bigger version of our award-winning Original Ocean Bottle - designed to come along, at home and beyond. It keeps your cold drinks cold and your hot drinks hot. Ice, coffee, cocktails and smoothies are all good, thanks to its double lid, dual opening that lets you sip, fill, pour and clean with joy.

ANTI-LEAK SEAL

HOT AND COLD STAINLESS STEEL VACUUM INSULATION

NO SWEAT SURFACE

DISHWASHER SAFE

EASY CARRY LOOP

DUAL OPENING FOR EASY CLEAN AND ICE

RECYCLED STAINLESS STEEL

SMART CHIP ACTIVATED FOR MORE IMPACT

The elegantly designed Ocean Bottle © Ocean Bottle

Fussy have done something similar in the world of deodorant. Single-use, plastic-free, natural deodorant could have been quite a functional offering designed to appeal to the sustainability crowd but instead they've created something that the BBC's *Dragons' Den*' star Stephen Bartlett described as 'The Apple of the bathroom world'. 'We wanted to design sustainable products that didn't look or function like sustainable products had historically,' founder Matt Kennedy explains. 'Our research also showed that as much as people cared about saving the planet that couldn't come at the cost of a product that wasn't beautiful to look at and hold let alone one that just didn't work.' They leveraged high-end photography to put the product on a pedestal and surrounded it with the beautiful natural ingredients that go into the refills. This approach certainly elevates the humble deodorant beyond a functional item and appeals to the audience's desire to improve their status. 'It was very much part of our marketing strategy to create a "deodorant for the Instagram generation" that would encourage sharing online. We see this in our high referral rates and of course winning awards such as the prestigious Red Dot for design. That was a really proud moment given the intent behind the product and brand.'

Fussy – 'The Apple of the bathroom world' © Fussy

The Triple-Win

As what people value in society changes, what they are looking for from brands also changes. As discussed in Part One of this book, there is a growing desire to take action to address the world's problems so the Change Brands that are setting out to do this carve out a bit of a competitive advantage. They appeal to the excitement goal as a solution to a problem they care about but it's vital never to forget that the brands people buy also say a lot about the individual buying them. People's desire to improve their status in the hierarchy by buying things that are perceived as high value isn't going away so by creating a Change Brand that is a high-status item that also says something good about the buyer as a thoughtful consumer, that brand is on a positive path. Increasingly sustainable behaviour has become intertwined with high-status behaviour, with more and more celebrities and influencers leaning into and celebrating their sustainable decisions. But if that brand is beautiful at the same time, you can't go wrong.

In an ideal world, a Change Brand should look to cater for each of the big three motivations: solving a problem people care about, improving the status of the buyer and being easy and effortless to buy. This makes them what I call a 'Triple-Win Brand'. Vinted is the perfect example of this. The circular fashion marketplace could have focused on the facts of the problem. The British Fashion Council recently highlighted that 'we have enough clothes in existence to dress the entire human race for the next one hundred years' or to put it another way, the next six generations. Seventy-three per cent of the 53 million tonnes of clothing created each year end up being incinerated or thrown into landfill[*] and only some 10–30 per cent of clothes donated to thrift stores and charity shops in the US and UK end up on the shop floor.[†] Some compelling statistics that shine a light on a problem that Vinted, as the biggest second-hand clothes marketplace, is setting out to make a major dent in.

But their sustainability messaging sits secondary to the other benefits of the platform in their communications. Vinted allows you to get great clothes at great value. Clothes from designer labels at a fraction of the new price imbues status on the buyer, at the same time both stylish and savvy. And the ability to get them cheaper appeals to that desire for ease of the security motivation.

---

[*] https://www.ellenmacarthurfoundation.org/a-new-textiles-economy
[†] https://www.weardonaterecycle.org/images/clothing-life-cycle.png

'Triple-win' brands that appeal to each of the big three motivations put themselves in a strong position. A brand that improves the status of the buyer, while addressing a problem they care about and requiring little effort to buy, is the holy grail for Change Brands and what they should strive for. The brands people buy should say something positive about them and they should be symbols for positive change in the world. As the need for sustainable choice and social change becomes more prominent in society, quick shortcuts that help people communicate that they are thoughtful individuals who consider the ramifications of what they buy does a job of communicating their high status. If you can make it affordable and accessible at the same time, you're on the fast track to mainstream adoption.

Brain Power

So many of the legacy brands that control the status quo were created before we had the deep understanding of human behaviour that we do now. By understanding the inner workings of our brain, we can create Change Brands that are tailored to how we interact with the world. This is a powerful thought and another crucial competitive advantage for Change Brands that it's important to make the most of and build into the brand worlds we're creating. Understanding that people make decisions emotionally and then post rationalize subtly changes the way we do things to focus on the emotional reaction of people over the rational one. Powerful individual stories over intangible statistics strike a chord with the brain and draw people in rather than scaring them away.

Leveraging the power of the crowd is a vital step in supercharging the growth of your brand. Making it feel like an emerging norm within people's lives, with people like them buying it and talking about it, quickly embeds that brand in society. Building social proof into the experience and also finding spaces where the brand can feel bigger than it is becomes a powerful tactic.

Finally, not forgetting that people buy brands because of what that brand says about them. One of the big three goals is to improve our status in the hierarchy. Change Brands should be a powerful shortcut for positive change, but also one that makes the buyer feel high-status and part of something bigger. Get this right and you're on the path to becoming a triple-win brand.

This chapter has barely scratched the surface of what behavioural science can do for brands. There are over 200 cognitive biases that can come in useful in thinking about all aspects of the customer experience and we're learning more about the inner workings of our brain every day. If you're interested in finding out more, writings by the likes of Rory Sutherland[*] and Richard Shotton[†] will come in useful. There is no doubt that behavioural science is an incredibly powerful toolkit that is already being used by all sorts of businesses, political parties and tech platforms to get us to behave in a certain way. It's vital we harness this toolkit to help people make better choices and grow the brands that are changing the world for the better.

---

[*] Sutherland, R (2019) *Alchemy: The Surprising Power of Ideas That Don't Make Sense*. Penguin

[†] Shotton, R (2018) *The Choice Factory: 25 behavioural biases that influence what we buy*. Harriman House Limited

CHAPTER NINE

Aim for Fame

'Don't do things because that's the way things have always been done. Be interesting. Most brands are excruciatingly boring, which is perfect because it makes it easier for other brands, the exciting ones, to stand out.'

John Schoolcraft, Chief Creative Officer, Oatly

What do the best Change Brands have in common with the Hollywood actor Hugh Jackman? No, it's got nothing to do with Wolverine. The brands we've discussed at length such as Oatly, Liquid Death and Tony's Chocolonely all like to channel their inner PT Barnum, just like Hugh in *The Greatest Showman*.

For the uninitiated, Phineas T. Barnum was a showman of great renown and notoriety in 1800s America. He was perhaps most famous for being the driving force behind the three-ring circus and the 'greatest show on earth', but that didn't come about until he was in his sixties. Before that, he was known for a series of more and more audacious stunts to get people talking and bring them to his shows: 'Bring them in with din and tinsel... then give them as much as possible for their money.'* Early (highly questionable) stunts included the Feejee Mermaid, an object created by sewing together the torso and head of a monkey with the tail of a fish, and General Tom Thumb, a boy with Dwarfism who he taught to sing, dance

---

* Cook, James W. (Ed.) (2005), *The Colossal P. T. Barnum Reader: Nothing Else Like It in the Universe*, University of Illinois Press

and impersonate historical figures, who became a cultural sensation across the US.

Nowadays, Barnum would be described as a 'hype machine' – creating stunts and using showmanship to get people talking. To get a product on the radar and create fame for it. The truth is that there is a lot of commercial power in showmanship and more and more brands are cottoning on to this. Elon Musk channelled his inner P.T. Barnum during the earlier years at Tesla. In 2018 he sent his personal Tesla Roadster into space, driven by a mannequin called Starman, to become the first car in orbit and generated significant publicity for both Tesla and Space X with the live stream of launch reaching 2.3 million concurrent viewers, making it the second most-watched live event behind another great piece of showmanship, Red Bull's Felix Baumgartner's jump from the stratosphere.*

He's done this time and time again. Tesla cars don't require a lightshow feature built in that makes the car look like it's dancing, but it goes down well with the kids and really does add to the fame of the brand. Even when, to test the unbreakable glass of the new Tesla Cybertruck, a baseball shattered the glass, it still generated headlines all over the world and made sure that product launch wasn't missed by anyone. The hype and fame Musk has created behind Tesla, Space X and his other businesses through his own sense of showmanship have all played a large part in their success.

The good news is that you don't need to send a car into space or buy Twitter to increase the fame of a brand. This chapter will show a range of fame-driving activity, both big and small, to demonstrate how Change Brands have leveraged a little bit of showmanship along the way.

---

* Singleton, Micah (6 February 2018), 'SpaceX's Falcon Heavy launch was YouTube's second biggest live stream ever'. *The Verge*

It's a classic example of the 'application of guile' strategy from a few chapters ago. Major brands, with huge war chests to spend on advertising, can afford to buy people's attention with their media spend. They buy TV and outdoor advertising to get their brand in front of people so that they have a large Share of Voice in the category. It's been proven that Share of Voice correlates with sales and drives growth. In buying broadcast media channels they are buying the stage on which to perform and get their message in front of millions of people. It's brand growth by the numbers. Maintain share of voice each year and your brand will continue to grow, or at least maintain its share.

But this option simply isn't open to Change Brands, at least not at the start of their journey. It costs serious money to make a TV ad and that's before you buy the amount of media required to make an impact so these brands need to find another way to get their brand in front of people and this is where the toolbox of *The Greatest Showman* comes in. You must earn the stage to perform on, draw people in with something so interesting and entertaining that it's impossible to look away.

We've talked a little bit about a concept called Mental Availability throughout the book. This vital principle from Byron Sharp's book *How Brands Grow* proves that brands with the highest Mental Availability are those that grow the fastest because they are most likely to be bought in buying situations. A brand with high Mental Availability is likely to be the first one that comes to mind when you think of certain buying situations or contexts.[*] A brand like Coca-Cola would have sky-high mental availability owing to the multitude of different situations where they are the first brand that comes to mind.

---

[*] Sharp, B. (2013), *How Brands Grow: What Marketers Don't Know*, Oxford University Press

Mental Availability is another way of saying fame. It's a psychological construct, whereas fame is a social construct. And in the words of legendary ad man Paul Feldwick, 'nobody ever wrote a hit musical called Mental Availability'.* By striving for fame, a brand creates higher mental availability and this fuels its growth. Fame is one of the most powerful marketing strategies there is and should be top of the list for anyone tasked with growing a Change Brand.

It's all too easy to get tied up in the rational reasons why someone should buy your brand over the status quo. After all, you've spent a lot of time creating the product to ensure you are an improvement on what's come before. You've formulated the product, you've got certifications you want to talk about. You have a great rational story of why people should buy your brand and this will work with certain people actively looking for that. But to really achieve the scale needed to make sure those product improvements have a major impact, it's time to get the brand out there and reach a much bigger audience who are more passive in their buying behaviour.

You've done the hard work to get to this point. You've brought a product to market that is making a genuine improvement in a category people care about. This has allowed you to make an emotional connection by talking about the problem. You've connected on a macro level, in terms of scale of the issue and impact of the solution. You've connected on a micro level, showing the difference it can make to one person, and you've made the difference that one person can make by changing their behaviour feel tangible.

Now comes the fun bit. Where you can take it up a few notches and force the world to sit up and take notice. This is where you can take risks. You need to have a few fails before you know what succeeds. Fly close to the sun and if it doesn't work, well, you can

---

* Feldwick, P. (2021), *Why Does the Pedlar Sing? What Creativity Really Means*, Matador

move on. At the very least, its good content for the loyal fan base you've been building so far. Showmanship is proven to be good for business. Fame truly is the name of the game if you want to take your brand to the next level.

How to Build Fame

Brand fame is a bit like a scene from an American High School movie. When a brand becomes famous, it's like being the cool kid at school. Walking down the school corridor, it's the cool kid who is the centre of attention. Popular and well liked, with lots of friends in different groups, they spark conversation and gossip around school. The other kids are always talking about them. People notice what they're wearing and they have the potential to start fashion trends. And people will remember that kid long after they've all left school. Brand fame is basically like *Mean Girls*, but with a proper strategy sitting behind it.

Campaigns that generate fame are proven to be the most effective way to have a commercial impact on a brand. *The Long and Short of It*, a major piece of analysis into over 30 years of the UK's best campaigns by Les Binet and Peter Field, showed that those campaigns that aim for fame are the most effective in generating large results.[*] They create the greatest profit growth over time and lead to very large improvements in all metrics, including sales, market share, price sensitivity, loyalty and penetration.

Fame can also create room for the brand to step over into adjacent categories. Oatly initially carved out a space in people's minds as an alternative milk, but their mission to help people move to a plant-based lifestyle has opened the door for other products including 'oatgurt' and their 'soft-serve' ice cream-like product. Liquid Death

---

[*] Binet, L. & Field, P. (2013), *The Long and Short of It: Balancing Short and Long-Term Marketing Strategies*, Institute of Practitioners in Advertising

have stepped into iced tea. Fame opens doors and creates new possibilities.

Paul Feldwick talks about the four aspects of fame.[*] The first two we have covered already. First, creating something that people want to own that gives them some sort of satisfaction. In the case of a Change Brand, that means providing a meaningful alternative to a status-quo brand in a category they buy and trying to have an impact on a problem they care about. Taking moral leadership of a category and making it satisfying for people to be a part of your journey. This is discussed at length earlier in Chapters 5 and 6 (*see also* pp. 119–172).

Second, it's about creating the most distinctive brand possible as covered in Chapter 7 (*see also* pp. 173–194). Developing a brand world that 'uniquely identifies the famous object' means that when the brand is seen, it's unlikely to be forgotten or confused with another brand. You really don't want to be going to the trouble of generating a load of attention for your brand only to have it misattributed to a competitor.

The first element of fame we haven't covered yet is the ability to reach mass audiences. Market traction and fame are two very different things. You can generate traction within a category by catering to a specific audience need but fame is a different kettle of fish entirely. This means going from small audiences to targeting the largest possible audience. It means tipping from a group of people predisposed to like your product into the mainstream.

The traditional way of reaching mass audiences has been broadcast media. Spending a serious amount of cash to get on TV, radio, billboards or in national newspapers. This is still a valid strategy and TV still offers the most efficient way to reach 90 per cent of the population in a short time period. But when this is out of reach for Change Brands at the start of their journey, what do they do to generate fame?

---

[*] Feldwick, P. (2021), *Why Does the Pedlar Sing? What Creativity Really Means*, Matador

If this book had been written 20 years ago before social media, brands then would have been far more restricted in what they could do to reach mass audiences and generate fame. Basically, mass media, celebrity endorsement or perhaps the odd Barnum-style stunt for the press. But now there are numerous options available and social platforms do create opportunity for Change Brands. They provide the conditions for ideas to spread quickly and while the idea of 'going viral' is attractive and still possible, it's much harder than it initially was, with social platforms prioritizing paid content over organic.

The final thing to aim for, which links in with the above, is creating space for the involvement of the public. Providing ways for the public to get involved and to talk about it. Feldwick describes this as 'social diffusion'. He goes on, 'It's not enough that we know about it... but rather than we also know that other people know about it. Something cannot be famous to a single person.' This means creating ways for people to get involved, comment on it, share it. Space to agree or disagree, to take a side. A way for people to show allegiance. It's basically creating reasons for people to talk about and engage with your brand in ways they hadn't thought about before. Again, social platforms are a useful instrument here as they allow interesting ideas to spread and the range of platforms, from TikTok and Instagram to LinkedIn, Facebook, Twitter (X) and YouTube provide all sorts of different ways to get people involved.

Winning the Fame Game

Liquid Death have created a Country Club for their members with all sorts of exclusive benefits including free product and exclusive access to merchandise and events. But being Liquid Death, they're doing it a little differently than the average loyalty programme. Yes, you can join, but it will cost you the small matter of $125,000. Or you can make the decision to join the 225,000 members who have decided to legally sell their soul to a canned water company. Now that is loyalty. And it even extends to the data disclaimer: 'By selecting "Sell My Soul" I agree to receive important info and offers from Liquid Death since they will own my soul for eternity.'

Actor Joe Manganiello sells his soul to Liquid Death © Liquid Death

Tony's Chocolonely's first advent calendar was a piece of genius in creating fame and getting people engaged with the mission. To illustrate the inequality in the chocolate industry, they left the window behind the number eight empty. An elegant way to get across their message, but it also meant that thousands of children who were excited to open their advent on 8 December were left confused and upset – and they got lots of complaints. Perhaps it walked close to the line and no one wants to see kids crying in the run-up to Christmas, but it certainly did a major job for the brand.

The uproar generated national press coverage, a seriously impressive feat for an advent calendar. If you didn't have a Tony's calendar, you certainly knew about the message they were landing. One parent said the empty calendar window was a 'devastating blow', adding: 'My children are also confused, my youngest close to tears.

I don't think this was a great teachable moment.' Another said: 'I'm amazed at some of the responses – 1.56 million children working in illegal conditions, but the complaints are about a child missing one day's chocolate from an advent calendar. Shambles! Never change Tony!' They did go on to explain that on 9 and 24 December, the calendar window contained two chocolates to demonstrate the inequality of the industry, so in the end children were getting 25 chocolates over 24 days, rather than missing out.* After the initial year, they've made the missing window a key part of the calendar, and it's become a much loved part of the product. All's well that ends well, and a masterclass in generating fame for a Change Brand.

Who Gives A Crap's Emergency Roll is also a fun and interesting way to get some social involvement. The last roll in the box is wrapped in bright orange and described as the emergency roll. It's a bit of fun. We've all been there and no one wants to run out of toilet roll at the wrong moment. It also serves the important purpose of reminding people to order their next box.

The Who Gives a Crap Emergency Roll © Who Gives A Crap

---

* https://www.independent.co.uk/life-style/food-and-drink/tonys-chocolonely-advert-calendar-missing-chocolate-b1974956.html

Fame as Pure Entertainment

Fame driving work can just be pure entertainment. Creating something that makes people laugh or is so 'out there' that they have to talk about it. As Paul Feldwick says, 'You just need to put on a show that keeps people in their seats and puts them in a good mood. They'll like you better and then they'll buy more of your stuff.'

But how do you do this with a limited budget? It's not easy or cheap to create cultural cut-through, is it? Tim Keaveney from Homethings introduced me to the idea of 'big budget energy' based on a slightly different and well-known saying that alludes to effortless confidence, likeability and positivity towards others.* While you might not have the same budgets as the big players, you can certainly behave like you have. Content is easier and more affordable to produce than it once was and so long as you're not trying to compete at the Super Bowl, it is possible to create great film and photography that has 'Big Budget Energy' but without the price tag.

Surreal, the brand disrupting the cereal category with their zero-sugar high protein offering, did this to great effect. They had seen that working with celebrities was a great way of borrowing some of their fame and hoping it would rub off on the brand. But with nothing like the budget required for big-name endorsements, they had to find another way. Instead, they pulled out the phone book (or probably more accurately, searched on social platforms) and found people with famous names. A billboard proudly stated that Surreal was 'Dwayne Johnson's favourite cereal', but this Dwayne Johnson is a bus driver from London. Serena Williams eats the cereal too. The student from London, rather than the record-breaking tennis player. It's the 'official cereal of Ronaldo' too, but not the Ronaldo you're thinking about. Cleverly placed across a handful of billboards in London and then posted online, the campaign went stratospheric

---

* Big Dick Energy

with 28 million views. 'It went nuts,' said co-founder Jac Chetland. 'And Michael Jordan is still a subscriber!'

Surreal's 'celebrity' campaign © Surreal

For Valentine's Day, the plant-based meat brand THIS™ created a bacon-scented perfume based on their research that showed almost one in three Brits found the smell of sizzling bacon sexy. After issuing a press release describing the fragrance as featuring 'smoky, woody and savoury scents', which are guaranteed to seduce even the most carnivorous people, the new scent sold out in just 20 minutes with 25,000 further requests for the perfume.*

Bacon-scented perfume from THIS™ © THIS™

---

* https://plantbasednews.org/culture/this-vegan-bacon-perfume/

To draw attention to the staggering findings that there are nearly a quarter of a million invisible pieces of tiny nanoplastics in the average litre of bottled water,[*] Ocean Bottle launched their own fake bottled water brand 'Acqua Sordida' that translates as Filthy Water. 'Recent studies have shown the alarming rate at which we are absorbing microplastics into our bodies and how this has the potential to affect our health and reproductive systems due to it's toxicity. It's been shown one of the sources is bottled water, so we launched this campaign to bring attention to the findings.' founder Pearson explains. It contains pieces of brightly coloured microplastic to show the reality of what people are drinking when they pick up a plastic bottled water. Despite the knowledge that it's terrible for the planet and the health impact of microplastics becoming increasingly common knowledge, 27 per cent of the UK still regularly buy plastic bottled water.

Liquid Death are masters at creating fame. Founder Mike Cessario says, 'We want to be one of the best things that consumers see that day because we have to compete with hilarious influencers, fitness athletes and movie trailers. The bar to earn someone's attention is really high now.'[†] Andy Pearson, their VP of Creative, goes on, 'Our competition is not other brands in the category. It's other things that you see in your social feed. That's our competition.'[‡]

This approach has led them to create an incredible amount of entertainment under the guise of growing the brand. Someone online said, 'I'd rather lick sweat off a fat guy's back than drink Liquid Death.' So, naturally, they ran the taste test for real and unsurprisingly, Liquid Death came out on top. For Halloween, they worked with home and lifestyle guru Martha Stewart to launch a

---

[*] https://www.pbs.org/newshour/science/scientists-find-about-a-quarter-million -invisible-microplastic-particles-in-a-liter-of-bottled-water

[†] https://www.contagious.com/iq/article/dead-in-the-water

[‡] Confessions of a Creative Director podcast, January 2024

candle in the shape of a severed hand. They created Voodoo dolls with Steve-O from MTV's *Jackass* that even included a little bit of his hair and skateboards with American skateboarder and entrepreneur Tony Hawk that used some of his blood in the paint. They made a full slasher movie, where teens camping in the woods were attacked by cans of Liquid Death, and they've partnered with all sorts of brands that are popular with their community, from gaming brands to skate and streetwear brands. This approach shows no signs of stopping. They play in culture, understand their community and push the limits. Pearson states, 'We have started thinking less of Liquid Death the brand and more of Liquid Death the character. And we write for the character.'

Does Liquid Death taste better than back sweat? © Liquid Death

Have fun with your brand. It's important to understand the role it plays in your audience's life, where it is far from the be-all and end-all. What is important to them? What makes them laugh? What other brands do they like and buy? Be playful and use this to bring a little bit of entertainment into their lives alongside all the other sources of fun and you'll go a long way towards building a relationship that will go the distance.

Take Aim at the Competition

Another tried-and-tested way of generating fame is to pick a fight with someone bigger than you. I'm not talking in the schoolyard sense, although getting a black eye is a quick way of gaining a bit of notoriety at school. I mean looking at the bigger players in the sector and calling them out. We've already spoken about how most Change Brands are looking to address a category problem; tackling an injustice and setting out to do things differently and better. This could be a change of ingredients, a change in packaging, a supply chain shift or the forward impact of the brand. 'Minimum footprint and maximum impact' is the mantra of lots of great Change Brands.

Everyone loves a plucky David figure taking on the industry's Goliath. Almost every established category and major manufacturer has things they could do better. The problem is they're tied into it with their current supply chain and the millions in sunk costs that they cannot walk away from. Change Brands are operating at a much smaller scale so they can afford to do things differently.

Brands that call out the elephant in the room can create a real stir. Oatly have perhaps been the biggest exponent of this over the last decade and the 'Milk Wars' have been raging. When they rebranded in 2012, they realigned their brand mission to encourage and help people to move towards a plant-based lifestyle. The sides of their packaging included copy that explained their beliefs (which also ran as full-page advertising) and a call for people to join the 'Post Milk Generation'. Along the way they've used lines like 'Wow, no cow' and 'It's like milk but made for humans', which has led to an ongoing battle with the dairy industry.

Chief Creative Officer John Schoolcraft provides an insight into their thinking at the time: 'If you want to explain oat milk to someone, you first have to explain the concept of milk. It's like an electric car. How would someone explain the concept of an electric car without first explaining the car? So, we wrote some very direct copy that explained the differences between oat and dairy milk. Apparently, that wasn't legal. They claimed we had discredited milk, so they filed a lawsuit against us.'

He continued, 'Most companies would immediately back down, but because we felt we had just spoken the truth, we published the entire 172-page lawsuit on our website and let the public decide. We had no idea what public opinion would be, but it quickly became a David versus Goliath situation, where thousands of people began to support us because they could see it was a bully tactic. We then took a full-page ad out in the morning papers that explained that we had been sued and why and suddenly the milk vs oat war is making headline news. We went from niche to mainstream in part because of that lawsuit so in one sense we were quite fortunate.'*

A pointed headline from Oatly © Oatly

The legal ding-dong has continued ever since and while Oatly are no longer able to use the word 'milk' and must describe their product as 'oat drink', the hard work has been done and consumers and baristas across the world still call it 'oat milk'. They registered the term 'Post Milk Generation' in 2019 and this became the subject of a legal battle

---

* https://thechallengerproject.com/blog/2016/oatly

with Dairy UK. In 2023, Oatly won their case to still be able to use the trademark because it 'describes the likely consumer rather than the product'. The judge ruled that the slogan made it clear that the products are 'for consumers who no longer consume dairy milk'.*

It hasn't all been one way either. Oatly have brought the transparency of their climate footprint to the fore in a multichannel campaign that calls out their own climate footprint numbers and leaves space for the dairy industry to do the same with cows' milk. They've even gone so far as to lobby governments calling for mandatory reporting of climate footprint on food packaging to turn the tables.

The climate impact of plant-based milk is much smaller when compared to dairy milk in terms of emissions, land use and water use. Dairy requires almost 12 times more land than oat milk and is responsible for 3.5 times more greenhouse gas emissions.† Armed with this data, and knowing that the dairy industry can't really respond, they are calling out the elephant in the room and making a virtue of the lower impact of their products.

An Oatly campaign calling out the dairy industry © Oatly

---

* https://plantbasednews.org/news/economics/oatly-legal-battle-post-milk-generation/
† Joseph Poore and Thomas Nemecek (2018). ourworldindata.org/environmental-impacts-of-food

I asked Schoolcraft how the behaviour of Big Dairy has changed since Oatly started causing a stir. He said, 'They've changed radically. First, they tried all the traditional bully tactics like trying to sue us. Now they are much smarter and more covert and fund a lot of misinformation on the internet about plant-based food and oatmilk because they know that their time has come and we don't need farm animals to make nutritious milk, certainly not if we want a planet to live on going forward.'

This approach can really cause a stir and it is possible to do it without ending up in a lengthy and no doubt expensive legal battle. Cano Water in the UK spotted an opportunity at the 2023 Wimbledon Tennis Championships. While Wimbledon has made a major commitment to sustainability, it generates a staggering 250,000 single-use plastic bottles each year and has a long-standing relationship with Evian.* Cano Water, the UK canned water brand, called on Wimbledon to #breakupwithplastic. They were at the event every day during the fortnight of the Championships with an electric billboard that called out the 'toxic relationship'.

Josh White, founder of Cano Water, said, 'At Cano Water we know that consumers are constantly lied to about the difference between recyclable and recycled. Only 9 per cent of plastic is successfully recycled and most of it ends up in landfill or leaking into the environment. Aluminium is the most recyclable material on the planet and that's why we created Cano Water. The recycling rate of aluminium cans is nearly 75 per cent in the UK and growing. We must come together to call out brands to not bottle

---

* https://lbbonline.com/news/cano-water-boldly-urges-wimbledon-to-break-up-with-plastic

it and break up with plastic! Large brands such as Wimbledon should lead by example.'

Cano Water call out Wimbledon on their relationship
with Evian © Cano Water

Tony's Chocolonely called out their competitors in a way designed to raise a few eyebrows and address the category problem. In 2021, they launched a range of products called 'Sweet Solution bars' that borrowed the branding of famous competitors like Nestlé's KitKat, Mars Inc's Twix, Mondelez's Toblerone and Ferrero Rocher balls. Ben Greensmith, Tony's UK lead at the time of the campaign, said, 'You've got 1.56 million children working illegally to provide cocoa and effectively the big chocolate companies aren't doing anything about it. These products are so iconic... they're something that anyone who like chocolate will have tried and recognized. We wanted to show that these bars – people's favourite bars – can be made differently.'*

---

* https://www.foodnavigator.com/Article/2021/01/26/Tony-s-Chocolonely-launches -look-alikes-in-ethical-cocoa-campaign

Tony's Chocolonely 'Sweet Solution' Bars © Tony's Chocolonely

This was intended to bring the brand's mission to end exploitation in the chocolate supply chain to the fore, but after only one day, the bars were pulled from Sainsbury's stores across the UK after pressure from two chocolate giants.* The limited edition bars may not have lasted long on shelves, but they did their job in registering with the audience and getting a statement from each of the big players acknowledging the presence of the elephant in the room that they don't normally talk about. For example, Nestlé said: 'This is an eye-catching stunt from Tony's but behind the marketing lies a very serious reality. Child labour exists within the cocoa industry and, at Nestlé, we have been working for many years to help tackle it.'

When they ran an updated version of the campaign in early 2024 to align with their launch in Germany and Austria, Mondelez, owners of the Milka brand that they had mimicked, started legal action over the use of the colour purple. Tony's then recreated the bar with the packaging in grey, rather than purple. If anything, the legal injunction from Mondelez added more fuel to the fire and gave the campaign added publicity with mainstream media coverage.

---

* https://www.foodnavigator.com/Article/2021/01/26/Tony-s-Chocolonely-launches-look-alikes-in-ethical-cocoa-campaign

It also provided a gift of a call to action, with the headline 'Pay Farmers, Not Lawyers' to highlight the need to pay cocoa farmers more to end exploitation in the supply chain.

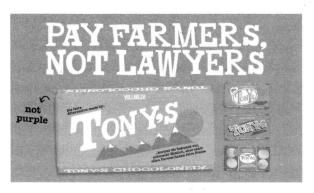

Tony's brilliant response to a legal challenge © Tony's Chocolonely

In summer 2021, when Fussy, the sustainable, refillable deodorant brand, ran a couple of social ads comparing their product to the Unilever brands Dove, Vaseline and Simple, they received a letter from Unilever's lawyers claiming the adverts were misleading in some of the things that were implied. Fussy held their hands up and fully admitted they were in the wrong. As a token of their apology, they extended both a metaphorical and real olive branch to Unilever by delivering an olive tree to Unilever's HQ in London's Blackfriars with a letter attached. As a small team they had made a mistake and said in their letter: 'that if we had a marketing department, we'd fire them, but as it's just us, we'll have to make sure we don't slip up again.'

Never ones to miss out on an opportunity for some publicity, they filmed themselves delivering the tree and posted the film and the letter across their social channels. 'Everything is an opportunity. And don't ask for permission ask for forgiveness, at least while you are small,' founder Matt Kennedy explains. 'As companies grow, they lose their bottle because they have more on the line. I think trying to preserve some of that risk taking is important. Stunts play a key role as a way to build the brand without spending big bucks on above the line media. They are also important internally too. They cultivate the right start up culture and they are fun. I spent years of clients saying no to ideas [referring to his previous career in advertising]. Now I get to say yes let's try it.'

Their olive-tree stunt even elicited a response from Unilever's CEO at the time, Alan Jope, on LinkedIn. He said: 'Thanks Matt for the olive tree. We'll take good care of it. And don't sweat it.' Kennedy admitted to *Campaign* that he might be open to the idea of selling Fussy to Unilever – a common move in recent years for personal care start-ups with an ethical dimension, given their commitment to sustainability. 'Maybe me and Alan will meet at a future date,' he speculated. 'We want to make sure whoever we work with aligns with our goals. For all the flack Unilever get, they've got some ambitious targets.' He added: 'Alan has my number now.'*

Fussy founder Matt Kennedy apologizes to Unilever on LinkedIn and receives a response from then CEO Alan Jope © Fussy

---

* https://www.campaignlive.co.uk/article/deodorant-start-up-fussy-makes-peace -unilever-violating-ad-rules/1724198

When is It Time to Go Mainstream?

There is a whole raft of opportunities out there for brands to generate fame. Early in the journey, shows like *Dragons' Den* or *Shark Tank* provide the opportunity to explain the story of the product to millions of people on mainstream TV. While the thought of stepping onto these shows is frankly a little bit terrifying, the shot in the arm it can give the business is significant. Fussy, Nuud, Tentree and Homethings have all been on *Dragons' Den* and seen a major uplift in interest and sales. Gener8 Ads caused a major stir, with Founder Sam Jones' pitch being described as 'the best in *Dragons'* history'. Their user base grew ten times overnight and raised their profile within the investor community at the same time. Every time there is a repeat of the show, the brands see an uplift in sales. Matt Kennedy from Fussy might be a little tired of seeing repeats of the clip of him jumping out of a giant wheelie bin on 'The Den', but the jump in sales probably makes up for that. 'Without doubt it accelerated the business along. I think at least 12 months compared to where we would have gotten without it. It is the best organic TV marketing you can get, for whatever amount you are willing to sell part of your business,' Kennedy explains. 'And this is before you even consider the benefit the right Dragon might bring in terms of value add and the ability to extend the impact through messaging and ads. We still use *Dragons' Den* content in ads two years on.'

While it might seem scary to many and it's certainly an intimidating environment to walk into, the benefits are well worth the anxiety. 'At an early stage, no one even knows your brand so better to be known for something than nothing at all,' Kennedy continues. 'If you have confidence in your product, the problem you are solving, have some traction and know your stuff then what are you worried about?'

Media owners are also keen to support up-and-coming brands. They see them as important for the future of the platform because these new brands who are making waves are likely to be the ones buying media in the future. These 'new to TV' or 'new to radio' brands are an important part of the strategy. A little bit like a drug dealer offering your first hit for free, media owners will often offer incredible deals to new brands to bring them onto the platform and show that it drives sales, to get you hooked on the potential results. It's in their interests to make it work (and they're a lot friendlier than drug dealers!). If they can demonstrate the effectiveness of their TV, radio, outdoor or digital campaign in growing that brand, they can showcase that in future conversations with similar brands.

There are also often competitions open to brands that are having a positive impact on the world. Sky run an incredible competition called the Sky Zero Footprint Fund, which is designed to help brands that are helping the UK move towards Net Zero. They give away £2 million in media value every year, with four prizes of £250,000 and a £1 million Grand Prix. Here We Flo, Serious Tissues and Grub Club have all won the £1 million Grand Prix and seen a major shift in brand fame and an impact on sales. Being on TV raises a brand's profile overnight and has a knock-on effect on B2B and retailer relationships as well as direct sales. Other Change Brands including Homethings, Milliways, Ocean Saver, WUKA, Ecosia, Ocean Bottle, Upcircle, Pura and Olio have all won the £250,000 to give their business a shot in the arm. It's worth keeping an eye out for similar competitions and initiatives other media owners have to sprinkle a little more fame onto your brand. Credit to Sky for putting this together and partnering with a whole host of brands who will hopefully go on to achieve success and appreciate the power of TV to drive their brand forward.

Media outlets are always looking for stories they can cover. The way Change Brands provide solutions for problems that lots of people care about creates a great opportunity for PR coverage, media appearances and column inches. People are interested in the stories of these brands, so journalists are keen to write about them. Toast came out of an idea pitched to Jamie Oliver's team and got such a huge reaction when it was on Channel 4's *Friday Night Feast* in 2016 that it turbocharged the brand from day one and it's now coming up to eight years since launch and shows no signs of slowing down. Change Please achieved major coverage at launch across all the key media outlets and continues to make regular appearances on mainstream TV. Liquid Death, Allbirds and Warby Parker are often featured beyond the business pages. The opportunity is there to tap into the media's appetite for good news stories at the intersection of social change and business so cultivate your brand with this in mind. A bit of well-placed PR can go a long way in dialling up the fame dial a little further and giving you something else to talk to your audience about.

The term 'fake it till you make it' has both good and bad elements to it, but this is one trick that Change Brand owners can use, particularly when it comes to billboards. Scrolling through LinkedIn or other social platforms, you might think that some of these brands have almost infinite outdoor advertising budgets, appearing on high-profile, large-format sites on a regular basis. The reality is that while some might have made it into the real world, plenty more will have been created for the impact they will have on social media platforms. This is another example of 'big budget energy' behaving like a much bigger brand to increase fame. Often the impact of a well-placed billboard leveraged on social media can reach a much bigger audience than the number of people walking past the physical site. You've got to ask yourself the question 'If a billboard never appeared in the real world and no one was there to see it, did it make a sound?' The answer is a resounding yes if it strikes a chord with your audience online.

There does come a time when Change Brands need to step beyond digital platforms and start to leverage mainstream broadcast media. Social media has proved itself an incredibly effective tool at finding the right audience for your brand, with algorithms optimizing to find the people who are most likely to buy. It can help a fame-driving idea to spread organically across the platform. Search also does a powerful job in making your brand easy to find online, but there does come a time when brands reach a plateau in terms of the growth that they can unlock through digital platforms alone and they need to start adding brand-building activity to continue their growth and attract new customers. Dr Grace Kite and Tom Roach describe this as the 'performance plateau',* where previously fast-growing brands exhaust the sales channels they are using, cost per acquisition goes up and the time comes to step beyond just advertising on social media and to start looking at broadcast media. Growth starts to flatline. Adding a layer of brand-building activity, as shown in the diagram below, gives the brand much bigger reach and helps build a demand pool of future customers who will be ready to buy your brand when they enter the market. It also improves the efficiency of existing performance activity. This addition of brand-building activity, designed to increase the fame of the brand, helps to move past the 'performance plateau' and return to growth. Fame is a way of rising above the noise of social platforms, cutting through into culture and is the first step in making the brand a household name.

---

* https://thetomroach.com/2022/11/14/is-your-brand-stuck-on-the-performance
-plateau/

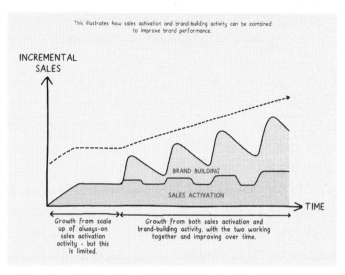

This illustrates how sales activation and brand-building activity can be combined to improve brand performance.

INCREMENTAL SALES

BRAND BUILDING

SALES ACTIVATION

TIME

Growth from scale up of always-on sales activation activity - but this is limited.

Growth from both sales activation and brand-building activity, with the two working together and improving over time.

Brand-building activity helps to escape the 'Performance Plateau'
© Dan White. Source: Tom Roach/Grace Kite, *The Wrong and the Short of It*

Play the Fame Game

So, there you have it. Proof that a bit of showmanship can reap serious rewards for your brand. Aim for fame and you'll be on the fast track to everlasting glory and immortality. If only it was as easy as all that. It's difficult to predict fame. It's been said before that fame is a tricky mistress. It comes from the interactions between people and we know how unpredictable they can be. It also comes from interactions between people and the media and timing can play a major part in what cuts through in the media.

We can create the conditions for fame, but it's impossible to fully control or predict. It comes from understanding your audience, being tapped into what's happening in culture and showing up consistently over time. By trying things and taking risks you give yourself the best chance of cutting through and achieving fame. It's important not to be afraid to fail. Some things just come together in the right way at the right time and catch a wave in culture. You can get lucky and be the beneficiary of a happy accident. Something you think is going to go big might flop and then the opposite could happen when there are lower expectations.

VP Andy Pearson at Liquid Death has a healthy perspective on this: 'We put out so much work continuously, which is how we learn. Not by being super constipated over the strategy of the thing. That is where agencies and brands need to unclench themselves. We are all overthinking it.'

As new Change Brands, you don't have a lot to lose and there's a lot of potential upside if you get it right. It's about experimenting and consistently putting things out into the world. Jac Chetland from Surreal took the view that, 'As long as it feels true to our brand, optimistic and full of joy, we'll put it out there and see what happens.' Thinking of your brand as a character without a rigid set of brand behaviours is a helpful way to see things. Have fun, try stuff and just don't do anything that's going to get you into any legal issues.

So, it's time to aim for fame. Pick a fight, address the elephant in the room, give people a way to get involved and just entertain them. At the very least, you'll learn something and bring some new people into the brand world. And best-case scenario, you could be getting on the radar of millions more people so that they think of you when they're next thinking about buying something.

CHAPTER TEN

Build a Rebel Alliance

'Individually, we are one drop. Together, we are an ocean.'

Ryunosuke Satoro, the father of Japanese literature

So, there you have it. The small matter of changing how people spend their money to change the world. Millions of tiny switches in consumer behaviour. Moving from Brand A to Brand B. From brands that are part of the problem to brands that are part of the solution. This has the potential to have an enormous positive effect on the world we all live in.

It's not about changing every single brand to a Change Brand and moving every single transaction in their direction (although that would be nice). The size of these categories means a couple of per cent moving in the right direction is seriously significant. Big FMCG companies constantly describe themselves as having 'the consumer at the heart' so if they start to see a shift in spending habits, they will take action to align themselves and their brands with this changing mindset.

Let's cast our minds back to earlier in the book. We talked about a 'magic number' of 3.5 per cent of the population needing to take part for real change to happen. That could mean hitting 3.5 per cent market share or we might think about it in terms of market penetration. This is an easier goal meaning that 3.5 per cent of the population have bought the product over the course of the year. This could mean one bar of Tony's, a coffee with oat milk in it, an eco-toilet roll, a meat alternative burger or a can of water. So many of the brands talked about in this book are a long way past this mark and as a result, we're already starting to see changes happening. Just 3.5 per cent of people making positive changes in the brands they buy to have a positive impact on the world is already making a real difference and big companies already have no choice but to sit up and take notice.

But winning market share is when it gets really serious for the incumbents because this is when it starts to hit the bottom line. That means lower sales, pressure on distribution in supermarkets, eroded margins, reduced profit and smaller bonus pots. It means fundamental shifts in strategy and supply chains. Gaining penetration is the start, but winning market share and getting people to buy not just once, but repeatedly, is the key.

The shift is already happening. Oatly turned over $783 million in 2023. Tony's Chocolonely hit $162 million in 2023 and are only just getting started in the US. Method and Ecover bring in over $110 million a year. Liquid Death reached $263 million in sales in 2023. Tesla, perhaps the most advanced Change Brand and one operating in a market with a very high price point, almost hit $100 billion in 2023.* These brands have proved that it's possible to sell a serious amount of product while making a positive impact on society.

If this shift continues, it would mean billions of dollars moving to brands that are making a positive impact on the world and the legacy players needing to take action quickly to keep up. But it's not going to be easy to hit that mark as Change Brands are outgunned by the established status quo. The advantage of size and scale is

---

* Sourced from the Oatly, Tony's, People against Dirty (Method and Ecover) and Tesla annual reports

significant. Deeper pockets and far greater resources make it hard for Change Brands to catch up.

Yes, there's a lot we can do to turn the situation to our advantage. Starting with a blank sheet of paper removes some of the challenges that come with every legacy business and you can pick an area of impact that matters to people while combining it with a category problem. You can then establish moral leadership of the category through the positioning and the key messages you use. Change Brands can move fast and take risks too. In fact, to be truly successful, I'd go so far as to say taking risks is a necessity and amounts to good business. This means throwing caution to the wind when it comes to established category conventions and aiming for fame in marketing activities. Legacy brands have been around a long time, before the invention of behavioural economics, so developing a brand story that plays to the way we know the brain works also moves the dial slightly in your favour.

But there's one thing we haven't talked about yet: the benefits of collaboration. With so many Change Brands gaining traction, building momentum and attracting new customers, there is the opportunity to work together collectively in order to grow each brand and the proportion of total consumer spend that is going to Change Brands as a whole.

Most of the brands we're competing with are part of a holding company of multiple brands, rather than being lone wolves out there in the marketplace. This means they can share resources when it comes to things like finance, IT, legal and HR. They're part of a supply chain that works for multiple brands. They can tap into specialist expertise for research, tech and New Product Development (NPD). They have better negotiating power with supermarkets and media owners. Whereas each Change Brand is effectively an island. A single entity competing against what feels like entire continents in comparison. Finding ways to work together is paramount in enabling these brands to meet their potential. By forming partnerships, both formal and informal, and working together as a collective, it might be possible to create a 'quasi-holding company' for Change Brands that has shared benefits for everyone involved. A Rebel Alliance of sorts, a collection of brands all looking to change things for the better.

Now it might feel like Change Brands are competing with each other, particularly for limited resources like venture capitalist (VC) investment, but the far bigger opportunity is to compete with the legacy players. Taking share off the status-quo brands who control vast swathes of the market and billions in consumer spend is where we need to collectively focus. While it obviously does make sense to think twice before collaborating with someone in direct competition, I believe the benefits of collaboration outweigh any concerns about competition between Change Brands. Ultimately, trying to create a world where all Change Brands rise collectively together would be the holy grail. Working together as a group of like-minded brands has the potential to level the playing field a little bit. We're all in this together, let's work together to drive social disruption and make brands that are not up to scratch obsolete – or at the very least, drive changes in their business model.

Collaboration is already happening informally within founder networks and having spoken to a number of founders while writing this book, developing something more formal is in the works. If you're interested in being part of a collective of Change Brands, please get in touch via the contact details at the back of the book (page 288).

There are a number of ways brands can work together to bring about better business results and wider change. While some of these benefits would make more sense with other Change Brands, there are also examples of Change Brands working with bigger players for a number of reasons. These opportunities for collaboration fall into three areas:

1. Knowledge and Network Sharing

The first way to collaborate is in sharing knowledge and connections. The journey a Change Brand goes on is reasonably well mapped out. There is a need to create a brand and product proposition, prove the concept by getting customers on board, increase routes to market and most likely, raise investment to fuel growth.

Sharing what has worked for brands as they look to attract customers is really useful. Has LinkedIn proved to be a useful channel to attract customers? Has radio worked better than social media? Is affiliate or influencer activity working best? It's also important to share failures so multiple brands don't make the same mistakes and waste vital working capital when the returns aren't there. Sharing both best practice and costly mistakes can be a useful shortcut to success for smaller brands following on the coat-tails of brands who are further along in the journey. When capital is at a premium, it's important to deploy it as effectively as possible and we should share knowledge to avoid making the same mistakes twice.

Recommendations for potential partners are also useful. A founder is likely to be inundated with sales messages from various agencies offering miracle results. It's almost impossible to know who is good and who is bad. Recommendations within a founder community for trusted suppliers, whether in brand development, social advertising, search, email, Amazon or finding a trusted Third-Party Logistics (3PL) supplier are really valuable and can again save people from making costly mistakes.

There are people you need help from along the way as well. Introductions to supermarket buyers, Venture Capital firms and potential investors are hard to come by. Any help that can be given from one part of the Change Brand community to another can make a really big difference.

Sharing of knowledge and connections creates an invaluable culture of reciprocity. This means that if you do something helpful for someone else, they feel compelled to return the favour and are always on the lookout for ways to help and vice versa. This concept is deeply ingrained in our society and underpins a lot of social norms like gift giving and sharing of resources. Trying to cultivate a culture of active reciprocity among Change Brands could be another marginal gain that could help all brands move in the right direction.

2. Marketing Partnerships

There are numerous opportunities for Change Brands to collaborate in their marketing efforts. It's quite likely that a consumer who has been attracted by the messaging of one brand that's trying to make a positive difference in the world would also be interested in the proposition of another brand. Lots of people are looking to make more sustainable swaps or make a positive impact with the money they spend so that is likely to involve multiple brands. Acquisition costs via social platforms like Facebook and Instagram have gone through the roof in recent years since the privacy changes to the Apple operating system so it seems foolish to just give more and more money to two of the richest companies in the world in Meta and Google to try and acquire customers when we could work together as Change Brands.

Partnership marketing can work in a variety of ways. The broad idea is that the activity should be beneficial to both brands. A win-win or a quid pro quo. We help you out and get something valuable in return. For D2C brands, it might mean product sampling in each other's boxes. It could be a competition or giveaway that goes out to the databases of two or more brands to reach a wider audience and get the other brand in front of new customers who are like-minded.

It could be an email swap with each brand sending a promo offer to their customers on behalf of the other brand.

Undoubtedly, Change Brands can learn something from the big holding companies. They pool their media spend together through one entity, often a media agency, so they can access better deals from media owners and get more bang from their considerable buck. Pooling that spend increases buying power. Could Change Brands do the same to get more from that spend?

Similarly, if you give your data to one holding company brand, it's not unlikely that you'll receive communications from another brand from the same stable. Could Change Brands do something similar (while being sure to respect data privacy laws)? Creating lookalike audiences with shared data would prove helpful in making media targeting more effective.

These can go a step further into the real world as well. It might mean sharing exhibition space at events or collaborating on a pop-up shop. It could mean product collaborations, creating a unique flavour or perhaps a bundle that puts together food or household brands in the same box that's then sold across multiple brand websites. There are so many ways for brands to work together to achieve shared goals and it all starts with a conversation.

Partnerships shouldn't be limited to just working with other Change Brands as well. Change Please had a lot of success with a partnership called 'Driving for Change'. The majority of Change Please beneficiaries are defined as 'statutory homeless', which means they don't have a fixed address, but are unlikely to be full-time rough sleepers, spending a lot of time in hostels and other temporary accommodation. While they were stopping a lot of this group falling further through the cracks and helping them back on their feet, they wanted to do something to help rough sleepers.

Change Please founder Cemal Ezel said, 'The plan was to take two London buses and fit them out to work as mobile care centres for rough sleepers that we could take to where people are. They'd include showers, washing machines and access to doctors, dentists, therapy and financial help.' A big idea, but one that was proving expensive for a small business to get off the ground. 'I'd bought the buses, but had no idea how we were going to afford to fit them out. Then we had the idea to reach out to some big companies for support.' Colgate, HSBC and MasterCard all got on board with their own co-branded buses. HSBC and MasterCard helped with financial inclusion, with many homeless people struggling to secure a bank account, which makes it very difficult to claim benefits, rent accommodation and receive wages. Colgate helped with the provision of dental services, as oral hygiene is one of the first things to go when sleeping rough.

The buses are now out on the roads of London four days a week offering a co-branded presence for the big brands. What these brands paid for an annual partnership works out as a fraction of the price of a full bus wrap for the same time period and they have a great story to tell of how their brands are making a positive difference. Each brand has supported the partnership with additional media spend, with Colgate in particular taking the message to TV, and doing a great job for both Colgate and Change Please.

Driving for Change bus – a Change Please and Colgate partnership
© Change Please and Colgate

Change Please have gone a step further with this in announcing a partnership with one of the world's biggest coffee companies in Nespresso. This means that from summer 2024, Nespresso system owners will be able to buy Change Please coffee for the millions of machines across the world. Nespresso have committed to supporting the Change Please mission with a minimum donation of £1 million each year that will help grow their impact and training operations in the Republic of Ireland and one other key city yet to be determined. Nespresso have a big marketing campaign lined up to support the partnership, something that will continue to increase awareness about Change Please and help them to help more people off the streets.

Partnership marketing can be a powerful lever to pull, both with other Change Brands and bigger players looking for a positive story to tell their own customers. It all starts with a conversation and pushing the limits of what's possible.

3. Game-Changing Partnerships

When you're trying to tackle some of the major environmental and societal problems that Change Brands have set out to address, it is often too much to do it all on your own. To make bigger change happen, it's vital to find ways for more people and brands to join in and be part of the change. Some of the game-changing partnerships that Change Brands are spearheading are truly inspiring and have the potential to bring about industry-wide changes. Douglas Lamont, CEO of Tony's Chocolonely, said, 'It's sometimes not enough to just change what you do, you have to change the game entirely.'

Tentree, the Canadian clothing brand that plants ten trees with every item of clothing sold, wanted to have greater transparency of the tree planting process. They knew they were planting millions of trees annually but wanted to know more about their location and their survivability rates, among other things. They were also keen to be able to provide answers to sceptics querying how they could make sure trees weren't double-counted or assigned to more than one company who is planting trees. To address this, they created Veritree, a tech platform that verifies every tree planted with GPS tracking, photography and blockchain technology (to avoid double-counting). You can even see the paths taken by workers on their tree planting days, with photographic evidence of trees in the ground. This radical transparency is vital in supporting reforesting efforts and gives confidence to consumers that when companies say they're planting trees, they can see it happening with their own eyes. Veritree are already supporting thousands of businesses who are planting trees, including Serious Tissues, and this transparency is the new gold standard in genuinely fighting deforestation and capturing more carbon through tree planting.

Ocean Bottle have done something similar when it comes to ocean plastic recovery. Not content to have stopped over 12 million kilograms of ocean-bound plastic from reaching the ocean, they wanted to make it easier for other brands to be part of the solution too. So, they created Ocean Co, a platform that would help other brands collect ocean plastic as part of their mission and exponentially accelerate their own mission at the same time. Numerous brands use plastic in some way as part of their supply chain. This solution gives those same brands an affordable and transparent way to be part of the solution and to do something that their customers genuinely care about.

Alongside the brilliant consumer brand Tony's Chocolonely are building, they also have a B2B initiative called Tony's Open Chain that gives them the ability to change the entire industry and achieve their mission. They basically broke the number one rule in business, by inviting other chocolate companies to tap into their supply chain and competitive advantage. Douglas Lamont, Tony's CEO, said, 'What I really like about Tony's mission is that it is very focused about changing a whole industry. It's not just about can Tony's be a good company, care about the supply chain and its people and make a good profit? It's saying we need to do that as step one, but what we actually need to do is change the whole industry and we're not done until the whole industry is changed.'

Tony's Open Chain gives other chocolate brands the opportunity to source their cocoa beans through Tony's own supply chain, complete with fully traceable beans, guaranteeing farmers a better price that means they are in a stronger position for the long term and can afford to remove child labour from their production.

Lamont continues, 'Doing it this way means we can actually prove you can do it at scale in the supply chain. Our brand was never going to grow fast enough on its own to reach 5 per cent of the beans in West Africa, which would mean we would start to be taken seriously, rather than be seen as an experiment that wasn't scalable.'

They opened up the supply chain to what they call 'Mission Allies', other businesses aligned with the desire to remove exploitation from the cocoa supply chain. 'So, we decided to open it up and then when Ben & Jerry's and others come on board with you, suddenly that gives a whole lot more credibility. And where the loop really closes nicely is that private label brands are now coming on board. Waitrose have joined and we've got all the big Dutch supermarkets, Albert Heijn, Jumbo, Aldi, buying those beans off us. They're paying for those premium beans in their private label chocolate.'

This then goes on to have a knock-on effect on the whole category: 'These supermarkets are now asking themselves the question, hold on, Tony's as a brand is doing it. Me as a private label player at a cheaper price than the brands are doing it. Why are the brands in the middle not doing it?' It starts to put pressure on the way these brands operate and it changes what is considered the norm in the sector. This is the first step in delivering change. 'It shrinks the social license to operate. Retailers are saying, well, I've got my chocolate with these ethical beans in it, why the hell are you not doing this? Particularly as child labour and deforestation are two big red flashing lights on anyone's sustainability scorecard.'

This gives Lamont and the team at Tony's a different perspective than a normal brand might have. 'So when I'm sitting in my shoes as CEO, making decisions about what's more important, does that deliver more premium bean volume into West Africa or does it grow my top line? I'm less interested in Tony's Chocolonely's top line. I'm interested in scale of change. So if, in the end, I had to prioritize volume because we suddenly won two or three big other equivalents to Ben & Jerry's and it meant that we couldn't quite grow as fast in Tony's Chocolonely, but it meant that the whole was going to grow faster, I would make that choice because my job is to grow the impact not to grow Tony's Chocolonely the chocolate brand.'

This is not something you'd expect a traditional CEO of a multinational company to say. It marks a major shift away from the idea of shareholder primacy and business returns to prioritize wider impact. While clearly Tony's are the exception rather than the rule, it only takes a few trailblazing organizations to show that growing a business and having a positive impact on the world we all live in can be complementary rather than contradictory. This mindset can unlock growth rather than being merely an inconvenient cost to deal with.

Growing and transforming the whole system, rather than merely the individual brand, makes a big difference because it makes a future with slavery-free chocolate more affordable. It unlocks major economies of scale: 'Once that increased cost is spread across a lot of beans, the cost of that can really be quite small. And therefore, the differential of doing it your way versus doing it the old way turns out not to be that big, especially when the cocoa in a bar of chocolate is only around 15 per cent of the cost.'

Lamont firmly believes a tipping point is coming: 'This is going to change, it's just a question of when, and I don't know whether that's in three years' time or 10 years' time, but I take a pretty big bet it's not going to be 20 years. It just needs one of the big players to show some moral leadership and then everyone else will follow. They've dragged their feet for 20 years. Changes are coming. Now it's just a question of when, but Tony's is here to make that as soon as possible because the sooner it comes, the better it is for the people of West Africa.'

One Team, One Dream

It's clear the world has a lot of problems and they're not going to be straightforward to solve. Refreshingly, there are a growing number of parties trying to make a positive difference. People making changes to what they buy and companies looking to make changes to how they operate to bring about good outcomes. Capitalism is based on relentless competition, with the market determining the winners. But by getting brands and the companies with a shared worldview to work together in concert, rather than in competition, to address these major issues, we have the best possible chance of achieving large-scale and lasting change.

It's not about throwing commercial considerations out of the window either. Solving problems people care about is good business. It improves brand perception, increases employee engagement and helps with attracting talent. Brands can both compete and collaborate at the same time and there is a competitive first-mover advantage on being the first to take action in a sector. Let's work together and look for opportunities to collaborate. In turn, this will help to multiply the impact brands can have on the biggest problems facing humanity. Brands of all shapes and sizes can genuinely change the world if we try and pull in the same direction a little more often.

The success to date and future potential of Tony's Open Chain is testament to the power of collaboration in driving positive change and it shows Change Brands can have an impact far beyond just increasing their own sales. It's incredible to think that a humble Dutch chocolate brand, started by accident by a journalist, could be responsible for transforming the chocolate industry and improving the lives of millions of children and their families across West Africa, and change the destiny of millions of children who haven't even been born yet.

Change like this tastes great, doesn't it?

CHAPTER ELEVEN

What if I'm not a Change Brand?

'The best way to predict the future is to create it.'

Peter Drucker, father of modern management and visionary author

One thing is clear: things are changing. People are increasingly looking for and expecting more from the brands they buy and the companies they work for. This isn't a short-lived fad to be dismissed as something not to worry about, it is a paradigm shift and will change how business is done for ever.

Change can be viewed through two different frames. Our natural tendency as humans is to fear change. Our ancestors who had carved out a modicum of comfort in their lives would treat all change with a healthy dose of scepticism. When food, water and shelter were all taken care of, anything that might change their circumstances would be seen in a negative light. It could upset the carefully created balance and threaten the status quo. Whether that was changes in the seasons, a new predator on the horizon or a new tribe edging into the periphery of their territory, these things were all seen as a threat first and foremost. Our loss aversion takes the lead. We act to minimize potential losses and protect what we already have. The potential opportunities that might come with collaborating with the other tribe or hunting the predator as an additional source of food fade into the background.

This is the mindset that we often see in legacy businesses. Something new on the horizon is seen as a threat to be managed rather than an opportunity to be grasped. A risk to be mitigated against. When a brand is doing millions or even billions in sales, any change in a category is seen as a potential threat. A shift to a new brand, new packaging, new ingredients or a new way of doing things is a shift away from the status quo and could add costs to a finely oiled machine.

Businesses have become very good at risk mitigation. They have invested heavily into systems and processes under the labels of Corporate Social Responsibility (CSR) and Environmental, Social and Governance (ESG) that enable them to measure and be transparent about all elements of their business and the impact on society and the environment. This is an important exercise but does it mean they're spending all their time and money looking backwards, rather than forwards? Leo Rayman of EdenLab says, 'We're at risk of creating the perfect rear-view mirror, potentially at the expense of keeping our eyes on the road and spotting opportunities to redesign and reimagine the future.' CSR and ESG create a tsunami of reporting, but is it just a case of counting the deckchairs on the *Titanic*? What Rayman describes is a Catch-22 situation: 'If you prioritize action over reporting, you get criticized for not being transparent. But if you spend too much time on reporting, you get criticized for not taking action.'

Where you're sat is likely to change the frame of how you look at the changes affecting our world. If you're sat in the camp of a Change Brand, it's highly likely you'll see this shift in consumer attitudes and buying behaviour as a major opportunity. The next ten years will bring a decade of disruption and things will never be the same again. You have nothing to lose and the opportunity is there to grasp in front of you. To carpe the diem.

But if you're sat on the side of the legacy brands, you will see things differently. This consumer shift isn't an opportunity, it's a threat – to your market share, to your bottom line and your bonus. While you've got more resources at your disposal, smaller brands can move faster and break things. They can eat away at your market share and suddenly your bosses and shareholders are asking awkward questions that are difficult to answer.

Looking at it this way puts you on the defensive. It's the same mindset that saw Kodak fail to take advantage of digital photography or Nokia and the smartphone. As with almost any circumstance we find ourselves in, there's a quote from Winston Churchill that is especially apt:

A pessimist sees the difficulty in every opportunity.

An optimist sees opportunity in every difficulty.

If this defensive mindset persists in every large organization as we move forward, it will be another case of missed opportunity on a grand scale. Slow to make decisions, managing losses rather than maximizing gains. Guarding against becoming obsolete, rather than seeing opportunity. But if we change the frame we look at the world through there is tremendous opportunity to be grasped. If we view the world through the eyes of the optimist, we see possibilities rather than pitfalls. The transition to more sustainable behaviours across society and the desire to make a positive impact on problems are perhaps the biggest opportunity on the planet for the next generation of businesses, both big and small.

The big companies that move the fastest and point their considerable resources towards maximizing opportunity rather than minimizing losses stand to win big. And given their slow-moving nature, there is the opportunity for one or two companies to steal a march on the others if they think fast and act smart. All bets are off and what came before is no indication of what the future might look like. To quote Chinese general and strategist Sun Tzu, 'In the midst of chaos, there is opportunity.'

Redraw the battle lines in a category that you weren't in before. Steal share. Win new audiences. Just because something has always been done that way, doesn't mean it always has to be. Strive for moral leadership. The world increasingly wants to change and people expect more from business. There is the opportunity to step up and be the hero in this story. The driving force behind a change that everyone wants to see, rather than the faceless entity standing in the way of progress. The company or companies that move first have a big advantage. They set themselves up to look beyond the next sales quarter and win not just today, but tomorrow too.

This book has discussed at length the benefits of being small, but we haven't talked about the benefits of being big. Here's five ways people in big companies can make the most of the opportunity that's been created by the emergence of Change Brands in the world.

A Five-Point Plan

The following is a five-point plan for bringing the Change Brand mindset to your brand and company:

1. Think Like a Change Brand

Where status-quo players see threats and losses to be managed, Change Brands see opportunity. Just because a category has always operated in a certain way doesn't mean it always has to, especially when there might be a better way of doing things, or a way that a change of the brand purchased in that category might make a positive difference to an environmental or social issue.

The decade of disruption we're embarking upon presents opportunity for brands and businesses of all shapes and sizes. If a particular category is dominated by one of your competitors, social disruption offers an opportunity to disrupt their market share in a way that hadn't seemed obvious before. If the chance is there to establish moral leadership in a category by shifting the way you operate or establishing a new brand that wins new customers from your competition. There is a first mover advantage of being quickest off the blocks and committing to the strategy. There might be a way to fundamentally alter the dynamics of a stale category and steal a march on the competition.

Asking the question 'what would your competition least like you to do?' is a useful way to unlock the sort of disruptive thinking that can lead to big gains in categories at the expense of your competition. Change Brands take risks, they draw a line in the sand and they stand for some sort of positive change in the world. There is absolutely no reason why big established brands can't also stand for something positive and there are a handful that have done this successfully. But the key here is making sure that it's genuine and there is a commitment to making a real difference to the problem. Actions speak much louder than words and as a major brand, even tiny changes in how you operate can have an impact on a huge scale.

The great purpose debate is over. Trying to find a slightly spurious brand purpose, Sellotape it to your brand and then create a vague manifesto style advert that shows your commitment to said purpose won't move the needle at all and is just as likely to backfire as make a positive difference to your brand's metrics. We're now in the age of impact. It's time to use the power at your disposal as a major brand with millions of customers to actually make a meaningful difference in the world. If you can't change the product or donate to a charity, why not encourage your customers to do something positive?

There is one other key thing to consider when thinking like a Change Brand. The concept of time. In big companies, planning happens on an annual basis against annual sales targets. Sales numbers are reported quarterly to shareholders. How will they deploy the annual budget to achieve their objectives? It is a short-term focus and if a change in strategy doesn't generate a serious chunk of change in year one, is it worth getting out of bed for? Marketers and brand managers operate on short-term cycles. Deliver a good campaign, hit your numbers and then move on to the next brand.

Change Brands have a different point of view. They see an opportunity to disrupt a category and realize it may take three to five years to make significant strides in that journey. But because the opportunity is big enough and they believe the category is well poised to change, they can take a slightly longer view. Finding a way to inject a little bit of longer-term planning into the normal brand management process might allow bigger brands to unlock the opportunities Change Brands are gunning for.

Clearly this is difficult to do for big companies with short sales cycles and shareholders to keep happy. Setting money aside to achieve five-year objectives at first seems admirable and strategically smart, but if sales aren't on track, it won't take long for brand managers to divert funds to the present day. It's the business equivalent of a politician focusing policy and spending taxpayer money on short-term vote winners, while kicking the can down the road on the bigger things that would really make a difference in the long term. The problem is, there's only so long you can kick the can down the road before someone else comes along and grasps the opportunity that you were best placed to act upon.

2. Link Positive Change to Business Metrics

Not everything in business is about sales. Understanding how the business really works and what other metrics the business truly values are important because they can help you to make a strong business case for change, rather than just relying on people's desire to do the right thing.

For example, customer data is an important commodity in almost every company out there and there are many ways you can use it to drive the business forward, while respecting privacy legislation. Launching a new proposition, inspired by Change Brand thinking, might allow you to open up an entirely new audience segment for the wider business. If you have good data, you can build a one-to-one relationship with the customer, rather than having to go via retailers, potentially opening up direct sales as a channel. You can use this relationship to gather customer insight and test new creative ideas, products and propositions. It can help with your media targeting. If you can make the case that your new strategy can grow your relationship with a new audience to the business, or those people who previously bought a competitor brand, it becomes a very easy sell to the business.

Not everything you do needs to generate sales instantly so long as it contributes to other metrics that the company values. New audience relationships can be a source of insight into attitudes, campaign creative and new product development. Improving brand metrics is always sound business because a stronger brand is a proven way of generating future sales. Growing an online community also has value over time. It builds mental availability so makes sure your brand is the first they think of when in the market.

By creating an indelible link between positive shifts and the metrics the business values, it is possible to prove that doing the right thing can also be a strong commercial differentiator, so in times when the business is under pressure, it isn't the first thing that is cut from the budget.

3. Partner with Change Brands
As the previous chapter shows, there are numerous ways to partner with Change Brands that are mutually beneficial. Change Brands have collectively set out to make a positive change in the world but trying to change things from a minority market share is often a challenge and partnerships can help Change Brands enhance their reach and impact. This means that there is ample opportunity to

partner with Change Brands to align on their mission and bring about the change they're fighting for faster.

But it's not just about partnering for the sake of it. It needs to make sense. Alignment between the two brands in terms of either product offering or mission alignment is key. If this is in place, it's easy for a partnership to take shape and make sense in the world. Tony's Open Chain are trying to drive the shift to exploitation-free chocolate, so anyone who is a big buyer of cocoa beans is an obvious ally and potential partner.

Nespresso could see Change Please as a competitor because they operate in the same category, but instead they saw the opportunity to widen their impact and contribute to a positive social mission that they believe in. It also gives them a great story to talk about in their communications. The same could also be said about the Change Please and Colgate partnership. Toothpaste ads have certain category conventions and formulas that we're used to seeing and the format was probably getting a little tired. The relationship between the two brands gave Colgate a way of talking about dental hygiene in an entirely new way that made the brand stand out.

With a little bit of imagination, there is likely to be a Change Brand out there who it makes sense to partner with. Whether that's in terms of mission alignment or a crossover in the categories you both operate in, the opportunity to work together to make something good happen in the world is right there. Time to reach out and start a conversation.

4. Disrupt from Within

One of the key recommendations of *The Innovator's Dilemma* by Clayton Christensen is to establish separate innovation units within big businesses. The business as usual operations are great at small innovations that move things forward a little bit and open up new revenue. Christensen calls this 'sustaining innovations'. But when it comes to disruptive innovations, those that fundamentally change categories, this is more of a challenge for the day-to-day business and big companies are notoriously bad at this.

Resources tend to be allocated towards projects that generate the most immediate returns or align with the current business model. They also have a fear of cannibalizing their existing revenue streams. They fear that introducing a disruptive product might eat into their current sales and routes to market, so they delay making moves, even if it's crucial for their long-term success and survival. The tendency of big companies to be customer-led, as discussed by Agent Change earlier (*see also* p. 37), helps with small, iterative changes but rarely leads to the visionary leadership that drives real disruption.

By establishing separate innovation units, that operate outside of the traditional confines of the organization, there is the opportunity to create the best of both worlds. You can create an environment that has the mindset of a Change Brand but the resources of a multinational organization. Done well, this could be a potent force for change in a major company. Disrupting yourself from the inside by tapping into the opportunities for innovation that don't necessarily sit easily with the existing brand portfolio and having the ability to start small, rather than deliver millions in revenue from day one. You can target key competitor brands, rather than your own, to make sure that when seismic shifts happen in categories, you are best placed to take advantage.

If you take the key strengths of Change Brands, visionary leadership, the ability to take risks and the ability to act fast, but play the long game, and then combine these with the key strengths of a major company, you create something that could be transformative for the business. Risk taking meets scale. Disruptive ideas meet expertise and proper budgets. Exciting brands combined with deep retailer relationships. This could be a very powerful force for change in both society and within major multinationals who are perhaps a little stuck in their ways and slow to move. This approach means you can move things forward faster. It's better to eat your own lunch than be left hungry and starving as the world moves on and consumer behaviour shifts.

Procter & Gamble have done this very well with the 2019 launch of EC30, a water-free personal and home care brand. It offers an 'Enlightened Clean' because they've removed the water from the products. They have created a beautiful brand that feels like a start-up with a clever piece of technology behind the product. It is a genuine Change Brand, but one created by one of the biggest companies in the world.

The statistic they use on their site, that 'every year 800,000 million gallons of unnecessary water is shipped' to get cleaning and personal care products into people's homes, is a powerful number that would be likely to strike a chord with consumers. But it's also a statistic that would be difficult for P&G to get behind because brands they own like Pantene, Head & Shoulders, Flash, Fairy and Ariel all contain a lot of 'unnecessary water'. The ability to position the EC30 brand as outside of P&G is an important part of the strategy. It allows them to appeal to the eco-conscious consumer without damaging their own brands and they can compete in the Direct to Consumer marketplace rather than via retailers. It's a smart piece of thinking on their behalf and is evidence this 'best of both worlds' approach can work well for big players. In fact, they've done such a good job hiding their involvement that the only way you know it is a P&G brand is that when the site asks you to sign up to join the EC30 Community and you can see in the disclaimer that you 'agree to receive emails from EC30 and other trusted P&G brands'.

This is a visionary approach from P&G and time will tell if other companies try to create something similar to disrupt themselves from within and make the most of the opportunities that changes in consumer behaviour will present in the next decade.

EC30 – a 'Change Brand' created by Procter & Gamble
© EC30 and Procter & Gamble

5. Buy a Change Brand

Finally, if you can't beat 'em, join 'em. Change Brands have built powerful traction in markets for a reason. The world is changing and people expect more from the brands they buy. These brands are successful businesses in their own right and have built a loyal following and have momentum behind them. Adding Change Brands to the portfolio can allow you to turn up the pressure on a competitor or enter a category that you weren't previously operating in.

While the scrappy nature of Change Brands means they might not be absolutely perfect and hugely profitable during the early part of their journey, what matters is the brand they're building and the heat they're creating in the market. If they've built a powerful brand with a loyal following that means they've demonstrated market traction and they could represent a major opportunity for an established business to come along and take things to the next level.

By buying a Change Brand and applying big company practices to it, it's possible to supercharge that brand and the impact it has on the world. There are so many ways the combination of a Change Brand and a major company can be hugely powerful and beneficial for all involved.

There are big supply chain efficiencies that come from being part of a bigger machine. That might come from unlocking much-improved margins that come from using a big company's factories and distribution at cost. This could instantly unlock a 20–30 per cent jump in margins just through that access to the greater scale these companies have through their operations. There is also the opportunity to leverage established retailer relationships to secure a bigger presence in store and more distribution. A Change Brand might be in 50 per cent of the big retailers in any given country, but by being part of a big player, this can quickly transform to 100 per cent and drive a significant jump in sales. A Change Brand could be a home for New Product Development within the organization that doesn't quite fit with any of the current house of brands, allowing you to test something with a different audience.

If a brand has built major traction in a handful of markets, but is yet to go truly global, the opportunity is there to take that hard-fought traction and enter new markets that are attitudinally aligned to the brand's mission and impact. Again, the hard work has already been done and with operations on the ground, it is relatively straightforward to use the disruptive presence of the Change Brand to unlock more growth.

One important thing to remember is to treat them well. Change Brands are unique in that they've carved out a meaningful position in people's hearts and minds through the positive impact they're having on the world so it's important to respect this. Making material changes to this, whether through formulations or operations, would jeopardize what made them special in the first place and risks undermining the value of the investment. A football manager wouldn't get very far if they tried to convert Lionel Messi into a goalkeeper. It's like asking Tom Brady to play linebacker. It's important to appreciate what you've got and give it the backing it deserves to help it to grow. Do this and what are small brands in the grand scheme of things now could become the power brands of the future.

Change Brands can protect themselves by taking steps to embed that mission front and centre in the organization for the future. Tony's Chocolonely have embedded a 'Mission Lock' into their business. This is a legal mechanism that secures their mission for the rest of eternity, regardless of shareholder structure. The Mission Lock has a golden share, which is a non-economic stake, that gives the Mission Guardians the power to prevent any legal changes to the definition of Tony's mission, the five sourcing principles or any other mission-related articles. Ben & Jerry's did something similar when they sold to Unilever in 2000 to make sure the values of the brand and business lived on.

Be the Optimist

This chapter shows that there are numerous ways for any brand to think like a Change Brand and grasp the opportunities in front of them. Consumers are increasingly wanting to see brands make a positive impact on the world and this will only become a bigger part of doing business over the next couple of decades.

You can look at the world through two different frames and see this coming social disruption as either a threat or an opportunity. The choice is yours.

You can look at the world as a pessimist. Viewing the shifts in society as a threat to be managed. A risk to be mitigated. A loss to be managed. Eyes firmly in the rear-view mirror and not seeing what's right there in front of you.

Or you can look at the world as an optimist. You can see this shift in behaviour as an opportunity to be grasped. A chance to win new customers. Deposition the competition. Enter new categories. Improve brand perception. An opportunity to create the future, rather than react to it. It is a chance to redraw the lines of the battlefield. You can be seen as the hero in the story and you can make a real difference in the world at the same time.

So, what's it going to be?

Epilogue: What Next? Move the Money, Change the World

'There is nothing more powerful than
an idea whose time has come.'

Victor Hugo

While the challenges these Change Brands are looking to address are hugely varied, there is an interesting common thread in the background of the founders. A high proportion of those featured in this book have come from within the creative sector, whether that is within an advertising or design agency or within a marketing role at one of the big companies who currently dominate these categories.

Looking beyond my own 20 years in strategy at advertising agencies, working on brands big and small and the whole raft of social problems from climate change to knife crime and obesity, there are numerous other founders who've come from this space. Mike Cessario, the Liquid Death founder, and Matt Kennedy from Fussy were both creatives in advertising before starting their respective ventures. Eric Ryan, the founder of Method, was an advertising strategist before starting Method with Adam Lowry and Richard Reed, the Innocent founder, started in advertising. My Serious Tissues co-founder Martin McAllister was also a highly awarded creative director before jumping on the Change Brand train.

John Schoolcraft, the Oatly CCO who had such a transformational effect on the Oatly brand and business, spent 20 years as a creative working in advertising agencies and became so frustrated with the limitations of marketing departments that his one condition when joining Oatly was that they wouldn't have a marketing department. Instead they would bake creative into the very heart of the business.

'You're trained to come up with creative solutions to problems,' Matt Kennedy from Fussy explains. 'So, it was logical that eventually I'd end up keeping one of those and doing it myself. It was always the ambition to be honest. I heard someone once say, "stop giving away your best ideas" and that certainly resonates.'

Mike Cessario, the Liquid Death founder, saw the potential in involving creative people in the very early stages of creating brands: 'Typically, what happens is business people, with MBAs, are the ones who want to start businesses. They create the brand and end up having this product that isn't that interesting and then when they have money, they hire creative agencies to build campaigns around this uninteresting thing. But when you have advertising people involved at the beginning, people who understand culture and psychology, you're starting from a way more powerful position than any product typically is.'*

In the words of Andy Pearson, Creative VP at Liquid Death, 'We are an industry of almost limitless talent and ambition. Can you imagine if we all directed that at businesses that were actually good for the world or the people in it? Can you imagine if we all actually gave a real shit about the brands we worked on?'†

Numerous other founders came from within large FMCG companies. The founders of SURI, an eco-electric toothbrush brand, Mark Rushmore and Gyve Safavi, both spent time at Procter & Gamble and within agencies. Nuud Chewing gum founder Keir Carnie spent over ten years working at Heineken in sales roles. Freddy Ward and Charlie Bowes-Lyon of Wild both worked in marketing for a long

---

* Uncensored CMO podcast, March 2024

† https://www.thedrum.com/opinion/2024/03/20/wondering-what-s-wrong-with-the -ad-industry-eventually-led-me-liquid-death

time before starting their own thing, with Freddy being the head of marketing behind the rapid growth of Hello Fresh.

Both smol founders, Paula Quazi and Nick Green, spent at least a decade each at Unilever and while they found it incredibly beneficial, they became frustrated with the constraints that come with being part of a big machine and are relishing life at a Change Brand. Green said, 'Unilever was an amazing company to work for. I learned so much about brands and general business and so have a lot to be grateful for. Without doubt, this has helped in building a start-up company. Ultimately, working in a large multinational became frustrating. As an independent small business, there is freedom and clarity of decision-making that is exciting and means we can be more nimble, focused and agile.'

This is a group of people who passionately believe in the power of an idea to change the world. Creative, lateral thinkers, they see opportunity where others see barriers. They deeply understand shifting trends and consumer preferences and have the ability to develop propositions that they know will resonate and then bring them together in a compelling way.

They are also likely to have become frustrated by the day-to-day reality of their previous lives. There are a lot of people working in this space who want to use their skills to change the world but the brands they work on can quickly become a limit on those ambitions. If a brand is trying to bolster its sustainability creds but has nothing meaningful to talk about, then that brief quickly becomes an exercise in greenwashing. If a business isn't moving quickly enough at adopting new practices because it might eat away at their margin, it might be time to jump ship and do it yourself.

They figured out there was a better way and set out to create the brands of the future, taking their belief in ideas and the power of creativity into building their own brands and grasping the opportunity they saw ahead of them. There's also something incredibly liberating about being the 'client' and being responsible for every decision; the good, the bad and the stressful. It's an incredibly vibrant sector with huge creative energy and the ability to bring breakthrough ideas to life. I'm sure there's hundreds of ideas sat in bottom drawers and notebooks across the world and I for one am keen to see them become a reality. And do get in touch if you need a hand along the way!

One Final Question

If you asked me if I think advertising, or even marketing, could genuinely change the world on their own, I'd have some big reservations.

Yes, there have been some incredibly powerful campaigns over the years that have gone a long way towards changing attitudes. Meet the Superhumans. This Girl Can. Dove's Campaign for Real Beauty. Numerous campaigns against school shootings.

There have been campaigns that have changed behaviour leading to huge shifts in what we do in regard to recycling, quitting smoking, eating better, exercising more, drinking less, driving carefully and so on. I've loved being part of behaviour change driving campaigns, but it's unbelievably hard to change behaviour in both the short and the long term. And even harder to track whether it's led to lasting change.

There have been impactful campaigns for charities or governments. Campaigns that have cut through, moved people and made them think differently about the world. But charities and governments often lack the financial muscle to maintain activity for long enough to permanently change behaviour. Political priorities change, elections come around, charitable budgets shift to the next challenge.

There have certainly been very powerful campaigns for brands. At their best they use their powerful platform to try and make a difference. At worst, they're using an issue people care about and a 'purpose' to improve brand perceptions, increase fame and ultimately sell products. Creative agencies love this because it means they've got a good shot at winning awards, but does talking about purpose really make a difference to the problem? They act to build positive brand associations through a problem people care about but rarely do anything tangible to be part of the solution. Actions will always speak louder than words. And while some of their intentions may be good, has any big brand really changed the world?

Yet?

But if you asked me if I thought brands could change the world, the answer would be a 100 per cent, unequivocal, yes.

And specifically, Change Brands.

Brands who are looking to represent a positive shift from the status quo in terms of their footprint, who have a positive forward impact and often stand for something bigger than themselves. Minimum footprint, maximum impact.

Coming back to the original question about whether advertising can change the world, I think if the advertising is for the right brands, then it absolutely can. The power is with the brands we're advertising for and what these brands represent, not advertising itself. The right cohort of brands growing and becoming the dominant players in multiple sectors has the potential to make a significant and lasting change to society. And those brands that don't make the required changes almost deserve to become obsolete and fade into history.

Brands have a big footprint, so changes to that and their impact can be seismic when rolled out across millions of purchases. They have sizeable, self-sustaining business models so when they're functioning well, they can continue to bang the drum for change in a particular area year after year after year. Something that isn't the case with government, charities or traditional brands.

So yes, the right brands can change the world. And all you've got to do to help is change where you spend your money.

A brand is an idea. A representation of how the world could change for the better. And one that you can buy into and support as easily as tapping your card. You don't need to wait four years for an election or attend a rally, you can do it while sat in your pants with your phone in your hand.

Brands transcend politics. They don't need to solve every problem known to man and navigate complex political landscapes and vested interests. They can focus on a single issue that they and their audience care about. They can drive progress in one area. Roll that peanut forward just a little bit. And then do it again. And again.

Brands can drive change with a tone of voice that charities or politicians can't touch. Liquid Death bring a dose of heavy metal to the sustainability landscape. And guess what, it's working. Tony's Chocolonely tackle child exploitation with a lightness of touch and a tongue firmly in cheek that is surprisingly effective given the gravity of the problem they're facing. Change Brands can have a unique voice that cuts through the negativity and divisive discourse. They can make positive change fun, rather than worthy. They give people an easy option to be part of a solution by just picking up a different product from the shelf.

Change Brands can be status symbols too. People buy brands because of what it says about them. How it reflects on their identity. By buying the brands we've talked about within the pages of this book you're not damaging your status in the eyes of others, you're actively improving it, particularly as attitudes shift towards positive environmental and social change. Brands like Oatly, Patagonia, Tesla, Allbirds and Ocean Bottle are firmly established as status symbols. The great thing about the best Change Brands is they make positive change aspirational. A chance to trade up for a product with a great story, rather than that positive change being something you need to compromise on.

There's room for a lot more Change Brands out there taking on the plethora of problems we face. There's room for progress in so many areas and launching a brand could well be the best way to make a difference to something you care about. There's never been an easier time to launch a brand with the tools on offer. Simple ecommerce site builders, AI tools to build great content, social media marketing to find that audience... The door is firmly ajar due to the trailblazers we've talked about in this book and people's increasing willingness to try new brands, particularly ones connected with problems they care about.

The opportunity is there for new brands to come to market and make a positive difference by using the toolbox of business. All you need is an idea to get the ball rolling. You don't need to quit your job from day one to make a start. You can launch alongside the other things that are going on in your life, so you get a chance to test those hunches and see if it strikes a chord with people before taking the big leap.

The inspiring founders and brand stories featured throughout the book show that it can be done, and it is possible to make a real difference to some of the biggest problem we face by launching a brand.

And if you don't do it, who will?

So, let's say it one more time for the people in the back...

If we can change how people spend their money, we can change the world.

Acknowledgements

The last decade has been an absolute rollercoaster. From leaving a (relatively) comfortable advertising job to dive headlong into start-ups that are trying to change the world. All while getting married and becoming a father to three wonderful children. It's fair to say the hair has got a lot greyer but I wouldn't change a thing.

I've spent twenty years working in the biggest agencies in the world, touching all of the 'Big Six' holding companies, while working on hundreds of brands across every category. I've also worked across the full spectrum of society's problems, from climate change, health and education, to knife crime, illiteracy, homelessness and poverty.

I believe in the power of ideas to bring about change in the world – either commercially or socially – and it increasingly feels like the two things are converging. There's so much talent within the creative sector. Passionate, hardworking people who give a shit about the biggest problems facing society. They're a frustrated bunch, limited by the ambitions of their clients and seeing their best ideas consigned to the bin. So many game changing ideas just waiting for a client. This frustration inspired the idea that the best way to change the world is to launch a brand. I'd like to thank everyone I've worked with for inspiring that thought. It's been hard work, but an absolute pleasure and privilege to work with so many interesting people. Just imagine what would happen if we channelled all that energy towards changing the world.

Special mention goes to a few influential people. Derry Simpson was a key mentor for me early in my career, encouraging me to think laterally and was a big help on the original APG award paper that was the spark for Change Please. Cheers Des.

All the team at FCB Inferno during those great years leading the way in creative that made the world a better place. The agency played a big part in the birth of Change Please, created great work for Barnardo's, UNICEF, NSPCC and Project Literacy, tackled knife crime for the Home Office and created the cultural force of nature 'This Girl Can'. Big thanks to Al, Owen, Tim, Frazer, Sharon, Simon, Vicki, Katy, Ben, Laura and Nic.

To the teams at Change Please and Serious Tissues I say a huge thank you. Since meeting Cemal in a Peckham café in 2015 I've been constantly amazed by the journey and huge jumps along the way, with the next crazy scheme always bubbling away. Your total lack of fear and ability to see the bigger picture, while dealing with constant challenges has been truly inspirational. Being awarded an OBE in 2024 is richly deserved. That idea of 'change how people drink their coffee, change the world' dates back to our earliest conversations and you're certainly walking the walk. Thanks hero.

Serious Tissues is a Serious team. We've faced numerous challenges and have come out stronger on the other side. Anne, Andy, Rich, Martin and Cemal have met every challenge with a smile on their face. Anne and Andy, you're the glue that holds us together and I don't know what we'd do without you. Massive thanks to our tree planting partners, The Tree Council, Eden Reforestation and Veritree, you're incredible.

Special mention goes to Martin. From those early days at FCB to the present day, you're always there to come up with the next idea that could change the world. All of this is just the beginning.

Enormous thanks goes to all the incredible brands featured in the book, and in particular to those leaders who took the time to talk to me. So many brilliant businesses created to bring about positive change in the world. You're a constant source of inspiration. Everyday I'm amazed by your ingenuity and ability to grow against insurmountable odds. It gives me enormous hope for the future. I'd also like to extend a big thanks to Agent Change for providing an invaluable counterpoint that's been crucial in building a balanced argument.

Thanks to the team at Kantar. Their data is the benchmark for understanding the role of brands in the world and it's brilliant to see a number of Change Brands starting to register – with more to come soon. Particular thanks go to Dom Boyd, Nicki Morley and William Birtwhistle for their help.

Big thanks to Jonathan Hayden, my literary agent. Getting a book deal is not easy. Your patience and ability to always offer constructive notes have been invaluable. An enormous thanks to the brilliant people at Bloomsbury who've helped bring the book to life. Ian, Allie and Amy in particular. Your wisdom and guidance have made a big difference.

Thanks to my sister Amy Baker, a brilliant author who showed me that getting published wasn't a total pipe dream and that patience and persistence is an undervalued trait. You're an inspiration and a total legend. Best sister ever!

To mum and dad. What can I say? You've been incredibly supportive of everything I've done in life and have been absolute rocks throughout. Thanks for always being there for me and 'never letting me down.' Thanks to mum for instilling that love of reading from an early age leading to both your children getting published. Hope I can instil that same love of reading in my kids. Love you both so much.

Thanks also go to Helen and Steve who've been tremendously supportive along the way and potentially being the first people to buy a copy of the book after extensive Google research!

To my amazing dog Bear who kept me company throughout those dark January mornings writing before the kids woke up, but unfortunately didn't make it to one last summer. I'd love to hear you scratching at the window one last time little man.

The biggest thank you goes to my wonderful wife Katy. For your endless patience and encouragement. What a ten years it's been. It's certainly never boring with our three little customers. Thanks for always fighting my corner and believing in me no matter what (and never once describing anything as a 'vanity project'). Love you so much my little Popsy.

And to my kids Maggie, Jasper and Delphi. You changed things forever when you came along with your cute little faces and funny way of looking at the world. You make me smile every single day. If I ever needed a reason to try and change things for the better, you guys are a pretty good one. Love you all so much and I'll do all I can to make you proud. Love Daddy xxx

Contact the Author

If you'd like to get in touch with me then drop me an email on the address below or find me on LinkedIn.

chris@serioustissues.com

To find out more about the world of Change Brands, join the collective, and for more information on the brands featured in the book, scan the QR code below. You might find the odd promotion too.

Index

Note: page numbers in **bold** refer to illustrations.